Changing Scotland

To my grandson Innes,
born on 24 September 2024,
and who will inherit this land

this is my country,
the land that begat me
these windy spaces
are surely my own.

'Scotland' by Alexander Gray (1928)

Changing Scotland
Society, Politics and Identity

David McCrone

EDINBURGH
University Press

Edinburgh University Press is one of the leading university presses in the UK. Publishing new research in the arts and humanities, EUP connects people and ideas to inspire creative thinking, open new perspectives and shape the world we live in. For more information, visit www.edinburghuniversitypress.com.

© David McCrone, 2025

Edinburgh University Press Ltd
13 Infirmary Street, Edinburgh EH1 1LT

Typeset in 10.5 on 12pt Sabon by
Cheshire Typesetting Ltd, Cuddington, Cheshire

A CIP record for this book is available from the British Library

ISBN 978 1 3995 3400 0 (hardback)
ISBN 978 1 3995 3401 7 (paperback)
ISBN 978 1 3995 3402 4 (webready PDF)
ISBN 978 1 3995 3403 1 (epub)

The right of David McCrone to be identified as the author of this work has been asserted in accordance with the Copyright, Designs and Patents Act 1988, and the Copyright and Related Rights Regulations 2003 (SI No. 2498).

EU Authorised Representative:
Easy Access System Europe
Mustamäe tee 50, 10621 Tallinn, Estonia
gpsr.requests@easproject.com

Contents

List of Figures and Tables	vii
Preface	xi
1. Social Change in Scotland	1
2. What *is* Scotland?	13
3. Transformations	39
4. Demography	71
5. Materiality	111
6. National Identity: Who Have We Become?	143
7. Politics in a Cold Country	173
8. The Cultural Turn	207
9. Where To Now?	241
Bibliography	272
Index	283

Figures and Tables

FIGURES

1.1	'You've never had it so good'	10
4.1	Natural increase and net migration per 1,000 population, Scotland, England and Wales, 1861–2011	73
4.2	Natural change and net migration	75
4.3	Net total migration, 1951–2021	76
4.4	Net migration to and from the rest of the UK, 1951–2021	77
4.5	Net migration international, 1951–2021	77
4.6	Immigrants as per cent of the population, Scotland, England and Wales, 1851–2011	78
4.7	Immigrants as per cent of Scottish, English and Welsh populations, 1851–2011	79
4.8	Scotland's population by age, 1951	80
4.9	Scotland's population by age, 2001	80
4.10	Number of births in Scotland, 1866–2022	81
4.11	Births by age group, 1951–2022	83
4.12	Number of births, Scotland, 1974–2022, by marital status of parent(s) registering birth	84
4.13	Economic activity by sex and age, 2022	87
4.14	Life expectancy at birth in Scotland by sex compared to other countries, 1981–2020	89
4.15	The changing causes of death and life expectancy	91
4.16	Life expectancy changes from 2017–19 to 2019–21 by cause, males	92
4.17	Life expectancy changes from 2017–19 to 2019–21 by cause, females	93

4.18	Life expectancies in Scotland and the UK	94
5.1	Percentage in work by occupation (SOC2020) by sex, 2022	129
6.1	'Best choice' identity: Scottish to British ratios by cohorts over time	155
6.2	Linz-Moreno national identity, 1986–2021	159
6.3	Ratio of 'mainly Scottish' to 'mainly British', 1986–2021	160
6.4	Percentage of 'Scottish not British' in favour of independence	162
7.1	British general elections in Scotland: % share of the vote, 1970–2024	174
7.2	Labour–Conservative gap comparing Scotland and Britain, general elections, 1945–2024	175
7.3	Scottish parliament elections constituency vote share %, 1999–2021	176
7.4	Liberal/Lib-Dem vote share at British general elections, 1945–2024: Scotland and England	183
7.5	Conservative vote share in Scotland at British general elections, 1970–2024	184
7.6	Labour vote share in Scotland at British general elections, 1970–2024	186
7.7	SNP vote share in Scotland at British general elections, 1970–2024	189
7.8	Measuring sovereignty by party supported	197
7.9	Where Labour supporters stand (Pareto chart)	197

TABLES

3.1	Percentage of each socio-economic group voting SNP in October 1974 general election	57
3.2	Percentage voting Conservative in Scotland (and in rest of GB) in October 1974	61
4.1	Population changes in and around Edinburgh and Glasgow, 2011–22	102
5.1	Father's social class by birth cohort of respondent	132
5.2	Respondent's own class, men (women in brackets)	133
6.1	Identity choices in Scotland, England and Wales, 2001	153
6.2	Ratio of 'best choice' Scottish to British identities	155
6.3	National identity and support for independence	161

6.4	Preferred national identity	164
6.5	Linz-Moreno five-point scale	164
6.6	Being European and Brexit vote, 2016	167
7.1	Constitutional preferences, 2010–19	190

Preface

Nations, like people, have 'imagining moments', points in their lives and histories which are way-markers in their progress, or lack of it. They are turning-points, derived from the ancient Greek term, κρῐ́σῐς, conventionally translated into English as *crisis*: 'a separating, power of distinguishing, decision, choice, election, judgement, dispute', according to the *Oxford English Dictionary*. To be sure, we may not mark moments as such until they are well and truly over, and only in retrospect. They represent decisions made, turnings taken, by no means willingly or even consciously, and not in any diminished sense of the term 'crisis' in use today.

In his classic book *Imagined Communities* Anderson observed that: 'The idea of a sociological organism moving calendrically through homogeneous, empty time is a precise analogue of the idea of the nation, which also is conceived as a solid community moving steadily down (or up) history' (Anderson, 1996: 26). In the narrative of Scotland, 'moving calendrically through time', there are a number of 'imagining moments', historically, Bannockburn and its aftermath in 1314, the Arbroath Declaration in 1320 and the negotiated Union with England in 1707.

When I wrote *The New Sociology of Scotland* (2017), I thought it worth including an appendix, a timeline, 1900–2016, to give a narrative of what I took to be key events in recent history. Inevitably, it was smoothed-out, and personal, assuming a temporal sequence, with the intention of providing signposts in a calendrical transition through history. It goes without saying that life, even that of nations, is not like that. It is a messy jumble of complex processes, frequently contradictory and at odds, through which, much like our personal lives, we weave retrospectively some meaningful thread so as to make sense of it.

The focus in this book is the complex process in Scotland of social, economic and cultural change dating from the last few decades of the twentieth century. Those of us who have lived through that process largely took it for granted, thinking that it was somehow inevitable, more gradual and less transformative than it now looks to be with the benefit of hindsight. But transformative it was, and remains so. We can see how people's lives, including our own, changed quite radically, as social changes made their mark.

So what is this book trying to do? It explores how the warfare/welfare nexus which had stitched Scotland into the British state for much of the twentieth century began to come apart in the final quarter. It argues that, while the 1970s can be seen conventionally as a 'political-cultural' rupture, reflected in the rise of 'nationalism' in different forms, the driving momentum came from social change: demographic, material, socio-economic. These took on political-cultural forms but these were, fundamentally, expressions of *social* change.

This is a good time to take stock of the new Scotland. Writing such a book in the second decade of the twenty-first century coincides with the 25th anniversary of the setting up of the Scottish parliament, and the process of 'devolution' which, arguably, has reached the limits of what is possible within the British state. Social change in that period, however, is not to be understood simply in terms of this new political institution. Rather, the new institution is the reflection of a new Scotland. We need to see it in the round: social, political and cultural. The book draws upon a wealth of empirical material so that we can 'read' the changing Scotland. The timeframe is crucial. We can now see, in retrospect, that the transformative moment lay in the long decade of the late 1960s/1970s, when social, economic and political processes in particular began to transform Scotland in a radical way. Fifty years on, we live in a quite different country. This book explains how that came about, and because we now have better data and evidence, the tale is told in a more sophisticated and social scientific way. The book uses this rich material not to overwhelm the account by numbers, but to distil the account by their judicious use.

It is a sociologist's book which draws upon other disciplines such as history, politics and literature, given the confluence of these around a sociological perspective on the grounds that this discipline brings to bear, almost uniquely, an account of social change in Scotland.

The book has nine chapters. Chapter 1, Social Change in Scotland, spells out the book's thesis: that until the 1970s the sinews which held Scotland in the British state were those of 'warfare' and 'welfare', in the course of the twentieth century in which they were dovetailed, and reflected in the lack of structural differences between Scotland and the rest of the UK. The long process of dis-integration was driven above all by *social* change, that is, by changes in demographic, industrial, and socio-economic structures which were common throughout the western industrial world. These impacted on societies with quite different political, institutional and cultural forms which came to terms in their different ways with social change.

Chapter 2 asks what kind of place Scotland is, and why it is that way. This chapter reviews the analytical terms which we need to understand Scotland; only then can we carry out the task of analysing social change in order to understand why generic social change had a particular impact. Scotland sits at the nexus of three key concepts: civil society, nation and state; in other words, it is framed by societal, cultural and political dimensions. We explore the origins of the idea of Scotland, and its subsequent transformation, and review how best to comprehend Scotland in analytical terms, given that it is not a conventional 'nation-state'. Rather than being a curious anomaly in the modern world, historically, a 'stateless nation', Scotland is a territory in which debates about civil society, nation-ness and state sovereignty are played out, reflecting transformations in the modern world at large.

Chapter 3 sketches out these transformations in summary, seeking to understand what drove social change in the final quarter of the twentieth century, and how social processes articulate to produce a new Scotland. The answer lies in the complex interaction of demographic, material, identity, political and cultural changes. The chapter focuses on the long decade from the 1960s and through the 1970s, and articulates the ways in which social change in modern industrial societies were transformative, and in which Scotland shared. The image is of a common wave of social change washing over societies differentially in this long decade, reflecting their social and institutional histories such that the transformative process was unique to each. It explores the interactions of demography, materiality, identity, politics and culture in Scotland which have helped to create a new Scotland that has broken free of the nexus of warfare and welfare which defined its pre-1970 social, economic and political forms.

The key transformations in the subsequent decades are then traced and analysed in the chapters which follow, starting with *demographic change* in Chapter 4. This chapter examines how and why demographic changes came about in Scotland with regard to (1) the transformation of migration practices such that Scotland ceased to be a place of *ex*-migration, to one of *in*-migration; (2) changing family forms in processes of shrinking family size, complex family re-formations, and patterns of increased geographical mobility. The chapter also explores how 'mobile privatism' emerged, and the relative decline of community solidarities which resulted.

Chapter 5 deals with 'materiality', shifts in economy, industry and social class, the means whereby people make a living. Arguably, the transformation of Scotland derives from the changing material base of society: in particular, the economy, industry, occupational and social class structure. The chapter focuses on this 'materiality', not to argue that there is an automatic transformation of the social, political and cultural bases in a predictable way, but that these changes work their way through in complex institutional and cultural ways to bring about social change. The chapter will also explore how changes in the Scottish economy and its material base generated shifts in the nature and meaning of social class, and patterns of social mobility and diversity.

What kind of people have we become? There are few more obvious transformations relating to Scotland than those relating to *national identity*; and yet few which are more misunderstood. Chapter 6 explores whether people in Scotland have become more Scottish, and less British, and in which respects, if at all. It argues that change is more nuanced and complex than we might expect, and depends much more on the social and cultural meanings attaching to national identity rather than treating it as a straightforward system of cultural classification. The chapter also explores how 'national' identity relates not only to 'state' identity (being British) but to other forms of social identity such as social class, gender, ethnicity, age and religion, and how these change through time.

And so to *politics*. How did political processes both reflect and account for the new Scotland? What role did devolution and the Scottish parliament play in transforming the country? Chapter 7 explores the transformation in political behaviour and political attitudes since the 1970s, not simply in terms of party allegiances but in how social and political values connect up with how people 'do' politics. It examines the impact of creating a devolved parliament in 1999, how political behaviour relates to other forms of political expression, and whether 'devolution' has been transformative, and if so, in what ways.

Much of the debate about Scotland concerns its 'culture', ways of understanding who we are and how we make sense of the web of significance around us. Chapter 8 asks: to what extent have old forms of cultural expression been replaced by new ones? What happened to the dominant tropes of cultural cringe, tartanry and kailyard, historic ways of understanding Scotland in cultural terms? Social and political change in particular have swept away long-held notions of cultural inferiority. What new forms of cultural expression have emerged, and why? What is the relationship between new cultural forms and 'politics', if any? Are we able to identify the relationships between them? To what extent has the 'new' Scotland found expression in new forms of culture and literature? To what extent, if at all, is the new politics of Scotland culture-lite?

And finally, in Chapter 9, we examine Scotland's futures, especially in the light of twenty-five years of a devolved parliament. What are the options? Is 'independence' a meaningful goal in the twenty-first century? Does 'sovereignty' matter anymore? Is Scotland in the UK still feasible, and if so, on what, and whose, terms? How 'European' is Scotland? How do people in Scotland manage and manipulate being Scottish, British and European? To what extent have differences with England in particular defined the new politics of Scotland? Can we find analogues in the modern world which mirror Scotland's development?

Books do not make themselves. Above all, they are a collective endeavour, even if they have a single author. I have benefited greatly from the comments and suggestions of many friends and colleagues, formally and informally. The idea for the book came from the late Malcolm Anderson, emeritus Professor of Politics at Edinburgh, made as a passing comment at a mutual friend's house. I owe a lot to Michael Anderson, Neal Ascherson, Alan Alexander and Tony Cohen, the late Frank Bechhofer, Alice Brown, Cairns Craig, John Hall, Jon Hearn, Michael Keating, the late Neil MacCormick, and Tom Nairn, Lindsay Paterson, Michael Rosie, Jennifer Todd, and above all, my civil partner Jan Webb. Behind all this is the wise observation by the late Neil MacCormick, that we all play the hands we are dealt. To paraphrase Michael Marra's song, I have written this book with the ghost of Neil next to me. 'Listen Neil, your apprentice has begun.'

St Andrew's Day, 2024

1

Social Change in Scotland

> This is about who we are, how we carry ourselves.
> (Donald Dewar, at the opening of the
> Scottish parliament, 1 July 1999)

This book is about social change; how modern Scotland has been transformed since the 1970s, why that is so, and with what effects. The argument is that in the long decade which lasted from the late 1960s through the 1970s, Scotland was changed in such a way that what came after resembled little what had gone before. Above all, the warfare/welfare nexus which had shaped people's lives for much of the twentieth century was transformed. What came after that, though recognisable to us who lived through it, did not much resemble what our parents and grandparents had experienced. Their lives were dominated by two world wars, actual or virtual, the aftermath of one war, and the prelude to another. If you were born in the early years of the twentieth century, you would have been fifty years of age before there was anything resembling settled peace; and you would have had little time to enjoy it, given shorter life expectancies at the time.[1]

Welfare provisions emerged slowly from the early years of the century but especially after 1945, when the welfare state was society's price for mass mobilisation. The people's wars led to the people's peace. And for the next three decades that set the context for people's lives. Then, in the final quarter of the twentieth century most of that was transformed. The social bonds which held Scottish society together around warfare and welfare were loosened: people became more mobile, both socially and geographically; they took advantage of new educational opportunities; families were reconstituted and became smaller; and it was far less necessary to migrate out of Scotland to 'get on'.

UNDERSTANDING CHANGE

In truth, most of us do not notice social change very much; there is a continuity in our daily lives which masks change. Every now and again we are startled into realising how much has altered, because our lives have undergone major transformations which we have barely noticed until they are upon us or even past us. We are more likely to notice change over generations; that, compared with our parents and grandparents, as well as our children and grandchildren, we see and experience things differently. We also notice, as we get older, that things are not what they used to be. Nevertheless, to coin a phrase, the child is the mother of the woman as well as the father of the man. The point is that who we become as adults is prefigured when we are children; or, at least, so thought William Wordsworth who coined the saying. It is perfectly fair not to notice social change very much; we might say that our lives somewhat depend on *not* noticing, as we get on with our lives. And in any case, in the words of one of Eugene O'Neill's characters: 'The past is the present, isn't it? It's the future, too. We all try to lie out of that but life won't let us.' (from *Long Day's Journey into Night*, Act 2, Scene 2).

Time, and history, matter. I am reminded of Fernand Braudel's notion of the *longue durée*. He observed:

> If one wants to understand the world, one has to determine the hierarchy of forces, currents, and individual movements, and then put them together to form an overall constellation. Throughout, one must distinguish between long-term movements and momentary pressures, finding the immediate sources of the latter and the long-term thrust of the former. (Braudel, 2009: 182)

Sociologists are, rightly, taken to task by Braudel for neglecting 'time'. He comments:

> I return to time, to duration. And as an incorrigible historian, I remain astonished that sociologists have been able to escape it. But it is because their time is not my time: it is much less imperious, also less concrete, and never at the heart of their problems and

their reflections. The historian in fact never departs from historical time. Time sticks to his thought like soil to the gardener's spade. (ibid. 197)

'Historical time', *pace* Braudel, however, is not enough; it is necessary to distinguish between clock-time and social-time. The former is astronomical, time with a beginning, a middle and an end, as 'chronos' (Χρόνος) in Greek. The second is existential time, 'kairos' (καιρός), bound up with human, cyclical time. Thus, social-time is not continuous, but punctuated by critical and meaningful points of reference. Braudel, though, is correct in his criticism.

As John Hassard (1990) observed, time is the missing variable in modern sociological analysis; sociological research processes are synchronic rather than longitudinal. Famously, Benjamin Franklin stated that 'time is money' in his advice to young tradesmen in the middle of the eighteenth century, and so time became 'a major symbol for the production of economic wealth. No longer was it sacred and reproducible through the "myth of the eternal return". It represented instead an economic object, a symbol of production' (Hassard, 1990: 13). On the other hand, '... social-time refers to social processes, and to the intersubjective conceptualisation of social life, rather than to the mechanistic structuring of social events' (ibid. 6). We experience events through time as external to us, while at the same time as highly personal, as we seek to impose order in our lives.

This book seeks to show how Scotland was changed utterly in the final decades at the end of the twentieth century, in the period characterised, in France at least, as *Les Trente Glorieuses*. This was social change on a grand scale: demographic, social, economic, political and cultural, all interweaving, having what social statisticians call interactive effects, impacting one on the other. Nevertheless, those of us who have lived through this period hardly notice it.

That is because we are accustomed to routines and predictability, which we require in order to live and make sense of the world. The American sociologist C. Wright Mills juxtaposed 'biography' and 'society'; that people went about their lives almost not noticing 'external' events except when they had a direct bearing, such as war, economic depression, changing political fortunes and the like. Mills made a distinction between 'personal troubles' and 'public issues of social structure'. Being able to connect the two he called the 'sociological imagination'. He wrote:

> the statement and resolution of troubles properly lie within the individual as a biographical entity and within the scope of his (sic) immediate milieu – the social setting that is directly open to his personal experience and to some extent his wilful activity. A trouble is a private matter: values cherished by an individual are felt by him to be threatened. (Mills, 1959: 8)

That is what Mills meant by 'biography'. It is private and intimate. 'Society', or what he calls 'issues', is a different matter:

> they transcend these local environments of the individual and his inner life. They have to do with the organization of many such milieux into the institutions of a historical society as a whole, with the ways in which various milieux overlap and interpenetrate to form the larger structure of social and historical life. (ibid. 9)

Mills gave as examples: unemployment, war, marriage, city living, the economy. Biography and society connect up because

> what we experience in various and specific milieux ... is often caused by structural changes we are only dimly aware of. Accordingly, to understand the changes of many personal milieux we are required to look beyond them. And the number and variety of such structural changes increase as the institutions within which we live become more embracing and more intricately connected with one another. To be aware of the idea of social structure and to use it with sensibility is to be capable of tracing such linkages among a great variety of milieux. To be able to do that is to possess the sociological imagination. (ibid. 10–11)

Social structures, then, condition but do not determine what we experience. Thus, what Mills called 'public issues' and 'private troubles' are connected up in practice, while most of the time we are only dimly aware of the connection between them. Indeed, there may be political mileage to be had in personalising the connection such that what happens to people is deemed to be 'their own fault'. Losing your job, failing in marriage or becoming homeless may be blamed on a lack of moral fibre, but, objectively, these have far more to do with structural change – rising unemployment, or pressures on personal relationships, or housing shortages – than personal failings. We get the point that there are ways in which society is organised (or disorganised) which are experienced as 'personal troubles'. This is especially so in periods of rapid social change when what we are used to alters fundamentally and opens up new opportunities as well as new challenges. So our task is to identify those structural changes which set the frameworks for people's lives.

What kinds of social change are we talking about? In social science, we refer to 'structural' changes, broad patterned shifts in how social and economic life is organised. They are the backdrop to how we organise our lives. As Mills observed, these are external to individuals but are manifestations of how they behave in a systematic and usually unconscious fashion. Sociologists talk about 'demographic structures', 'occupational structures' and 'class structures'. These are called structures because they are routinised or objectified forms of behaviour which we take largely for granted, even though by our actions we contribute to them and thus lend them our support, and so help to embed, as well as embody, them. To reiterate the point, we are only dimly aware of changes in such social structures, and usually get them wrong because we can't see the big picture. We might, for example, be tempted to think that social class does not matter anymore, or, at any rate, is less important than it used to be, even though social statistics clearly show that we live in a world where social inequality is much greater than previously. There is no guarantee, then, that we 'see' things through official statistics, or that we faithfully follow what they tell us. We go about our lives, and are engrossed in our 'personal troubles' rather than the 'public issues', even though the latter provide the framework through which we live our troubles.

Social change, more accurately social structural change, refers to those routinised and taken-for-granted forms which are created by people's actions, but which are, relatively, predictable background through which we make sense of the world around us. We only experience these dimly as we go about our lives. I am, then, using the term 'social change' to refer to changing structures of work, employment, industry, social class and demography – how family and household life is organised and structured. Such are the institutions within which people operate, experienced mainly as givens, or more probably, as constraints on their behaviour. It is perfectly reasonable that we are unaware of these most of the time, but they are, fundamentally, determinants of the ways we live.

Identifying these aspects of social – structural – change is one side of the equation. The other is how these aspects are refracted through prisms of social understanding: politics, identity and culture. There is, then, no expectation that these structural changes will impact on societies in the same, or even, similar ways. To take an example: there is an interesting and developing literature, mainly by historians of the late twentieth-century, exploring how social change feeds through into 'popular individualism' dating from the 1970s (Lawrence, 2019; Robinson et al., 2017; and Sutcliffe-Braithwaite, 2018).

This, though, is a literature almost entirely about England. Why so? One of these authors, Jon Lawrence whose book he titled *'Me, Me, Me: The Search for Community in Post-war England'* justifies it thus:

> Why England rather than Britain? Well, partly this is because I did not find good surviving field-notes from Welsh and Scottish studies when planning the project. But more fundamentally, it is because many of the issues at the heart of 'me, me, me' played out differently across the four nations of the United Kingdom. (2019: 10)

Lawrence points to 'the deep-rooted traditions of individualism within English culture' (ibid. 11). This he is perfectly entitled to do, but this is asserted rather than proven.

Similarly, Florence Sutcliffe-Braithwaite in her book, *Class, Politics and the Decline of Deference in England, 1968–2000* also justifies the English focus, that 'the complexity of class in a "four nations" context makes it necessary to confine substantive discussion to one nation [England]' (2018: 14). Both authors are at liberty to confine their accounts to England; but it is the *specificity* of England which is the key question. We might ask them, what is it about England that allegedly makes that so, and why does structural change generate 'popular individualism' in that manner? A third historian, Emily Robinson, shares this perspective, and takes it, revealingly, further. Writing with her colleagues, one of whom is Sutcliffe-Braithwaite, her article 'Telling Stories about Post-War Britain (sic): Popular Individualism and the "Crisis" of the 1970s' observes that: 'This popular individualism was not the result of Thatcher; if anything, it was a *cause* of Thatcherism' (2017: 268). Refining that a few pages later, they say '... rather, it was a trend Thatcher managed, through luck as well as political skill, to exploit' (2017: 272).

What is interesting, sociologically, about this genre of recent historical writing is the not-unreasonable assumption that England is different, at least from Scotland and Wales. The 'normal' view is that it is Scotland and Wales which are aberrant; England being the 'norm'. It is premised on a vein of writing that is trying to account for the rise of Thatcher and her subsequent 'ism' in terms of more deeply rooted social values – popular individualism – in *England*. It is not a cultural-political framework which 'explains' developments in Scotland, nor arguably in Wales, at least in terms of political outcomes.

This is a key point. Social structural change – with regard to demography and materiality in particular – does not have the same, even similar, outcomes within the 'home nations' of England, Scotland and Wales, still less Northern Ireland,[2] although they currently belong to the same unitary state, the United Kingdom. Social change, in other words, is refracted through prisms of comprehension, political, cultural and identity, and my task in this book is to account for that process – in Scotland. Social structural changes opened up new ways of seeing, and indeed being, north of the border since, roughly, the 1970s. I will endeavour to spell out the specificities of Scotland such that the ways in which quite similar aspects of social change, demographic and material, produced a quite different 'society' than the one which preceded it.

My argument in this book, then, is that in the final quarter of the 20th century these structural determinants altered in a dramatic way such that new opportunities, even new ways of seeing, were opened up for a post-war generation coming to adulthood. These opportunities related to new ways of earning a living, even new ways of living, new educational and social opportunities, new ways of 'getting on', different from those of our parents and grandparents, new patterns of mobility, both geographical and social, and new forms of social solidarity. What this book tries to do is show how those structural changes brought about new ways of making sense of the world, new perspectives, new ways of seeing.

That is why the book is in two halves: the first outlines shifting social structures, and the second, how these work through national identity, politics and culture. The point is not that 'structure' causes 'cultural change', but that there is a subtle interaction between them. For example, how we see ourselves, how we do our politics and culture, are reflections of social structural change, but that they also lay down the parameters whereby social change happens. Thus, because we see ourselves as 'different people' compared with our parents and grandparents, we weave those structural strands differently. 'Culture', then, in the broadest sense impacts upon structural change, making sense of who we are and try to be. In this context, being Scottish, or rather Scottish in a different way compared with our forebears, has come to matter more.

Nowadays we tend to think of ourselves as more in control of our lives, as individuals, than our forebears did, but we refract that through the political and cultural prisms available to us. We are not unique in this. This is not a 'nationalist' point; similar structural changes had, for example, different political outcomes north and south of the border. And if anything, culture and politics on each side of that border have become *more* different, not less. That is the key point of the book, to make sense of the different structure/culture nexus in Scotland.

There are alternative ways of accounting for change in Scotland, all of them acceptable. We could write a political account, focusing upon the transformations in voting habits and institutional change, most obviously the setting up of a Scottish parliament in 1999. We could trace cultural change, the means whereby people make sense of what is happening to them, amplified into literature and Culture (with a capital C). We could explore identity change to show how and why people in Scotland do national identities, in particular being – more – Scottish rather than being British. I will try to do all of these, but will treat them as outcomes, as effects, of social change, rather than their cause. Why so? Because my argument is that social change as I have described it is what has been driving political, cultural and identity changes rather than the other way round. It is important, though, to grasp that all these aspects of social life are bound up together, and that there are considerable interactions between them so that in practice sorting out causes and effects becomes messy and complicated, but also intriguing. The key point of my argument remains: that social change – demographic, occupational, industrial and socio-economic[3] – is where we should look for causes as to how Scotland has been transformed. Put at its simplest, the argument is that we should start from the nuts and bolts of social life, what I call materialist factors, from which political and cultural changes derive.

It is, of course, not so simple, for material changes do not determine politics and culture; they interact with each other. We see things differently, and thus come to expect things to be different, and help them to become so by acting accordingly. To take an example: the generation coming to political adulthood in the 1970s began to leave the old politics of capital and labour behind, especially if they migrated to new communities such as New Towns and suburbs, and were no longer embedded in old ways of doing things.

This is not simply a function of age, but of cohorts. We might assume that chronological age, being, say, seventy years of age as opposed to thirty, is what matters. Only up to a point. If you are seventy, you appreciate that growing up and through your thirties – in the 1980s – was not the same as doing so in the 2020s. The opportunities, the constraints, but also the mindsets are different; we are socialised differently, we come to expect different things. Chronological age matters less, then, than the social, political, cultural contexts we inhabit. This book seeks to translate the ways in which people became different social creatures. There was a process of reinvention taking place in who we were, culturally and politically, who we aspired to be. In truth, this process was happening across much of the western world; I will explore how it took a Scottish turn, and how it transformed Scotland.

TRANSFORMING SOCIETY

Put at its most basic: I aim to explore how social change, thus defined, which is broadly shared among modern, industrial, western societies, ramified through them such as to be transformative of their politics, culture and forms of identity. I will explore how these had an impact in Scotland, on its politics, culture and senses of identity, not to make it the same as other societies which underwent similar social change, but to conjure up an image that social change operated like a tidal wave washing over such societies, but having different effects because of historical and institutional features and practices.

We have moved a long way from the view which was dominant in the social sciences in the 1960s that industrial societies were much of a muchness, that we were all becoming the same. That proved not to be so, and we realised that tides of social change did not reduce historical and institutional structures to irrelevance.

Consider, further, the term *Les Trente Glorieuses*, first used to describe the three decades from 1945 in France in particular, but applicable to most modern industrial societies. The term, invented by a demographer, Jean Fourastié, was designed to account for the transformation of France from rural to urban, and peasant to industrial, aided and abetted by the state (thus, the term *dirigisme* entered the political lexicon). We will see, however, that Scotland's thirty years from 1945 to 1975 were not especially glorious, not because it was not France, but because it was not even England, where economic transformations were more successful, and offered greater opportunities.

In 1957, the British Prime Minister Harold Macmillan uttered a phrase which became the strapline of the day: 'you never

Figure 1.1 'You've never had it so good'
Source: Courtesy of Mirrorpix/Trinity Mirror with the permission of *The Daily Mirror*, and British Cartoon Archive, University of Kent.

had it so good'. Like many iconic sayings, we discover that Macmillan didn't actually utter those precise words. Giving a speech at a Conservative rally, what Macmillan said was: 'you will see a state of prosperity such as we have never had in my lifetime – nor indeed in the history of this country. Indeed, let us be frank about it – most of our people have never had it so good.' (http://news.bbc.co.uk/onthisday/hi/dates/stories/july/20/newsid_3728000/3728225.stm)

Macmillan's words were pounced upon by critics as invoking complacency at a time of social disquiet, as in Vicky's cartoon in *The Daily Mirror*, 26 March 1958.

Rather like another Conservative Prime Minister, Mrs Thatcher, thirty years later, whose words 'There is no such thing as society' were also taken out of context, 'you've never had it so good' became iconic of the age, even if they were a distortion of what was said and implied. However, as the political scientist Bill Miller pointed out, Macmillan's sentiment 'sounded differently in Scotland and South-East England. It was too complacent, and all the stress on prosperity made regional variations that much less easy to bear' (Miller, 1981: 29).

The point was not that Scotland shared fully in this apparent prosperity – certainly compared with England to which many Scots migrated. Consider Corby in Northamptonshire, for example. By 1961, over one-third of its population had been born in Scotland, to such an extent that Corby became known as 'little Scotland';[4] an unusual example, but nevertheless, similar economic and social forces were at work to transform Scotland, which ultimately led to a significantly changed society.

That is what the book will try to do; to show how this complex process of social, political and cultural change came about such that the Scotland of the 2020s is quite unlike that of fifty years previously, and that something of a social revolution has taken place, and what it means for our lives today.

NOTES

1. In Scotland, men born in 1910–12 could expect to live until they were 50, and women, 53. Source: <https://www.statista.com/statistics/1040159/life-expectancy-united-kingdom-all-time/>.
2. The adverb 'still less' in that sentence reflects the historically contentious character of the Province and its division these days

largely into two separate and distinct political and ethnic cultures (see Todd, 2018).
3. I use 'socio-economic' rather than 'social class' to make the point that these might be broader than simply occupation-based.
4. <https://www.bbc.co.uk/news/magazine-28225325>.

2

What *is* Scotland?

This is my country,
The land that begat me.
These windy spaces
Are surely my own.
And those who here toil
In the sweat of their faces
Are flesh of my flesh,
And bone of my bone.
            (Alexander Gray, 1928)

Before we explore the impact of social change on Scotland, we need to sort out what kind of place Scotland is, and why, for it is not a conventional state; and we require some kind of descriptor for what it is. Why bother? Because the conventional wisdom is that 'societies' are nation-states, and those which are not 'independent' – like Scotland – cannot be considered as distinct societies. The problem, though, is that there are few genuine 'nation-states' in the world, where the cultural 'nation' maps neatly on to political 'state'. Furthermore, Scotland is a stateless nation, or at best, an under-stated nation. What analytical concepts do we need to comprehend it? This matters, because we need to know what kind of entity, sociological and political, we are dealing with.

This chapter argues that, in sociological terms, Scotland sits at the nexus of three key concepts: civil society, nation and state, that is, framed by the societal, cultural and political. If we say Scotland is a 'society', what does that mean? Simply put, it means that its institutions and social structures are relatively self-contained and meaningful to those who live in the place.

The key term in that sentence is 'relatively', for it is a question of degrees of self-containment. Having a separate system of law, education, religion (when it mattered more than it does today), institutionalised since 1999 in a parliament at Holyrood has helped to create a frame of reference within which people think of themselves as 'Scots'.

WHEN WAS SCOTLAND?

The historian Dauvit Broun has commented: 'However old this fundamental sense of people [Scots] and country [Scotland] may be, it must have begun sometime' (Broun, 2015: 164). So when did 'Scotland' as an idea begin? Broun observes: 'to insist that Scotland was not a meaningful concept, or that Scottish identity did not exist before the end of the 13th century, would surely be to allow our modern idea of Scotland to take precedence over the view of contemporaries' (Broun, 1994: 38).

Can we be at all sure, though, that there is a clear historical lineage from past to present? We might take the view that our notion of 'Scotland' is a modern one, reflecting contemporary political and constitutional concerns, which we then read back into history, by way of ideological justification.[1] We can use such justification for political purposes, to say, for example, that Scotland is one of Europe's oldest nations, but can we be sure that our ancestors thought of it as a nation, and, if so, in what senses? Hence Dauvit Broun's comment that we cannot assume that the 'Scotland' we have inherited is that of the Middle Ages; that *medieval* Scotland means the same as *modern* Scotland. Much more difficult, then, as Broun observes, to ask whether people in the thirteenth century had any notion of Scotland, and what it might have meant to them.

But why the *thirteenth* century? 'Scotland' might have existed as early as the first millennium, but it was the twelfth and thirteenth centuries, and above all the wars of independence at the beginning of the fourteenth century which arguably made Scotland in a way we now recognise. This is a topic which is the property of medieval historians. Dauvit Broun contends that: '... it was not until the period between 1260 and 1290 that the idea of country, people and kingdom coincided to form what we recognise as the beginning of modern Scotland' (Broun, 2015: 165). In other words, Scotland developed a sense of itself as not-England, at the point where regal authority south of the border was flexing its muscles. Not to be incorporated into England required active dissociation. In any case, by the 1180s we have the earliest indications that local lords thought of the Scottish kingdom as a land with common laws and customs, an unintended consequence of comparable legal and administrative reforms in England during their king Henry's reign.

By the middle of the thirteenth century, we have evidence of legal mechanisms in Scotland about the reporting of local land inquests to the king. Furthermore, the amount of money in circulation grew dramatically between 1250 and 1280, which was reflected in the creation of coinage mints from Inverness to Dumfries, as well as establishing sheriff courts throughout the land, both indicating jurisdictional expansion by the Crown. We might assume, then, that the Crown was mainly responsible for shaping and imposing national institutions on Scotland much as the monarchy did in France (Beaune, 1985). Dauvit Broun argues that Scotland came to be a phenomenon of the mind, an 'idea that, at some point, came to be thought of by its inhabitants as one-and-the-same as the kingdom they lived in' (Broun, 2015:164).

From the thirteenth century, those living south of the Forth began to see themselves as Scots living in a place we call Scotland, even if they viewed the northerners as somewhat unsavoury. Broun concluded:

> Overall ... we seem to have kingdom, country and people coalescing round the image north of the Forth as an island, an image rooted in an awareness of a genuine topographical barrier. By the late thirteenth century kingdom, country and people has coalesced anew around the dawning concept of sovereignty. The sense of ultimate secular authority shared by both had moved its centre of gravity from geography to jurisdiction. (Broun, 2015: 186)

Thus did kingdom/country/people coalesce imperceptibly into a new Scotland as an independent realm, a view shared by its people at large.

Who Were the Scots?

We have inherited a characterisation of Scots as a mongrel people, no pure race, but an amalgam of peoples united by territory, rather than ethnicity. Scotland has no ambitions to be pure bred: we are a mongrel people, at least in our conception of ourselves. It helps to convey the sense that being Scottish derived from what the historian Christopher Smout memorably called a 'sense of place', rather than a 'sense of tribe'. This is no claim to be morally superior to any other people; it was simply *realpolitik*: thus,

> If coherent government was to survive in the medieval and early modern past, it had, in a country that comprised gaelic-speaking Highlanders and Scots-speaking Lowlanders, already linguistically and ethnically diverse, to appeal beyond kin and ethnicity – to loyalty to the person of the monarch, then to the integrity of the territory over which the monarch ruled. The critical fact allowed the Scots ultimately to absorb all kinds of immigrants with relatively little fuss, including, most importantly, the Irish in the 19th century. (Smout, 1994:107)

This fitted in with how other historians made sense of the history of these islands. In many ways Scotland was less homogeneous culturally and linguistically than its Celtic neighbours. The historian Sandy Grant observed:

> during the Middle Ages the Welsh and the Irish surely had at least as strong a concept of racial or national solidarity as the Scots, and much more linguistic solidarity. Yet, between the eleventh and the thirteenth centuries, the whole of Wales and very substantial parts of Ireland were conquered by the English; subsequently both countries experienced many anti-English rebellions, but neither was ever liberated from foreign rule. The contrast with what happened to Scotland is obvious, and demonstrates that success or failure in maintaining independence cannot simply be explained in terms of racial consciousness, nationalist myths, common language and the like. (Grant, 1994: 75)

Grant's point is that territorial interests, reinforced by state authority in the shape of the Crown, held Scotland together despite its regional and ethnic diversity; or perhaps because of it, in the sense that national integrity had to be actively worked at to offset ethnic diversity on the ground.

Stating the Nation

It is in this context that we can appreciate what the iconic Declaration of Arbroath of 1320 signifies.[2] This was a political document from the Barons of Scotland to Pope John XXII, which begins with a re-writing of the history of the people, one that no modern historian could ever countenance. The Scots, the declaration averred, 'journeyed from Greater Scythia by way of the Tyrrhenian Sea and the Pillars of Hercules, and dwelt for a long course of time in Spain among the most savage tribes, but nowhere could they be subdued by any race, however barbarous'. Having reached their promised land, the 'Scots' single-mindedly pursued their goal: 'The Britons they first drove out, the Picts they utterly destroyed, and though very often assailed by the Norwegians, the Danes and the English, they took possession of that home with many victories and untold efforts.' So much for being a mongrel people, for live-and-let-live: the fourteenth century was not the time to make such an essentially modern, and liberal, claim.

We might take it for granted that this letter stands for a Scottish Declaration of Independence, but academics have been reluctant to call the document a 'declaration' in any sense, still less a 'Declaration of Independence', as this does not properly represent the history of the letter to the Pope (Harrison, 2017). The term 'Declaration of Arbroath' did not become routine until the latter period of the twentieth century, although it was a known term in the previous century. Laura Harrison observed: 'a document with relatively little impact during the time of its creation in the Middle Ages can take on delusions of grandeur in a later period' (Harrison, 2017: 450.).

The famous passage in the Declaration of Arbroath is well-known:[3]

> for, as long as but one hundred of us remain alive, never will we on any conditions be brought under English rule. It is in truth not for glory, nor riches, nor honours that we are fighting, but for freedom – for that alone, which no honest man gives up but with life itself.

Few, however, take note of what precedes these famous few lines. If 'our most tireless Prince, King and Lord, the Lord Robert' [that is, Bruce]

> should give up what he has begun, and agree to make us or our kingdom subject to the King of England or the English, we should exert ourselves at once to drive him out as our enemy and subverter of his own rights and ours, and make some other man who was well able to defend us our King.

These sentiments seem, in modern times, to be *lèse-majesté*, but reflected the contingencies of regal power in the twelfth and thirteenth centuries, in which someone was nominated as monarch as *primus inter pares*. Similar sentiments to those in Arbroath are found in the Aragonese oath of allegiance in the twelfth century: 'We who are as good as you are swear to you who are not better than us to obey and be loyal as long as the monarch honours our rights and laws, and if not, not (*y si no, no*)' (cited in Ascherson, 2022: 535).

The puzzle is that, as the historian Roger Mason observed, the Declaration of Arbroath is 'the *ur*-text of a tradition of Scottish political thought and practice that in turn defines Scotland's unique constitutional – and cultural – identity' (Mason, 2014: 266), and yet for over 350 years, no-one referred to it explicitly. Its re-emergence today is manifest to its resonance with modern political sentiments. As Dauvit Broun observed: 'It is almost impossible for us to read the most famous words of The Declaration of Arbroath without hearing in them the echo of our own modern notions of national self-determination' (Broun, 2003: 1).

The Declaration of Arbroath stands as Scotland's foundation myth: *this* is who we are, and where we have come from. An 'embarrassingly brazen piece of propaganda' (Broun, ibid.) it may have been, but its ideological power cannot be denied. A fourteenth-century letter from barons to the Pope asking him to restrain the King of the English has a claim to be 'one of the masterpieces of political rhetoric of all time', as the judge, Lord Cooper, wrote in 1951. Lord Cooper of Culross is probably better known for his ruling, as Lord President in the case *MacCormick* v. *Lord Advocate* in 1953 anent 'the numeral' describing 'Elizabeth the Second of the United Kingdom of Great Britain', on the grounds that in Scotland that there had never been an 'Elizabeth the First'.

In the course of his ruling, Lord Cooper observed:

> The principle of the unlimited sovereignty of Parliament is a distinctively English principle which has no counterpart in Scottish constitutional law. It derives its origin from Coke and Blackstone, and was widely popularised during the nineteenth century by Bagehot and Dicey, the latter having stated the doctrine in its classic form in his Law of the Constitution. Considering that the Union legislation extinguished the Parliaments of Scotland and England and replaced

them by a new Parliament, I have difficulty in seeing why it should have been supposed that the new Parliament of Great Britain must inherit all the peculiar characteristics of the English Parliament but none of the Scottish Parliament, as if all that happened in 1707 was that Scottish representatives were admitted to the Parliament of England. That is not what was done.[4]

Lord Cooper was no conventional 'nationalist', and indeed served as a unionist (in modern parlance, Conservative) member of parliament for Edinburgh West from 1935 until 1941 when he became Lord Justice Clerk, and in 1947 Lord Justice General and Lord President of the Court of Session.

SHAPING SCOTLAND

Why should a sociologist bother to look at this early history of Scotland? Does it really matter? First and foremost, it establishes where, and when, 'Scotland' came to be thought of as a nation, and makes the point that the nation was an 'imagined community' (Anderson, 1996) as early as the thirteenth century. We should not get too hung up on what being 'Scottish' meant at that time. Being able to establish Scotland in meaningful terms well before the modern period marks it as one of Europe's oldest nations. Second, this Scotland derived from diverse peoples and territories, which were united under the authority of the Crown, and yet without ceding absolute legitimacy to that institution. To be sure, all nations have diversity in common, even though it behoves them to claim unity in diversity. From such a reading of Scottish history derived the belief in the 'sovereignty of the people', set against the sovereignty of parliament, otherwise the English Crown.[5] To reinforce the point, the Crown was imagined as a legal entity, as the *state*; we are not referring to the person of the monarch.

Did people in the twelfth and thirteenth centuries actually think of themselves as 'Scots'? Surely this is to impose modern conceptions on a past we cannot know. The first thing to be said is that in modern Scotland we live quite happily with multiple meanings of what a Scot is: by birth, descent and residence, and we know that each of these is sufficiently distinct from each other, but they are also valid in their own right (McCrone and Bechhofer, 2015). National identity is a bit like a game of cards;

you play the hand you're dealt, according to the circumstances, and as best you can. In any case, being born in a country, the prime criterion for national membership, is not something any of us has chosen for ourselves. Broun's point (1998: 11) about the thirteenth century that 'Scotland and the Scots are, first and foremost, images which have been adapted and recreated according to the experiences and aspirations of the society to which they related' is just as valid in the twenty-first century.

Although it is a much more difficult task to know what the thirteenth-century peasant made of being Scottish, the historical consensus does seem to be that at least the 'middling folk' and foot soldiers of Scotland at that time certainly made something of it (Broun, 1998; Ferguson, 1998; Stringer and Grant, 1995). The concept of the 'community of the realm'[6] – *communitas regni* – appears to have been a sufficiently understood concept to rally the nation against the English foe, just as there is support for the existence of national consciousness in England in the Middle Ages (Greenfeld, 1993; Hastings, 1997). Think too of a modern example: the invasion of eastern Ukraine by the Russian state in 2022 has helped to 'make Ukrainians', to unite into a people a historic divide between east and west Ukraine (Hrytsak, 2023).

In short, the conditions for generating national awareness *contra* the 'other' were surely there for Scotland and England in mutual context, as Grant observed: 'in the two medieval kingdoms of the British Isles, the people were involved along with their elites in their countries' wars; in France, they were not' (1994: 95), which is why 'making Frenchmen' took so much longer (see Eugen Weber, who titled his book *Peasants into Frenchmen*, 1977). The point was also made by Adrian Hastings (1997) in his analysis of the development of national consciousness in these islands. Thus it was that the designs of the English state on its neighbours, particularly Scotland, helped to mould diverse peoples into a single nation in the face of this common threat; again, much like the invasion of the Ukraine by Russia in 2022. History repeats itself.

Origin Myth-stories

The Scots and English, however, did not settle down contentedly into 'mutual other' status, especially as far as England was concerned. Bill Ferguson's monumental study *The Identity of the Scottish Nation* (1998) showed that the ideological battle raged as fiercely as the military one, and for longer. To twenty-first century ears, debates about the ancient origins of peoples may seem arcane, even somewhat racist. The myth-stories, however, were deadly serious, because whether or not peoples had a right to exist depended on winning the ideological battle of origins. Much rested on who the founding peoples were judged to be. Geoffrey of Monmouth's *Historia Regum Britanniae* ('History of the Kings of Britain') written in the twelfth century was long accepted as the standard history of that realm, and helped to promote feelings of Englishness to the considerable advantage of the state. It was, in essence, ideological, promotional, history.

By the late eighteenth and early nineteenth centuries, 'Pictomania' had come to serve the views of those such as John Pinkerton that the true aboriginals were the Picts – Teutons, and, *ergo*, they were English. James Macpherson, who claimed to have discovered the Gaelic poems of Ossian, fell foul of anti-Scottish feeling in the eighteenth century which was aimed at denying a distinct origin-myth to the Scots at the point they entered the British Union. Best to put them in their place.

Lest we think that this sort of historiography is well and truly over, Bill Ferguson reminded us that the English historian Hugh Trevor-Roper was still employing Celtophobic arguments in the 1970s to undermine the claims to Scottish autonomy which were growing in that decade. Ferguson, on the other hand, says that 'there can be little doubt ... that the national identity of the Scots sprang from an early Gaelic tribal root that first flourished in Ireland' (1998: 306).

It is almost impossible to avoid much of this historiography from becoming subordinated to one political claim or another. Ferguson, for his part, concluded: '... Scottishness was never exclusive, but, on the contrary, has always been highly absorptive, a quality that it retains even in the vastly different circumstances of today' (1998: 305). There are echoes here of Willie McIlvanney's claim that Scots are a 'mongrel nation', drawn from many roots, but primarily concerned with the future rather than the past; a concern, to borrow Stuart Hall's nice play on words, with *routes* rather than *roots* (Hall, 1992). Those who wish to argue that an ethnically diverse Scotland is the morally correct one, and no barrier to common identity, are thus able to mobilise this reading of history to considerable effect. The debate about origins came to matter significantly when issues of relations between the peoples of these islands became salient.

The End of Scotland?

So why, in this context, should Scotland have acceded to union with England? There is a conventional historiography, largely nationalist, which saw the Union in the words of the Earl of Seafield, one of the signatories to the Treaty document, as *ane end of ane auld sang*. The answer, however, lies in *realpolitik*.

Above all, the British parliament was acceptable because it did not interfere, and thus guaranteed liberty, of both religious and civil sorts. The threat of an autocratic and Jacobite Stuart regime was seen off, and the incorporation – 'pacification' – of the Highland *Gàidhealtachd* after the battle of Culloden in 1746 ensured Protestant supremacy. The forceable incorporation of the Highlands was one of the few instances of the British state using its considerable military muscle at home rather than abroad.

Union meant that Scots had a national right to be treated as equals, and it is to that belief, more often than not, which modern nationalists have appealed (Broun, 2023). In the ensuing centuries 'unionists', like the judge Lord Cooper, went to great lengths to assert the theoretical independence of Scotland, while 'nationalists' went to similar lengths to argue for equal treatment under the Union. Unionism and nationalism are not polar opposites.

We have moved, almost inexorably in our own times, from a dominant view for much of the twentieth century that Scotland and England were partners in Union complementary not antithetical, to one in which the opposite is the case. This reflects the rise of political nationalism north of the border, but also in England, where English nationalism requires to be taken seriously, if critically (McCrone, 2023). In fact, sharing an island generated a much older pedigree, it seems, according to Dauvit Broun. He observes that John Mair's *History of Greater Britain, both England and Scotland*, published in 1521, is a history of Britain from a Scottish point of view:

> Although Scotland's British identity has been difficult to detect in late-medieval historiography, its presence is clear. It offers a fresh

perspective on John Mair's celebrated history that invites us to see it not only as a precursor to unionism but also as an expression of a long established—if infrequently articulated—Scottish identification with Britain. (Broun, 2023)

Furthermore, '... appropriating Britain as an extension of your country is not unique to England: the Scots did it, too'. This reinforces Colin Kidd's view that Union did not entail capitulation so much as a common acknowledgement of partnership and shared interests.

What Scotland got out of eventual union, first, in 1603, and then in 1707, this *'mariage de raison'* (roughly translated as a 'marriage of convenience'), was a solution to many of its most pressing economic problems, and a share in an expanding 'British' empire, so successful that many in England complained of 'Scots on the make'[8]. The defence of autonomous civil society with its institutions of law, education, religion and civil life was the achievement of union, and the reason it lasted for so long.

This independent civil society, however, was not a national expression in and of itself. That was to come much later, and is quite another story, but without understanding the union of 1707 for what it was, we cannot make sense of our politics in the twenty-first century. Even asserting that it was a 'treaty' of union,[9] rather than conquest (as in Wales and Ireland) makes a historical point with much political force. Thus did nationalists and unionists alike insist on the constitutional equality of Scotland with England.

BECOMING BRITISH

In spite of popular opposition to the Union in the early years of the eighteenth century, it proved in the nineteenth century to be relatively easy to re-fashion the Scots into British. The point was that Scots became British *as well as* continuing to be Scots, not *despite* that fact. The Jacobite legacy always had the power to be a potent nationalist myth, but, as Richard Finlay (1994) has observed, that was a step much too far. In the first place, Jacobite ideology could not be moulded into the Scottish Presbyterian spirit: it was too Catholic and Episcopalian for that. In the second place, Jacobite adherence to the divine right of kings could not be worked into meritocratic and liberal ideology. And finally, it contradicted the notion of a bloodless union. While Jacobitism has always had complex potential as an alternative Scottishness, although Christopher Smout judges that 'it is a sad misconstruction of Scottish history to see in the Jacobite movement some appeal to an archaic, anti-capitalist, anti-improvement, green past' (1994: 110), it was too far removed from the experiences of most Scots for the connection to be made.[10]

Rather, Scottishness in the nineteenth century was re-fashioned around three pillars of identity: church, state and empire. Protestantism helped to 'forge', in both senses of the word, the business of being British. Most people in Wales, Scotland and England, Linda Colley has observed, 'defined themselves as Protestants struggling for survival against the foremost Catholic power. They defined themselves against the French as they imagined them to be, superstitious, militarist, decadent and unfree' (Colley, 1992: 5). That, in essence, is why most people in Ireland could not consider themselves British, nor were they permitted to be in any case. Scottish Protestantism proved to be an important seedbed for the three dominant political creeds from the nineteenth century onwards: Liberalism, Unionism, and latterly, Labourism.

RECOVERING SCOTLAND

The 'Scottish question', however, did not go away. 'When was Scotland?' became highly salient again in the final quarter of the twentieth century, our third 'narrative moment'. With hindsight, and in the light of political developments in the twenty-first century, the recovery of a parliament and the rise and rise of the Scottish National Party (SNP), it might seem strange to assert that Scotland 'died' as a meaningful entity after the Union of 1707. Nevertheless, a high degree of cultural pessimism has permeated Scottish thought for much of the last two hundred years. Pessimists argued that Scotland was 'over' as a self-governing civil society, having thrown its lot in with England. David Hume deliberately titled his mid-eighteenth-century book *A History of England* (and not a *History of Britain*). He was not making a category error, but implying that 'England' was culturally and politically dominant because it was one of the most progressive societies on earth. England was conceived of as a 'mature, all-round thought-world' (Nairn, 1977: 156–7) of which Scotland aspired to be part.

Cultural Pessimism

And so cultural pessimism has run deep among Scottish intellectuals, as we shall explore in Chapter 8. The perceived absence of a rounded culture, reflecting the Scottish/British split, mapping as it does on to the culture/politics split, long had an appeal. Writing in the 1930s Edwin Muir saw a Scotland 'gradually being emptied of its population, its spirit, its wealth, industry, art, intellect, and innate character' (Muir, 1980 [1935]: 3).

The most powerful and dominant analysis of Scottish culture was Tom Nairn's *The Break-Up of Britain* published first in 1977. This is a view of Scottish culture, epitomised in Walter Scott, divided between 'heart' (representing the past, romance, 'civil society') and 'head' (the present and future, reason, and, by dint of that, the British state). There is the Caledonian Antisyzygy, a term borrowed by Hugh MacDiarmid from Gregory Smith's 1919 characterisation of Scottish literature as containing an antithesis of the real and the fantastic; a concept without which no modern version of Scotland is complete.

Thus, the image of Scotland as a divided and unhealthy society became a common one in Scottish literature which acted as a key carrier of Scottish identity. Scottish culture could never, in this conventional wisdom, be an 'organic whole'. Instead, as Cairns Craig observes, it was common to see Scotland's as 'fundamentally a dead literature, the literature of a nation which once existed but now has no independent identity' (Craig, 1999: 16). Much of the commentary was, hence, elegiac.

Why should any of this be connected to the question: when was Scotland? – because if, to all intents and purposes, Scotland was 'over', then the crucial link between culture and politics had been irrevocably broken. Does this matter? It does, because it seemed to explain why political nationalism in Scotland did not take the classical form.

So here we have an intriguing puzzle. Scotland does not fit conventional accounts of the rise of nationalism, at least in terms of classical timings. It was not until the final quarter of the twentieth century that a strong nationalist party challenged for political power. Furthermore, it seemed to be strong on 'politics' and weak on 'culture'.

We can, however, turn the argument on its head. Far from being divided, even schizophrenic, without a cultural whole,

Scotland can be deemed normal. That claim has been controversial for many decades now: at least since the nationalist cultural revival of the 1920s, the belief has gained currency that Scotland in the nineteenth century was subservient to England. This belief assumes that the only sure sign of not being subservient would have been a developed demand for an independent parliament. Lindsay Paterson's argument is to the contrary: '... it is close to the image that middle-class Scots of the nineteenth century had of themselves. They had real autonomy' (1994: 70).

Imagining Moments

Let us take stock of the argument so far. I have chosen three iconic moments in Scottish history to show the following:

First, 'Scotland' was a meaningful entity as early as the thirteenth century, reflected in the wars of independence, which helped to shape Scots as a people. This is not to imply that thirteenth-century peasants relate to Scotland in the same way as twenty-first century Scots; in any case, how would we ever know? The most we can say is that, like many peoples in the world, war against an Other helped to make Scots. The process of Othering is vital to imagining any nation. Being invaded by that Other, whether Russia in the twenty-first century or England in the thirteenth century, mobilises the population to stand against them, and in the course of things, discover who they are, and who they are not. It is a forging process. So it is a testament to the ideological success of a document like the Declaration of Arbroath in 1320 that many have seen it as the precursor for later such declarations (of independence).

The second iconic moment was the Treaty of Union in 1707, at which point Scotland technically ceased to exist as a state; but then, for that matter, so did England – in theoretical terms. It mattered more to Scotland as the smaller country because the Union was, by and large, an incorporating one, although Scotland retained hold of its civil society institutions. These were to provide the bases for civil autonomy, and ultimately, the recovery of a law-making parliament in 1999. Indubitably, Scotland continued to exist after the Union. Its national identity was underwritten by institutional autonomy; the recovery of state-ness came later. Whatever the outcome of the Union, we can say that Scotland was *not* over. As the oldest elected member of the 1999 Scottish parliament, Winnie Ewing opened the session with the words: 'I want to start with the words that I have always wanted either to say or to hear someone else say – the Scottish Parliament, which adjourned on March 25, 1707, is hereby reconvened.' Scotland, she was saying, had simply been paused.

The final moment came in the last quarter of the twentieth century. Despite claims that Scottish culture had ceased to exist, and hence could not underwrite the recovery of statehood, even short of independence, the re-connection of culture and politics could not be denied. As Cairns Craig commented:

> In academic terms, the re-imagining of Scotland took the form of the recovery of the sense of the Scottish past as precisely the opposite of the history of negation inherited from the early part of the 20th century. Scottish history and culture were reconceived in terms not of negations but in terms of fundamental continuities. (Craig, 2001: 19–20)

It is this 'moment' which will concern us here, the final quarter of the twentieth century.

UNDERSTANDING SCOTLAND

So how are we to understand Scotland in terms of its sociology? What analytical tools do we need? Let us focus on three interconnected concepts: nation, society and state.

Scotland as Nation?

Following Benedict Anderson (1996), 'nation' usefully as an 'imagined community' has four dimensions:

- It is *imagined* because the members of even the smallest nation will never know most of their fellow-members, meet them, or even hear of them, yet in the minds of each lives the image of their communion.
- The nation is imagined as *limited* because even the largest of them, encompassing perhaps a billion living human beings, has finite, if elastic boundaries, beyond which lie other nations.
- It is imagined as *sovereign* because the concept was born in an age in which Enlightenment and Revolution were destroying

the legitimacy of the divinely ordained hierarchical dynastic realm.
- ... it is imagined as a *community*, because, regardless of the actual inequality and exploitation that may prevail in each, the nation is always conceived as a deep, horizontal comradeship.

Anderson talked of nations being 'imagined communities' because they require a sense of belonging which is both horizontal and vertical, in place and in time. The nation not only implies an affinity with those currently living, but with dead generations. The idea of the nation is to be conceived of, says Anderson, 'as a solid community moving steadily down (or up) history' (1996: 26); calendrically, so to speak. This idea of historical continuity is a vitally important part of the nation as imagined community. It implies links with long-dead ancestors, echoing Anthony Smith's words 'the nation becomes the constant renewal and retelling of our tale by each generation of our descendants' (Smith, 1986: 208). That is why paying attention to the process of imagining Scotland as far back as the thirteenth century makes sense; it is a process of recovering the past in the pursuit of a future; roots into routes again.

There can be little doubting the ideological power of Scotland as a nation in cultural terms. It implies that Scotland is not simply a collection of rocks, earth and water, but a transcendent idea which runs through history, reinterpreting that history to fit the concerns of each present. To be sure, it is not unique. To say that Scotland (and Wales, Ireland or England for that matter) are figments of the imagination is not to imply that they are false, but that they require to be interpreted as ideas, made and re-made, rather than treated simply as actual places.

Scotland as Society?

Our second concept is that of 'society'. Thus, it is not simply equated with the 'state', with 'political society' but rather, with '*civil*' society'. Civil society refers to these relatively dense networks of organisations and institutions resulting from, and in turn, framing the day-to-day interactions of people. As Ernest Gellner (1994: 7–8) put it, civil society is the social space located between the *tyranny of kin* and the *tyranny of kings*; between the intimacy of family life and the impersonal power of the state. It is related to the state, the political level, but is not coterminous with it. Neither does civil society equate with the nation, for a sense of nation-ness is sustained by institutional autonomy, not the other way round (McCrone, 2010: 184).

We can see, then, how the assertion of nationalism derives not from elemental emotions based on historic memories, but from the day-to-day contemporary social associations between people. It arises from patterns of sociality structured by organisational life, in essence with civility. A nation is an 'imagined community' *because* of its associational and institutional distinctiveness, and, as a result, it follows Durkheim's definition that: 'a society is not constituted by the mass who comprise it ... but above all by the idea it has of itself' (Fournier, 2013: 625–6).

This sense of being a nation is sustained by its sociality, and together, nation and society may encourage a quest for some kind of state-like characteristics even if these fall short of what conventionally is called independence. There is considerable, and repeated, interaction between 'society', 'nation' and 'state' – the social, cultural and political levels, but they remain distinct levels; we cannot subsume one into the other. We can argue that the assertion of nationalism in Scotland, of nation-ness, derives not from some elemental set of emotions based on historic memories – ethnicity, if you prefer – but on the day-to-day contemporary social associations of people, on patterns of sociability structured by organisational life –in education, law, etc. – what I have called 'civility'.

Civil society, then, comes to refer to the relatively dense networks of organisations and institutions resulting from, and in turn, framing day-to-day interactions of people. That is the meaning of Gellner's distinction, between the 'tyranny of kin' (the familial, the intimate) and the 'tyranny of kings' (the state and its apparatus). Society is the key intermediate realm, and is held together by the everyday relations of people and institutions as they go about their lives. It also invokes *demos*, the sense that people are bound together by sharing common procedures and manners of thought, in contrast to *ethnos*, which places the focus much more on cultural homogeneity, and tribal identity.

Despite subsequently being hijacked in the cause of extreme individualism and private self-interest, Adam Smith was at pains to stress that much of the authority of the social order derived from 'society' rather than 'government'. As Jonathan Hearn observed: 'we can see the formation of a familiarly modern conception of "society" as a reality *sui generis*, as a system with its own emergent rules and order, not created from above, and also more than "the sum of its parts"' (Hearn, 2015: 15).

Thus, 'society' is not the state, nor, indeed, the economy, but sustains both state and economy because it operates on the basis of social trust between people. Society, then, *precedes* the political and the economic. Without social trust, state and economy cannot hold. Hearn observes: 'Very far from suggesting a world of individual atoms artificially bounded by constraining states, [Smith] suggests that "nations" and their states map onto the underlying principles of propinquity and sympathy, providing a certain intractable aspect of social structure.' (ibid. 7).

Civil Society and Nationalism

The idea of 'civil society' is vested with normative and analytical significance to explain the rise of neo-nationalism, challenges to the British state (in Scotland and Wales), the Spanish state (in Catalonia and Euskadi (Basque Country)), as well as in France, the classic bastion of the Jacobin state. Whether badged as 'nationalism' or 'regionalism', it became clear that the more developed and autonomous associational structures in these territories, the greater the challenges to central state legitimacy.

Scotland – and to a lesser extent, Wales – had a framework of autonomous institutions, of law, religion, social governance dating from the Treaty of Union with England in 1707, and much developed subsequently. Since that Union, Scotland has continued its separate system of law, jealously guarded by its judges and legal establishment (recall Lord Cooper's comments on the nature of the Union between Scotland and England); also part of 'the state', or more precisely the 'semi-state', that collection of government and quasi-government departments in the Scottish Office, which was, at least nominally, until 1999 governed by ministers from the ruling party at Westminster.

The Scottish Semi-state

Nowadays, Scotland has a parliament and its own directly elected ministers in control of the bureaucracy of state, if not a 'state' in the orthodox sense of the term, enough to describe Scotland as an understated nation, but a state nonetheless in high degree. We can, then, think in terms of *degrees* of stateness, and Scotland has more of that than it used to have pre-1999, though not as much as most of its people would like, if we gauge that by public opinion.[11] We can conclude that the precise dividing line between 'state' and '(civil) society' is unclear, but there is little doubt that they are not synonyms of each other.

Civil society, then, is the social hinge between economic capital and the political apparatus of the state. As Craig Calhoun observed: '... from the point of view of democracy, it is essential to retain in the notion of civil society some idea of a social realm which is neither dominated by state power nor simply responsive to the systematic features of capitalism' (1993: 310–1).

If 'civil society' is neither state nor market, is it simply a synonym for the nation? Not quite. If anything, feeling and being 'national' is the *outcome* of the process of civil societalisation, sustained by patterns of sociability which teach us how to behave appropriately. The feeling of being a national, of belonging to a community, is the result of the channels and mechanisms which shape us and make us feel that way rather than the other way round. As Bernard Crick pointed out in his classic book *In Defence of Politics*, there has to be a public sphere for negotiation between political organisations which are neither the hidebound creatures of the state nor of narrow social interests. In a telling comment, Crick observed: 'Democracy is one element in politics; if it seeks to be everything, it destroys politics, turning "harmony into mere unison", reducing "a theme to a single beat"' (1992: 73).

Autonomous Civil Society

To sum up so far: 'civil society' is related to, but not the creature of the state, the market and the nation. It cannot be reduced to the level of the political (state), to the economic (market), or the cultural (nation). It stands in contradistinction to these even though it might appear to be their creature. Still less is civil society reducible to the private sphere. Civil society can also claim to precede rather than derive from the state and political realm, can unmake political authority and re-fashion it. That is why the concept was pressed into political service in Scotland (as well as eastern Europe) in the 1980s and 1990s, and why doctrines of popular sovereignty in the 'People's Claim of Right' were re-imagined.

Re-fashioning the State

In late twentieth-century Scotland, it became plain that the political realm was at odds with the informal and quasi-formal networks of civil society; in short, the British state was perceived to be unresponsive to Scotland's needs and demands across the socio-economic spectrum, from professional bodies, voluntary groups, to trades unions. There was what was labelled the 'democratic deficit', the fact that no matter how people in Scotland voted at Westminster elections, they got a government elected by people in England; not unreasonable, given that they represented 85 per cent of the UK population.

The task, however, was not to overthrow the state, but to re-fashion one – parliament and government – more in keeping with the wishes of the electorate. Thus, people think of themselves as Scots because they have been educated, governed and embedded in a Scottish way. It is a matter of government, not of sentiment; and, if anything, the latter derives from the former. In any case, Scotland had never been short of 'government'.

The remarkable growth of separate political administration for Scotland since 1886 has undoubtedly helped to reinforce this sense of 'Scotland'. It is easier to visualise what a separate Scotland would look like precisely because by the 1980s the Scottish Office had become a Scottish semi-state with a powerful administrative apparatus. The proponents of devolution in the 1979 referendum could set out their case for political autonomy in terms of the need to extend democratic accountability over this bureaucratic structure; and the 2014 referendum on independence was an argument about how much 'sovereignty' modern Scotland required while remaining within the European Union (McCrone and Keating, 2021).

Throughout the twentieth century, increased agitation for reform in Scotland resulted in increased responsibilities accruing to the Scottish Office to the extent that *de facto* Scottish self-government, or 'limited sovereignty' as Paterson called it, resulted. The demands for democratic accountability over this Scottish semi-state in the late twentieth century represented recognition of the limits which bureaucratic devolution had reached, and in turn helped to bring about the devolved parliament in 1999.

At this level, Scotland plainly existed as a political-administrative unit, as a governed system defined by the remit of the Scottish Office. In just over one hundred years of its existence, the Scottish Office had given a political meaning to Scotland. There is irony in this, because by treating Scotland as an object of administration, the Westminster government had to live with its political consequences. If the Scottish Office had never been created, it would have been much more difficult to address 'Scotland' as a meaningful political unit. The northern territory could have been handled as the North British regional province of the central British state, much like Wales until 1965 when the Labour government created the Welsh Office, although the power and influence of civil society could never be ignored. It is significant that attempts to refer to Scotland as 'North Britain' and England and Wales as 'South Britain'[12] after the Union of Crowns in 1603 came to nothing.[13] This was reflected in the creation of the Scottish Office in 1885, and the building of St Andrews House in Edinburgh in 1939.

The Exceptions Prove the Rule

What of the hyphenated 'nation-state' which is in common currency in political as well as sociological thought? States are described as such in a fairly unthinking manner; indeed, the terms 'nation' and 'state' are frequently linguistically interchangeable. Strictly speaking, however, the nation-state implies that the cultural concept 'nation' maps neatly on to the political one, 'state'; in other words, that a 'people' with a common culture and a sense of imagined community seek self-determination in having an independent state.

In effect, there are few states to which the description applies. Even taking a simple linguistic measure, there is a distinct lack of correspondence between nation and state. Thus, the same language will be spoken in different states (English, German, French to take but three), and within states there will be multiple languages spoken (Belgium, Canada, Spain). The classic case of a multilingual state is Switzerland, usually treated as 'an anomaly', the case which proves the rule that every state needs a cultural nation, or rather, a dominant ethnicity. Andreas Wimmer makes the point: 'Switzerland ... presents a good example of a fully nationalised modern state built on an ethnically heterogeneous basis – contradicting the idea that industrialism or democracy demand cultural and linguistic homogeneity to work properly' (Wimmer, 2002: 223). The point he is making is that matters of language and ethnicity never became politicised, and that Switzerland became a 'nation by will' (*Willensnation*). Wimmer observes:

> this small and somewhat bizarre country, surrounded by powerful states each ruling in the name of a single, distinct language community, was in fact revealing what these other states were hiding: the true nature of the national bond, made out of political spirit rather than cultural essence; out of the perception of commonality rather than objective distinctiveness. (Wimmer, 2011: 720)

The point is not that Scotland is some analogue of Switzerland, but that similar principles applied as early as the thirteenth century; that the national bond is made out of 'political spirit' and not 'cultural essence'.

So why is the term 'nation-state' in such common currency? – largely because it represents an ideological – aspirational – claim, that states which represent nations are somehow natural. Few states are nationally cohesive; having made France, Germany, Italy, the USA, the UK and so on, it was necessary to 'make' nationals. Even if we do not adopt linguistic criteria for nationness, it is hard to find the appropriate correspondence between nation and state. Thus, the UK is not a nation-state, for it contains distinct nations – England, Scotland, Wales and Northern Ireland[14] – and was constructed as a state-nation, rather than vice versa. Or rather we might see the UK as a plurinational state. As Michael Keating observed: 'The UK is not a state, unitary or federal, but a union and as such does not need a hard core or sovereignty or purpose' (Keating, 2021, 50).

It is a reflection of the dominance of the nation-state idea, however, that it has such common currency in academic writing. Critics like Wimmer and Glick Schiller argue that 'nationally bounded societies are taken to be the naturally given entities to study'; that 'methodological nationalism' abounds. Thus, 'the social sciences were captured by the apparent naturalness and givenness of a world divided into societies along the lines of nation-states' (Wimmer and Glick Schiller, 2002: 304). Note, however, the unproblematic use of the term 'nation-states' in their comment. States have lost some of their power to transnational corporations and supranational organisations; they have been transformed by in-migration, and yet, the authors claim, social science continues to treat them as the unit of analysis. There is irony in the argument that we should avoid 'methodological nationalism' on the grounds that the nation-state has internal cultural and social unity. The irony rests on the fact that understanding sub-state nationalism (in, for example, Scotland, Wales, Euskadi, Catalonia, Quebec) runs far less risk of methodological nationalism than the implicit variety attaching to self-styled nation-states of western Europe, Britain included.

Societies which are not states have a perceived fragility which conventional nation-states do not have. Indeed, they are frequently deemed to be 'over', to belong to the detritus of history (see Norman Davies's book *Vanished Kingdoms: the History of Half-Forgotten Europe*, 2011) with little or no future. This matters because what is deemed the 'proper' study of particular societies depends on what we consider a 'society' to be; and much of writing about Scotland has had to take this premise into account.

CONCLUSION

Scotland, we can now see, never really ended, but survived and developed as a civil society within a state whose major focus was on imperial ventures in which Scots played a major, and often shameful, part. Airbrushing out awkward history, such as slavery, has been part of that process.[15] The fact that this empire itself is now 'history', and new processes of cultural and political revival are transparent have made the old pessimistic order *passé*. The interweaving of social, political, cultural and economic processes means that studying Scotland is not the simple preserve of sociologists, political scientists, cultural historians and economists. It is the fruitful interaction of disciplines and perspectives which have reinvigorated the study of Scotland.

The question to be tackled, then, is how Scotland was transformed in modern times. Our argument, now equipped with analytical tools as to what Scotland is, focuses on that key period, the long decade from the 1960s into the 1970s. It is to this that we now turn.

NOTES

1. Gywn Alf Williams wrote a book entitled *When Was Wales?* (1991) which explored the origin and idea of Wales. We can make a similar point about Scotland, and I am grateful to the late Gywn Alf for the suggestion.
2. My essay 'Declaring Arbroath: *atque supra cresidam*', appeared in Klaus Peter Müller (ed.), *Arbroath 1320–2020* (Frankfurt, Lang, 2020).
3. See National Archives of Scotland (<http://www.nas.gov.uk/downloads/declarationArbroath.pdf>). The Latin text reads: '*Quia quamdiu Centum ex nobis viui remanserint, nuncquam Anglorum dominio aliquatenus volumus subiugari. Non enim propter gloriam, diuicias aut honores pugnamus sed propter libertatem solummodo quam Nemo bonus nisi simul cum vita amittit.*'
4. <https://en.wikisource.org/wiki/MacCormick_v_Lord_Advocate>.
5. As in The Claim of Right, 1989 (<https://en.wikipedia.org/wiki/Claim_of_Right_1989>).
6. In the Middle Ages, the 'three estates' of prelates (bishops and abbots), nobles and burgh commissioners were known as the 'community of the realm', a term which translated into the Estates of Parliament, or '*Thrie Estaitis*' in medieval Scots.
7. The Irish term *Gaeltacht* refers to the west of Ireland where Irish (Gaelic) is spoken. The term *Gàidhealtachd* refers more broadly to the area of Gaelic culture in the Scottish Highlands and Islands.
8. See, for example, David Stenhouse's book which uses it as a title, *On the Make* (2004).
9. 'Treaty' is preferred to 'Act' (of Union) because there were separate acts in Scotland and England in the respective parliaments.
10. The claim was made by Murray Pittock in his book *The Invention of Scotland: the Stuart Myth and the Scottish Identity* (1991).
11. At the time of writing (late 2024), almost half of people in Scotland support independence, despite the travails of its political carrier, the SNP (see <https://www.whatscotlandthinks.org>).
12. As for Ireland, the term 'West Brit' became one of mockery.
13. Apart, that is, from the 'North British' hotel in Edinburgh, opened in 1902, which had its name changed in 1991 to *The Balmoral*. Thus ended the last vestige of 'North Britain'.

14. Northern Ireland is included to make the general point, even though its people are 'nationally' divided along political-religious lines, one owing allegiance to Britain and the other to the Republic of Ireland.
15. Scottish historians have only lately woken up to the participation of Scots as enthusiastic slavers. See Tom Devine's edited book *Recovering Scotland's Slavery Past: The Caribbean Connection* (2015); and David Alston's *Slaves and Highlanders* (2021) for excellent accounts.

3

Transformations

A new generation comes up that will know them not, except as a memory in a song, they passed with the things that seemed good to them with loves and desires that grow dim and alien in the days to be.

Lewis Grassic Gibbon had the Rev. Colquhoun speak those words on Blawearie Brae, in the final pages of his novel *Sunset Song*.[1] They have wider implications for us, for they speak of fundamental social change, just as applicable to our own age.

With hindsight, we can identify how Scotland was transformed. Hindsight, of course, can mislead us into thinking that social change[2] was much more clear-cut than it was, that the new Scotland was significantly different from the old. Furthermore, dating it from the 1970s might lead us to believe that key changes suddenly happened in that decade, when, rather like a musical composition, the old and the new were interwoven in major and minor keys. Social changes are not date-precise; they are processual, but it is helpful to associate these with the *longue durée*, in this case, from about the late 1960s into the 1970s and beyond. A useful image is to see social change common to most western industrial societies washing over Scotland, impacting differentially over its social, economic and political landscape previously shaped by historical processes. The ways in which social change had an impact depended on what was there beforehand.

The purpose of this chapter is to sketch out briefly the key dimensions of social change which happened in Scotland, and how these connected up, with a view to exploring them in detail in the following chapters of the book.

COMPREHENDING SOCIAL CHANGE

So what were these changes? It is common to think of western societies as sharing in *Les Trente Glorieuses*, between 1945 to 1975. The term, coined by the French scholar Jean Fourastié as the title of his book,[3] explained the demographic, social and cultural transformations of France in the post-war years. This was a period of social and economic catch-up, following inter-war stagnation, and one in which demographic change, notably smaller family sizes, geographical mobility from countryside to city, coupled with economic transformation and new employment opportunities especially for women, re-shaped the family as a unit of consumption as well as production, and nicely captured by Annie Ernaux in her 2008 sociographic novel, *The Years*.[4]

France, of course, was not Scotland, nor Britain. The peasantry in Scotland had long been wiped out (Grassic Gibbon's lament in the quotation above concerns the demise of the peasant class in North-East Scotland after The Great War), but it is a moot point as to whether Scotland had, in relative terms, much of a *Trente Glorieuses*, at least compared with other countries, including England. The challenges to staple heavy industry had begun in the inter-war period, and only war had slowed that process down. Post-war, light engineering and white goods production largely passed Scotland by. The Scottish semi-state in the form of the Scottish Office had begun a programme to promote industrial modernisation in the 1930s, and in that regard, the British state, much more interventionist than anything imagined after the Thatcher years post-1979, took a strongly Scottish form, notably during the war years under the Scottish Secretary of State, Tom Johnston.

The lack of employment opportunities had encouraged many Scots to move, to the rest of the UK, or abroad. In Glasgow, for example, during the 1970s, it is estimated that three-quarters of total net migration went either elsewhere in the UK (mainly to England) or overseas, to Australia, New Zealand or Canada (M. Anderson, 2018, Table 9.4). Indeed, between 1946 and 1971 as many as three-quarters of a million people (in a population of only 5 million) left Scotland, either for England or abroad. That is, in proportional terms, 15 per cent of Scotland's population in only twenty-five years. In relative terms, Scotland's net out-migration rate was never less than two and a half times that of England and Wales. Furthermore, between 1968 and 1988, Scotland's rate of out-migration was three times that of Ireland, conventionally thought of as the classic emigrant state. As Michael Anderson observed: 'the Scottish diaspora is ... the most enduring and pervasive characteristic of Scotland's population history, and has been more for than 200 years' (Anderson, 2018: 124).

Indeed, we might conclude that Scotland's *Trente Glorieuses* was largely exported abroad. As rates of natural increase (births over deaths) flatlined and even fell, and out-migration continued especially among the young and skilled, there could have been little sense in Scotland of 'you've never had it so good'. Tom Nairn observed that: 'The British equivalent of France's post-war *trente glorieuses* produced restlessness and a desire for liberation among Scots too. A form of political nationalism appeared in the 1960s' (Nairn, 1998: 88). The question, of course, is how that came about, which is the task we have set ourselves here.

In any case, we can never tell whether British people actually thought that they had never had it so good, but as a political *zeitgeist* Macmillan's *bon mots* undoubtedly struck a chord. In Scotland that was a different matter. The British state did what it and development grants could do to persuade industry to relocate to Scotland, while attempting to shore up industries such as shipbuilding and coal mining, the historic staples of Scottish industry. The process of de-industrialisation, and the desperate attempts by government to persuade foreign companies to locate in Scotland is expertly told by Jim Phillips, Valerie Wright and Jim Tomlinson in their book *Deindustrialisation and the Moral Economy in Scotland since 1955* (2023). Note the reference to the moral economy, making the point that there is more to the process than a narrow accounting calculus. Emigration still beckoned; it was wired in to 'getting on' – which meant, by and large, getting out. 'In a country with a long tradition of emigration and where most people had family or other personal contacts in England and overseas, it was also a significant spur to high levels of migration' (Anderson, 2018: 429).

The Scottish arm of the state, meanwhile, embarked on a programme of re-housing, encouraging local authorities like Glasgow to 're-develop', which meant knocking down swathes of inner-city housing, deemed sub-standard, and relocating people to the peripheral housing schemes ('estates' did not quite describe the urban deserts, housing-at-all-costs, but with very little urban infrastructure). The novelist Willie McIlvanney captured that policy and its outcomes in his novel *Laidlaw*, speaking through his eponymous character:

> You think of Glasgow. At each of its four corners, this kind of housing-scheme. There's the Drum and Easterhouse and Pollock and Castlemilk. You've got the biggest housing-scheme in Europe here. And what's there? Hardly anything but houses. Just architectural dumps where they unload people like slurry. Penal Architecture. (McIlvanney, 1977: 32)

The building of huge housing schemes on the periphery rapidly led them to becoming clusters of multiple deprivation, with living conditions neither conducive to good social integration nor positive mental health:

> many of these areas and also many parts of the once-booming industrial heartlands of the West of Scotland, did not benefit to anything like the same extent from the greater security and higher living standards on offer elsewhere in Scotland and above all in the Midlands and South of England. (Anderson, 2018: 430)

Differential out-migration simply exacerbated the problem, because it was skilled workers who were most likely to get up and leave.

Industrial Transformation

Behind these demographic shifts lay a story of industrial decline. There is a view that Scotland suffered from being unduly specialised in terms of its economy, that membership of the British state required it to carry out particular industrial functions. It was, however, not the case that, in terms of its economic history, Scotland had an industrial structure which was particularly specialised with respect to the wider British economy. In fact, Scotland mirrored Britain's industrial structure, and was, if anything, more 'British' than other standard economic regions within the UK. We will explore the details of this argument in Chapter 5, but it is important to reinforce that important point here because it frames how we should understand Scotland.

The key to that understanding is that Scotland became an industrial capitalist society within the context of a *laissez-faire* British imperial state. Scotland was, for a time, especially well-adapted to benefit from Britain's highly advantageous structural position within a world economy, itself shaped around Britain's interests, and Scotland's capitalists took advantage of the economic opportunities which the empire afforded. Scotland was, in industrial terms, British. In fact, Scotland was so *over-adapted* to imperial opportunities in the nineteenth century that the collapse of the economy after the First World War was catastrophic for Scotland. Hence, we can explain the roots of Scotland's economic decline in the *surfeit* of imperialism rather than because of clientage or dependence.

The extreme localisation of the effects of this collapse within Scotland in the 1920s and 1930s stemmed from the degree of regional specialisation which had occurred *within* Scotland prior to the war, for significant specialisation had taken place within Scotland, notably in the nineteenth century. Thus, it was that counties dependent on engineering and shipbuilding such as Lanarkshire, Renfrewshire and Dunbartonshire suffered most from the economic downturn, as well as the coal mining communities of West Lothian, Fife and Stirlingshire. Industrial differentiation *within* Scotland was greater than the industrial differentiation of Scotland from the rest of Britain; the traditional specialisations of the nineteenth century remained in key industrial regions of Scotland well into the twentieth century. I will explore this in greater detail in Chapter 5.

In 'industrial' terms, then, Scotland was 'British'. The state had encouraged inward investment. As Douglas Fraser, business correspondent of BBC Scotland observed:

> The post-war period in Scotland saw sustained effort to restructure the economy, and in particular to induce foreign capital to come to Scotland. Governments and a succession of development agencies were proactive in attracting inward investment, and 'persuading' employers to set up plants and facilities. The 1960s wave of such facilities included the Hillman car plant at Linwood in Renfrewshire, the BMC/Leyland truck factory at Bathgate, the steel strip mill at Ravenscraig in Lanarkshire. By 1992, all these had closed. (McCrone, 2017: 216)

State Intervention

These factories were built largely for 'political' reasons, induced by UK governments to come to Scotland. Later in the twentieth century, many of these foreign companies had moved on, closing their Scottish plants: Massey Ferguson in Kilmarnock in 1978, Singer in 1980, the British Aluminium smelter at Invergordon in 1981; and staple industries such as shipbuilding (Upper Clyde Shipbuilders (UCS)) had gone into liquidation, a decade earlier, in 1971. These were the years when the British state, and its Scottish arm, the Scottish Office, practised 'corporatism' built upon state investment and direction (*dirigisme*, in its original French formulation).

After the Second World War, the search for legitimacy became a problem for western industrial states, for they had been drawn more and more into full participation in the economic and social life of societies. A 'corporate bias' was introduced into Britain as early as the second decade of this century, and it flourished after 1945, before falling into disrepute in the 1970s (Middlemas (1979; 1986). The need to coordinate production efforts and to resolve differences of interest between employers and employees laid many of the foundations for corporatist structures. The state, through its civil servants, mobilised groups on the basis of 'the national interest'. Keith Middlemas pointed out that 'those who aspire to and are able to compete at the "altruistic" level of the national interest enter the environs of the state' (1986: 10). Those who remained outside the invisible boundary were defined as self-interested lobbies or pressure groups. Almost regardless of political ideology, the state in the post-war period intervened actively in economic processes, and played a central role in directing economic resources. It was seen as the appropriate instrument for guaranteeing the individual life chances of its citizens, and ironing out social inequalities. In the post-war period, the state in western democracies endeavoured to hitch its star to the quest for economic growth. As Gianfranco Poggi commented:

> The state found a new and different response to the legitimacy problems; increasingly it treated industrial growth per se as possessing intrinsic and commanding political significance, as constituting a necessary and sufficient standard of each state's performance, and thus as justifying further displacement of the state/society line. (Poggi, 1978: 133)

In Britain, the failure of policies to promote economic growth at a fast enough rate had the effect of destabilising the political arrangements of the United Kingdom. The attack by the Left on corporatism was less incisive than that by the Right in the 1970s. It was the rise of Thatcherism and market liberalism which duly swept away state-led corporatism (see Young (1989) for a good account of that process).

The inward investment strategy pursued by the Scottish Development Agency (later, Scottish Enterprise) since the mid-1970s, following the Highlands and Islands Development Board (HIDB) a decade earlier, came to a halt. Both Labour and Conservative parties, albeit with slightly different political twists, had supported state intervention up until this point. The election of the Thatcher governments from 1979 sounded its ideological death-knell, but not before the last hurrah – Silicon Glen – which proved successful more as a marketing slogan than a sustained industrial strategy.

The disintegration of the post-war settlement occurred at a crucial conjuncture in Scotland's history. Scotland had undergone its own version of economic planning. The lessons of Keynesian economic management had been applied to Scotland by the Scottish Office, that 'semi-state' which had acquired more and more administrative power from Whitehall since its foundation in 1886 (Kellas, 1989: 32–3). Given the collapse of indigenous industry after the war, the Scottish Office had played a more directive role in restructuring the economy by means of direct employment, and by offering inducements to foreign capital to locate in Scotland. Like other declining industrial regions[5] of the UK, it relied more heavily on public initiative than on private enterprise. In its desire to act as the midwife of economic regeneration, the British state devolved a significant part of its administrative resources to Scotland.

In the absence of devolved government, the Scottish Office provided a powerful administrative apparatus, or 'negotiated order', as Chris Moore and Simon Booth termed it. They were 'not arguing that Scotland can be seen as a separate political system, but that there is a degree of decision-making and administrative autonomy in certain sectors, and over certain issues a Scottish interest emerges' (Moore and Booth, 1989: 15). Scotland represented a 'negotiated order' operating somewhere between corporatism and free-market pluralism, that the 'Scottish policy community' mediated through the Scottish Office – representing a 'meso-level of the British state' (ibid. 150). Note the echoes here of a 'moral economy' within which such manoeuvrings had to operate (Phillips, Wright and Tomlinson, 2023).

There operated in Scotland a set of policy communities, in which the values and culture of decision-making elites helped to sustain a distinctive set of institutions and relationships which influenced bargaining and policy outcomes. Such a 'community' stretched across government and outside groups who were involved in the implementation of policy, while there was no single policy community covering Scotland, and certainly nothing as formal as a 'Scottish government', the scale and administrative history of the country made this form of governance particularly apt. It also helps to explain why the Thatcherite strategy of cutting down the state and asserting the primacy of the market proved to be far less popular among the governing classes of Scotland, as well as among the population more generally, seen as an affront to a moral economy which sustained Scotland in the Union.

Labour's strategy in the 1960s was, according to Michael Keating and David Bleiman, largely pragmatic. Labour's attitude to the Scottish question was based upon the assumptions that the basis of any discontent was economic, and that the electorate was more concerned about the economic goods which they received than with the constitutional mechanism by which they were delivered (Keating and Bleiman, 1979: 151).

The post-war belief in 'equal citizenship' was mobilised as equal citizenship for Scots within the UK in such a way that the (British) nationalist assumptions built into the welfare state could be transferred in rhetorical form to Scottish nationalism. Even the concept of 'the economy' was a national, even nationalist, assumption. Certainly, the ability to transfer from one form of nationalism (British) to another (Scottish) occurred at the right moment for the nationalist party, as well as for many Scots. The perception of Scotland as a separate unit of political and economic management coincided with the arrival of North Sea Oil, which opened up the political possibility of an alternative Scottish future, and which the SNP was to exploit as 'Scotland's Oil' (Kemp, 2011; 2012). The SNP helped to make explicit, as well as problematic, the 'national' dimension of the post-war consensus, and provided a political alternative when the British settlement began to fail. Both the Conservative and Labour parties paid the electoral price, the former more profoundly than the latter, culminating in electoral wipe-out in the general election of 1997.

Labour's early success was based on a view of the state as a generator of economic growth. As Labour was seen to fail to deliver the economic goods in the 1970s, the SNP became increasingly the beneficiary. Ironically, when the next major ideological battle occurred later in the decade – between the radical Right with its anti-state project, and the defenders of the post-war settlement – Labour in Scotland was in a much better position than the SNP to switch the terms of the struggle on to a Left/Right dimension, while taking with it some of the nationalist mantle after 1979.[6] For Labour, this culminated in devolution in 1997. Seeing this as 'killing nationalism stone dead' proved to be far from the case.[7] From the early 1970s the SNP acted as a key electoral catalyst for change, and provided a political home for the socially mobile and the young, in search of a new political identity in a rapidly changing Scotland. It is in the systematic swing away from the Conservatives, however, that we have the most coherent manifestation of the emerging Scottish political system, a system increasingly incompatible with the ideology of that party's role as the British or, increasingly, the English, national party.

Scotland underwent industrial and occupational change along similar lines to the rest of the UK and western societies generally. The 'occupational transition' – the shift from manufacturing to service employment – occurred in all advanced industrial societies in the post-war period as reflected in the *Trente Glorieuses*, and accelerated from the 1970s. Thus, the increase in the share of jobs in the service sector – from 24 per cent in 1951, to 33 per cent in 1971, 66 per cent in 1991, 70 per cent by the turn of the century, and 80 per cent by 2024 – is undoubtedly the greatest shift in sectoral employment which Scotland has experienced in modern times. The growth of the service sector has been the greatest single driver of social change in Scotland since 1945. The changes in occupational structure, patterns of female employment and social mobility right through to household structure, demographic behaviour and political orientations can be traced back to this single transformation in the jobs people did.

SCOTLAND'S CLASS STRUCTURE

The other key piece in this jigsaw of social change concerns social class. We will see in Chapter 5 how social class cannot simply be read off industrial and occupational structures, nor is a social class simply a (social) category. The English historian E. P. Thompson in his classic study *The Making of the English Working Class* commented: 'class is a relationship and not a thing ... It does not exist, either to have an ideal interest or consciousness, or to lie as a patient on the Adjustor's table' (1963: 11). This is why Thompson deliberately titled his book, 'The Making of the *English* Working Class', explaining that he did not do so out of chauvinism, but because 'class is a cultural as much as an economic formation that I have been cautious as to generalizing beyond the English experience ... The Scottish record, in particular, is quite as dramatic, and as tormented, as our own' (Thompson, 1963:13–14). By that time, Thompson had written an important essay 'The Peculiarities of the English' in *The Socialist Register* in 1965 in which he took Tom Nairn and Perry Anderson to task for underplaying the cultural component of social class south of the border (Thompson, 1965). More recently, the work of historians of England makes a similar point. Thus, Sutcliffe-Braithwaite observed that from the late 1960s class remained important to people's narratives about social change and their own identities, even though strict class boundaries had become blurred in the post-war period, reflecting the decline of social deference (Sutcliffe-Braithwaite, 2018).

Even so, social classes are not static. As Göran Therborn pointed out: 'classes must be seen, not as veritable geological formations, once they have acquired their original shape, but as phenomena in a constant process of formation, reproduction, re-formulation and de-formation' (Therborn, 1983: 39). For most people, their life chances, the basis of social class, are determined by what they do for a living, what they work at, because that is the source of their income. It characterises their life security, gives them access to housing, education, social goods and so on. In modern market societies, then, there tend to be three main classes – a dominant class whose power is based on the capital it owns; an intermediate class whose power derives from the educational or organisational skills it possesses; and a subordinate class whose power, such as it is, tends to be based on its physical labour. It is this relationship to the labour market which determines to which social class people belong.

At the beginning of the twentieth century the Scottish class structure was a classic pyramid, with the bulk of the labour force in manual jobs, a small group of non-manual managers and professionals, and at the top, a self-contained elite, culturally and socially distinct. By the second half of the twentieth century, the manual working class had shrunk in size to less than one-half of people in employment, while the middle or service class had grown concomitantly. From the 1950s, what sociologists call the 'occupational transition', the shift from manufacturing employment to services, had occurred, in line with other advanced industrial societies. The growing share of employment in services, from 19 per cent in 1911, to 43 per cent by 1981, over 70 per cent by the turn of the century, 80 per cent by 2022, has been the major motor of economic and social change. In any case, what is meant by 'services' has changed considerably over the twentieth century, from domestic service employment to occupations concerned with state service functions like education and social services, and private sector ones such as banking and finance. The changing occupational structure and concomitant patterns of social mobility, coupled with new opportunities for women, have ushered in major social, and political, changes.

The trend for women to participate in the labour force has been a feature north and south of the border. In Scotland, however, as far as married women are concerned the trend has been one of convergence. Until well after 1945, the economic activity rate for married women in Scotland was only two-thirds that of the rest of Britain, and it was not until the late 1970s that Scotland caught up. By 1981, 57 per cent of married women in Scotland under 60 were economically active. The expansion of new occupations for women runs alongside the feminisation of certain occupations such as clerical work, in which the percentage of clerks who were female rose from about half in 1961 to three-quarters by 1981. Women were not, however, becoming 'middle class' by dint of being in non-manual jobs, because female pay and conditions remained substantially poorer than those of men.

By the 1970s, the trends, which Scotland shared with the rest of the UK, were for the expansion of white-collar work, notably professional employees, and intermediate non- manual workers (such as teachers, and non-managerial workers). Manual workers declined as a percentage of those in employment, from just over half (52 per cent) in 1961, to around 40 per cent in 1981. In comparison with the rest of the UK, Scotland had a higher share of manual workers in employment, but the general decline was in line with elsewhere. In comparison, Scotland had a lower share of non-manual workers, notably in the private sector, and of own-account workers. By the 2020s, all that was history.

The fact that Scotland's industrial structure has been close to the British mean for much of its industrial history suggests, however, that its occupational structure would be also, and so the data show. Only that of the north-west of England was closer to the British mean in the 1970s, and Scotland's proportion in most socio-economic groups occupied a fairly median position with respect to the other Standard Regions. Scotland did have the highest proportion of unskilled workers as well as the lowest proportion of petit bourgeois groups, employers and managers in small establishments, and own account workers. In terms of white-collar employment, however, the divide was not between Scotland and the rest, but between South-East England and the rest. In Scotland, as in other Standard Economic Regions of Britain, the expansion of white-collar employment has been by far the most important transformation since the Second World War.

The expansion in non-manual employment was occurring before 1961, but continued subsequently, notably for professional employees, intermediate non-manual workers (such as teachers, nurses and 'non-managerial' non-manual workers). Manual work continued to decline, especially the skilled manual group, down from 28 per cent in 1961 to 20 per cent twenty years later. However, Scotland was by no means an outlier, but in a middle band along with Wales and North-West England. We can conclude that, once again, Scotland's occupational structure had largely mirrored that of Britain as a whole.

Getting On in Scotland

The considerable divergence in political behaviour between Scotland and England since the 1970s cannot, then, be the result of the two countries having distinctively different class structures. The explanation lies far less in difference of class structure, and much more in the realm of the other dimensions of class, namely, culture and political action. The dominant impression from the analysis of social mobility patterns in the 1970s was one of similarity between Scotland and the rest of Britain, rather than difference. The significant differences occurred among the petty bourgeoisie (class IV), although it seems that fewer sons of class II fathers made it into the top class ('the service class'[8]) compared with England and Wales, and there was a higher degree of class retention in II (lower grade professionals and administrators, and technicians).

Given the differences in employment structures north and south of the border, the similarities in social mobility patterns are what is striking, not the differences. Goldthorpe's remark in this respect is correct: 'On the basis of such comparison, it would seem clear enough that, had our enquiry been extended to Scotland, no substantially different results would have been produced so far at least as the pattern of *de facto* intergenerational rates is concerned' (Goldthorpe, 1980: 291). He concluded that the mobility model for England and Wales had a tolerably good fit with the Scottish data, the model accounting for over 95 per cent of the association between class of origin and destination.

In the later edition (1987) of his social mobility study, Goldthorpe set the Scottish experience in the wider context of other industrial nations – England and Wales, France, West Germany, Republic of Ireland, Sweden, Hungary and Poland. As regards relative rates of mobility:

> England and Wales, together with France, turn out to be the most central nations with the configuration that emerges. Scotland and Northern Ireland, along with Hungary, fall into the intermediate band, and it is Poland, Sweden, West Germany and Ireland which, in that order, represent the most outlying cases. (1987: 309)

In structural terms, Scotland, England and Wales shared common characteristics by virtue of early industrialisation and the demise of the peasantry. Hence, in terms of social mobility patterns, and in particular, comparative inflow rates, Scotland, as well as England and Wales, had the highest percentage in classes I and II who originate from the manual working classes, and the lowest recruitment from farm origins (unlike the Republic of Ireland, for example). On the other hand, the British nations showed the highest proportions of self-recruitment into the manual working classes, with Poland and Hungary the lowest. These patterns are the result of a shared economic history of industrialisation. In Goldthorpe's words:

> Britain's early industrialisation and the unique path that it followed can be rather clearly associated, first, with a service class recruited to an unusual degree from among the sons of blue-collar workers, and secondly with a broadly defined industrial working class which is to an unusual degree self-recruited or which, one could alternatively say, is highly homogeneous in its composition in terms of its members' social origins. (1987: 316)

Britain, Goldthorpe concluded, does not possess any kind of historical legacy or institutional barriers, as reflected in these data, either to impede or to promote social fluidity. In this context, Scotland, together with England and Wales, are the nations in which the distributions of social origins and destinations differ least. On reflection, we should not be surprised at this finding, because Scotland, England and Wales share common features as industrialised countries. Plainly, it would be perverse to conclude from the general data on social mobility patterns, that Scotland had taken a different mobility route from the rest of the UK. The most we could say was that by the 1970s, Scotland had a slightly smaller middle class, and a slightly larger manual working class, but the processes of upward and downward social mobility which created these structures of opportunity are very similar on both sides of the Tweed.

The picture of inter-generational social mobility[9] in Scotland in the 1970s, then, was of a society similar to England and Wales, with a substantial proportion of the service class socially mobile out of manual working-class backgrounds. For example, fully one-third of the top salariat had fathers who had been in manual jobs, and for class II, the figure was 43 per cent. On the other hand, the manual working classes (VI and VII) were much more homogeneous and self-recruiting. This is because, while there was considerable upward mobility into the social classes at the top, there was little corresponding downward mobility into the lower social classes. This lack of correspondence was due to the fact that while the size of the manual working class had shrunk, that of the service classes had grown, thus allowing those who were already there to stay put, as well as permitting considerable upward social mobility from below. In other words, the changing shape and size of social classes within the class structure was permitting class retention at the top and class mobility from the bottom.

Education and Social Mobility

Crucial to this transformation was education. There were profound changes in secondary schooling after 1945, and post-1965, all secondary schools in the public sector were re-organised along 'comprehensive' lines. Much longer periods of young people's lives were spent in education, from 5 to 16 years of age. Furthermore, post-school education had become a mass system, and at the beginning of the twenty-first century, there were roughly as many undergraduates in higher education as there had been in the whole of secondary education in the 1930s (Paterson, in McCrone, 2017: 255). Whereas in the 1930s around 3 per cent of the relevant age cohort were in higher education, by 1960 it had doubled to 6 per cent; by 1980 it had trebled to 18 per cent, and by the end of the century, was almost 50 per cent. The Robbins report of 1963 had recommended university expansion throughout the UK, and new universities were created in Scotland: Strathclyde, Heriot Watt, Dundee and Stirling.[10] By the end of the twentieth century there had been a six-fold increase in the number of students in Scotland in the space of fifty years.

The motor for these changes lay in the demand for educated labour. 'The consequences for people's access to further learning, to good jobs, to social status, and to social influence have been profound' (Paterson, Bechhofer and McCrone, 2004: 106). Expansion, and particularly the unification of higher education after 1992 (when colleges of technology such as Paisley, Robert Gordon's in Aberdeen and Abertay in Dundee became universities), reduced social class differences. The ratio of middle-class to working-class school leavers in higher education fell from 5 to 1 in the 1970s, to 2 to 1 post-1992, reflecting how 'new' universities broadened social class appeal (Paterson in McCrone, 2017: 259). By the end of the century, as many as 62 per cent of those with a higher education degree had been upwardly mobile to a higher social class than their parents; while at the same time, 47 per cent of those in professional and managerial social classes had been upwardly mobile from working-class origins.

Scotland, of course, was not unique in these respects, but the process had particular social, cultural and even political outcomes north of the border. One peculiarly Scottish feature of the shift (relative to England) was the propensity of such upwardly mobile people to describe themselves as 'working class'. By the 1990s, as many as four in five of this upwardly mobile group saw themselves as 'working class', reflecting their class of origin rather than their class of destination. In terms of social mobility, the top 'service class' was much more socially diverse than ever before as it drew up the highly educated into its ranks. Thus, '... middle-class though it has become, Scotland still thinks of itself as being a working-class country' (Paterson, Bechhofer and McCrone 2004: 101). Furthermore, the decline of the Conservatives in Scotland was notable among this upwardly socially mobile group who continued to call themselves 'working class'. In a later chapter we will see that they also had a significant effect on the Yes vote in the 2014 referendum on Scottish independence, as well as providing the leadership cadre for the Yes movement.

The key point is this: social mobility fuelled by higher education has had a transformative effect, not only on re-forming the class structure in a functional way, but in terms of culture and politics. As the American writer Amy Gutmann observed:

> learning how to think carefully and critically about political problems, and to articulate one's views and defend them before people with whom one disagrees is a form of moral education to which young adults are more receptive ... and for which universities are well suited. (Gutmann, 1987: 173)[11]

In other words, the more education people have, the more liberal and respectful of diversity they are. Nor is this simply a Scottish phenomenon. In England, the dominant discriminator in accounting for how people voted in the Brexit referendum of 2016 was education; the more you had of it, the more likely you were to vote Remain. Thus, in both Scotland and England the vote to Remain among those with degrees was almost identical: 78 per cent in Scotland, and 77 per cent in England. On the other hand, those with little or no educational qualifications voting Remain were significantly different: 51 per cent in Scotland, and only 23 per cent in England. (McCrone, 2017: Table 4, 394). As John Curtice observed: 'support for Leave and a hard Brexit is much higher amongst those with few, if any, qualifications than it is among university graduates' (Curtice, 2017). We will return to these themes in a future chapter, while our purpose here is to flag the effects of educational expansion in the context of social mobility in the 1960s and 1970s.

Is Scotland Different?

The social mobility studies of the 1970s were depicting a post-war society in which the expansion of non-manual occupations reflected the growing public as well as private sectors. In that Scotland followed a similar trajectory in terms of industrial, occupational and social class features as did England and Wales, then we are left with a puzzle: how to account for the cultural and political differences which emerged post-1970s. That is the task of this book, as we bring our data to bear on the later decades, and explore in detail the dimension of social, economic, political and cultural change which have resulted. The point, to reiterate, is that 'structures' in themselves, whether industrial, occupational or social, do not determine what people think or how they behave. The key is what people make of them, and relate them to wider political and cultural contexts.

To take one example: if, as we have indicated, people in Scotland are significantly more likely to describe themselves as 'working class' than in England, that is a reflection of the 'culture' of class, and its social meanings, rather than its structure. The existence of social classes objectively does not determine how their members see themselves. Whether or not people use class categories, and what they mean when they do so, depends on an array of social and cultural forces impacting upon how they see and make sense of the world around them. It does, however, draw us back to important matters of culture which are underpinned by institutional differences. If, for example, we were studying social class in different societies, say in Germany and France, we would have little quarrel with the view that while their class structures are quite similar, the *meanings* of class, generated by distinct political cultures and histories, are different. We would acknowledge, for example, that these cultures are historically constructed and refracted through, for example, the political agendas in the two countries. While this might seem an obvious point to make in comparing and contrasting societies, it is frequently unobserved when looking at differences *within* the territories of these islands. We should not, therefore, expect that social class in Scotland will be interpreted and explained in the same way as in England, because key institutions such as the legal system, religion and the education system will evidently mediate structures and experiences to produce different political and social outcomes.

SOCIAL CHANGE AND SCOTTISH NATIONALISM

So how is social change related to the social base of nationalism? In the early phase of the Scottish National Party's electoral success, James Kellas observed:

> At all times, it seems to have attracted defectors equally from all parties, although this varies from constituency to constituency. Up to 1974 it seems to have appealed to first-time voters or previous abstainers. Its declining support after 1978 was particularly marked among young voters and New Town voters, many of whom had consistently supported the party since the late 1960s. (Kellas, 1989: 141)

The appeal of the party to such social groups was reflected in the volatility and unexpectedness of its successes and failures. The volatile appeal of the SNP to the young, the socially and geographically mobile, was reinforced by the absence of a significant class base. Hence, it performed uniformly across all social classes. The October 1974 election in which the SNP took 30 per cent of electoral support in Scotland proved to be the party's best performance in a British general election up to that point. In the October 1974 election the SNP did well across all classes, but especially among 'intermediate' non-manual and skilled manual workers (see Table 3.1), those groups who had become electorally detached from traditional social bases.

Further evidence suggested that the party's appeal was stronger among the 'new' working class – technicians and craftsmen – than it was among 'traditional' manual workers such as steelworkers and miners (Davis 1969). The Scottish Election Survey for October 1974, for example, pointed to the classless appeal of the SNP, which proved to be both its strength but also its weakness.

In contrast to its broad-based class appeal, in October 1974 the SNP attracted the young in high proportion. The age

Table 3.1 Percentage of each socio-economic group voting SNP in October 1974 general election

Employers and managers	27%
Professionals	30%
Intermediate	**40%**
Junior non-manual	26%
Foremen and supervisors	18%
Skilled manual	**35%**
Semi-skilled manual	23%
Unskilled manual	23%

Source: Scottish election survey, October 1974.

structure of SNP support was the mirror-image of Conservative strength. Among 18–24 year olds, 42 per cent voted SNP, and only 10 per cent Conservative. In contrast, among those 65 and over, the SNP managed only 16 per cent, while the Tories took more than double that, 38 per cent. The SNP also did proportionately well among those who were upwardly socially mobile from manual working class origins. For example, 32 per cent of SNP voters in non-manual jobs had fathers who were *manual* workers, compared with 24 per cent of SNP non-manual voters who had *non-manual* fathers, a difference of 8 percentage points. In other words, in terms of father's occupation, you were more likely to vote SNP if you came from a working-class background than a middle-class one. Hence, non-manual workers who had been upwardly socially mobile from the working class were especially susceptible to the appeal of the SNP, as were younger workers, and those buying a house with a mortgage. Since then, a new generation of voters has appeared, notably the children of those who were socially mobile in the 1960s. The fact that there is now a substantial fifty-year history of SNP voting provided a solid platform for later electoral success, and socialised people into nationalist voting habits across generations.

The Scottish National Party, then, was the beneficiary of key social changes in Scotland in the late 1960s and 1970s – rising affluence, full employment and upward social mobility. Groups who became less reliant on the support of kin as well as being more home-centred – Scotland's analogues of the classic 'affluent workers' studied in England[12] – found themselves drawn to the nationalists less for reasons of political ideology than because of their social detachment from their social class of origin.

This social base paid electoral dividends where Labour was historically weak, although there was nothing inevitable about this. For example, Peterhead, a town in North-East Scotland where the SNP made an early and lasting impact, and which Alex Salmond, who went on to lead the party, won in 1987 as part of the Banff and Buchan constituency, pointed up this important nationalist social base (Bealey and Sewel, 1981).

We can argue, then, that it was the *lack* of class connotations in the SNP which was the key appeal to this socially mobile group in the 1970s. Such people were susceptible to alternative frameworks of perception, for their traditional forms of social and political identities were weakening. It is important to underline the point that Scotland differed little from the rest of the UK with regard to social and cultural changes, but from the late 1960s, 'Scotland' was a frame of cultural reference in terms of which the political world could increasingly be interpreted.

Crucially, the SNP was a political party which could more easily capture this Scottish label, because it was a 'national' party, in much the same way as the Conservative Party had assumed an implicit national identity in England. In another important respect, the SNP was a party well suited to an increasingly volatile electorate. Just as the SNP came to rapid prominence, so it fell rapidly from electoral grace at a later stage, which makes the point about the lack of inevitability.

So the SNP appealed to the generation entering the electorate in the 1960s and 1970s who, in England, turned towards the non-Labour parties, to the Conservatives or the Liberals. The collapse of the SNP in the late 1970s shifted to Labour, who were happy to do 'nationalist' talk to a significant degree. By the late 1970s, the Scottish stage was set for a new – yet more traditional – battle over the role of the state, between Labour and Conservative, which the latter were singularly ill-equipped to fight in Scotland. This was a key element in the process of political divergence between Scotland and England. The slippage in Conservative support in Scotland began well before 1979 and the election of the first Thatcher government. But as the data also make plain, the 1980s drove a considerable wedge between the electoral performances of the two nations. Mrs Thatcher may not have created the divergence, but she gave it a flavour all her own. She told Michael Ancram, one of her

Scottish MPs and ministers: 'Michael, I am an English nationalist and never you forget it'.[13]

The more recent work by historians in England reinforces the point. Recall Emily Robinson's point that 'popular individualism', that is, greater personal autonomy and self-determination was a cause of Thatcherism, rather than its effect, or rather, that she gave it voice (Robinson et al., 2017). Jon Lawrence, in his book *Me, Me, Me* observes: 'I am clear that class resonated differently in England compared with the other home nations', specifically with regard to 'ingrained hierarchical and status-based models of social difference' (2019: 11).

And in Scotland? As long as the Scottish political dimension remained latent, it was perfectly possible for Conservative rhetoric about the nation to coexist with the everyday reality of Scottishness. And, of course, for much of the twentieth century the presence of an ideological affinity between Conservatism, Unionism and Protestantism was useful to the party. Latterly, however, alternative dimensions of Scottishness emerged, making Scotland as an ideological category incompatible with Conservative Anglo-British rhetoric. Nothing did more to make explicit this Conservative nationalism than the election of Mrs Thatcher in 1979.

A large part of Thatcher's success south of the border derived from harnessing conservative motifs. Much of the explanation for the rise of Thatcherism focussed on neo-liberal ideas of extending market power, but alongside these lay a powerful stream of ideas which were quite distinct. Its neo-conservative motif was authority not freedom, the desire to re-establish and extend the power of the state over many aspects of social, political and even personal life. If the notion of the 'citizen' derived from liberal ideas of the state, then the conservative idea of the 'subject' was drawn from an allegiance to the nation; the question was *which* nation. In post-war societies, politics operated by claiming the legitimacy of the 'national interest'. Clearly, Thatcherism represented a radical break with this consensual, corporatist style of government. Thus it was that nationalism – a key element in this discredited system – was re-mobilised by the radical Right in the new cause.

What Britain saw after 1979 was the re-assertion of nationalism under a new set of political and economic ideas. And it was a nationalism which was distinctly at odds with the new alternative variety north of the border. While the older unionist one was quite compatible with Anglo-British nationalism, the newer post-1979 version was not. Thatcher's unpopularity in Scotland was the downside of her electoral support in England. The political scientist Andrew Gamble (1988) pointed out that Thatcherism focused its appeal on the English, to the detriment of the Scots, the Welsh and even the Northern Irish.

In Scotland, the attack on state institutions – the nationalised industries, the education system, local government, the public sector generally, even the church,[14] institutions which carried much of Scotland's identity – was perceived as an attack on 'Scotland'. Essential to current Conservative appeal south of the border was an appeal to 'the nation' on whose behalf politicians and the state act. But Scots had a nation of their own, and the vision of recreating bourgeois England was out of kilter not only with Scottish material interests, but with this alternative sense of national identity.

Modern Conservatism spoke increasingly with a southern English voice. The populist, nationalist, anti-state appeal which sustained Thatcher in England for the whole of the 1980s had distinctively negative resonances north of the border. It is hard to envisage a political message more at odds with what had gone before, and one which has run against the grain of Scottish civil society.

Thus, the failure of the Conservative Party in Scotland was *not* the result of an unfavourable class structure. Scotland did not vote anti-Conservative because it was more 'working class' in a structural sense. Even among the middle classes, there was a distinct anti-Conservative differential, as these data (see Table 3.2) show for the October 1974 British general election (and recall that Mrs Thatcher did not become party leader until 1975).

Across *all* social classes there was an anti-Tory differential in Scotland in October 1974, and it has continued ever since. Among manual workers, the Conservative vote in Scotland is about a half what it is in the rest of Britain, while among professional and managerial classes it ranges from a high of 78 per cent of the similar class vote south of the border in 1979 to a low of 62 per cent in 1997 when all seats in Scotland were lost. That defeat ushered in the most fundamental transformation of Scottish governance in almost three hundred years.

Table 3.2 Percentage voting Conservative in Scotland (and in rest of GB) in October 1974

	% voting Conservative (Scotland)	% voting Conservative (rest of GB)	Differential (Sc minus rGB)
Professional and managerial	36	51	−15
Skilled non-manual	29	43	−14
Skilled manual	14	25	−11
Semi/unskilled manual	12	23	−11

Source: British general election survey, October 1974.

CHANGING NATIONAL IDENTITIES

And so social structural change impacted on national identities, explored more fully in Chapter 6. It comes in this sequence of our argument about transformations to make the point that the notion of 'national identity' is much misunderstood. It is not a 'thing' nor even, in social science-speak, a variable, but in essence the expression of relationships, above all a prism through which social change is refracted. The writer Willie McIlvanney understood this when he wrote: 'having a national identity is a bit like having an old insurance policy. You know you've got one somewhere but often you're not entirely sure where it is. And if you're honest, you would have to admit you're pretty vague about what the small print means' (*The Glasgow Herald*, 6 March 1999). In more academic terms, the social psychologist Michael Billig referred to nationalism as 'banal':

> In so many little ways, the citizenry are reminded of their national place in a world of nations. However, this reminding is so familiar, so continual, that it is not consciously recognized as reminding. The metonymic[15] image of banal nationalism is not a flag which is being consciously waved with fervent passion; it is the flag hanging unnoticed on the public building. National identity embraces all these forgotten reminders. (Billig, 1995: 8)

Both McIlvanney and Billig in their different ways are making the point that much of the time who we take ourselves to be is implicit, and depends on the context and purpose within which we make such a claim to be who we are. In the decade since the referendum on Scottish Independence (2014) and reinforced by the Brexit referendum of 2016, it is commonplace to assume that national identity in Scotland is primarily 'political'; that if you say you are Scottish, you are a nationalist, and if you say you are British, a unionist. That may have a greater degree of truth today, but the association between national identity and 'politics' in that straightforward form is relatively new, dating from the second decade of the twenty-first century, the decade of referendums.

In the 1970s, a survey question was adopted from the work of political scientist Juan Linz in Catalonia and Spain, following the re-emergence of democracy after the death of Franco. This took the form of a Likert scale, in Linz's formulation, juxtaposing 'Catalan' and 'Spanish'. In Scotland, it became known as the Moreno scale, after Luis Moreno who adapted it for Scottish use in that form in 1986; with five points, from 'Scottish not British', 'more Scottish than British', 'equally Scottish and British', 'more British than Scottish', and 'British not Scottish'. Previous survey work in the UK had asked simpler questions: 'Do you think of yourself as British, Scottish, European etc' as a multiple-choice question, and 'which (of these) best fits how you see yourself'. Subsequent studies used a variant of that on the grounds that 'Moreno' was frequently misunderstood as a measure of the *strength* of national feeling rather than simply a matter of relating two 'national' identities (see McCrone and Bechhofer, 2015 for a fuller discussion of these measures).

In the Scottish context, the import of the national identity question was clear: had people in Scotland simply shifted from being British to being Scottish? The old orthodoxy had been that people were Scottish *and* British, the former nested in the latter; that 'state' and 'national' identities were complementary rather than in competition, but that was an assumption, rather than being subject to empirical testing. Part of the issue was that we had little evidence of how people in Scotland did national identity before it became more problematic in the 1970s.

We do get a glimpse of how identities operated from the 1979 Scottish Election Survey where 56 per cent said their 'best' national identity was Scottish, and 38 per cent that it was British, a ratio of around 1.5 to 1. Subsequent studies, usually at the time of elections, put the ratio in favour of being Scottish over British much higher, at a ratio of at least 5 to 1. And the inference was that prior to 1979, Scottish and British were more in balance such that Scottish was a cultural identity and British more political, essentially a mark of citizenship. There was little hard survey evidence in the 1970s, although James Kellas (1984: 124) reported that *The Glasgow Herald* referred to surveys in Glasgow where 18 per cent said 'British' and 78 per cent 'Scottish', and in 'other large towns in central Scotland' 'British' ranged from 16 per cent to 24 per cent, and 'Scottish' from 75 per cent to 78 per cent, figures suggesting that respondents had to choose between being one or the other. Jack Brand, in his 1978 book on Scottish Nationalism,[16] also cited these figures, as well as Glasgow surveys at times of British general elections, in 1970, and in February and October 1974, which showed a strong Scottish identification.[17]

There is evidence that the Scottish Unionist Party, which changed its name to the Conservative and Unionist Party in Scotland only in 1965, had particular appeal to the Protestant working class, welded by a strong sense of British national and imperial identity, and metonymically symbolised by the Union Flag. This version of Scottishness drew upon a strong sense of militarism (warfare) which ran through Scottish society in the late nineteenth and early twentieth centuries, and especially in the two twentieth-century world wars. Furthermore, in 1973 James Kellas wrote that 'religion and voting behaviour are more closely connected in Scotland than in England' (1973:7). And in particular, '...the Catholic voter contributes in no small measure to the continuity of Labour support in Scotland and to the weakness of the SNP' (ibid. 110). By the end of the century, all that had changed. Steve Bruce observed:

> In 1970 only 4% of Catholics (as compared with 11% of the population at large) voted SNP. In 1987, these figures were 9 and 14%. Five years later the Catholic and general SNP were almost identical: 20% and 21%. And the collapse of the Labour vote in 2011 and again in 2014 confirmed the end of any lingering religious tinge to Scottish nationalism. (Bruce, 2017: 367)

Catholics were as likely as Protestants, and the non-religious, to prioritise being Scottish after the 1970s. The ancestral origins of Scottish Catholics, especially in the west of Scotland, were Irish. However, in a Glasgow survey of 2002, 81 per cent of Catholics chose 'Scottish', 23 per cent 'British' and only 8 per cent 'Irish'[18] (Bruce et al., 2004). By the turn of the century, three-quarters of Catholics in Scotland said they were only or mainly Scottish rather than British (compared with 60 per cent of Scots as a whole).

The conventional assumption, however, had been that British politics were pre-eminently those of social class (Pulzer, 1967) reinforced by first-past-the-post voting. In Scotland, surveys asked people whether they identified most with 'same class English', rather than 'opposite class Scots'. In 1979, marginally more identified on lines of class rather than nation (44 per cent to 38 per cent), but by 1992, it had switched around to 27 per cent to 45 per cent respectively. and that relationship has held ever since. By 1999, 41 per cent of Scotland's salariat identified with 'opposite class Scots', compared with 24 per cent with 'same class English' (among the manual working class the proportions were 47 per cent to 19 per cent). The political hard-line of the Labour Party had been that working class Scots had more in common with the English (and Welsh) working class, than with other-class fellow Scots. This no longer held, and Labour was ill-suited to play the national card when there was a nationalist party which positioned itself on the social democratic left.

It would be easy to assume that there had been a straightforward switch of national identity in Scotland from 'British' to 'Scottish', but much depends on how questions about national identity are asked. We cannot assume that if survey respondents prioritise being Scottish (say, for example, that they are 'more Scottish than British') that they do not feel strongly about being British, and so it proves by disaggregating the two identities on separate scales (see McCrone and Bechhofer, 2015). By the twenty-first century, whilst, unsurprisingly, most people in Scotland (nine out of ten) were strongly Scottish, as many as 50 per cent were also strongly British; proof that it is possible to be strongly both,[19] and we will explore that in Chapter 7. What we do not have, however, are data relating to the earlier period, the 1970s, the cusp of social change in Scotland.

What is key is that national identity is a prism through which events and power structures are perceived and through which openings for change are refracted (McCrone and Bechhofer, 2015: 7). It is the mode in which historical narratives, religious divisions and cultural boundaries are personalised and practised (A. Cohen, 1986). National identity shifts are at once litmus tests of important changes in social, economic and political relationships, and point to popular re-orientations, relocations of meaning, and prospects of further change. Thus, national identities are long-established, and the categories in which they are expressed – Scottish, British, Irish, Welsh, English – have not changed much over centuries. The configurations and meanings, however, *have* changed considerably. Scottish national identity, traditionally consistent with the Union and nested within it, has taken a sharper political edge in recent decades. Being British has also been challenged by the politicising of being English, notably in the context of the Brexit referendum of 2016 (McCrone and Keating, 2021).

How 'political' has being Scottish become? In 1992, only a minority (48 per cent) of those describing themselves as 'Scottish not British' supported independence for Scotland. In the Scottish independence referendum of 2014, 88 per cent of people describing themselves as 'Scottish not British' voted Yes to independence (British Election Study, 2019). While the broad categories of Scottish to British have remained consistent over time (five or six times as many prioritise being Scottish over being British), it is far more that the *meaning* of those categories has altered such as to politicise them. To take a non-Scottish case, that of England, saying you were 'English' (rather than 'British') was a strong predictor of voting Leave in the Brexit referendum of 2016 (McCrone, 2017). By and large, in England there has been little surface change in the proportions saying they are English vis-à-vis British over time. What *has* changed, however, is what these terms have come to signify in political terms.

In Britain, a politicisation of Scottish identity has come to restrict British identity to being, in large part, a 'state' identity; the Scottish challenge to the Union being informed by a strong political-national identity. In a similar fashion, the transformation of national identity in England has taken the form of politicising being English in the context of the 2016 Brexit referendum, rather than an aggregate shift of national identity from 'British' to 'English'.

As long as the British state recognised the attenuated nature of Union, and notions of Scottish self-government, Scots were content to recognise the complementary and nested nature of being Scottish *and* British. When the relationship between culture/nation and politics/state altered definitively in the final quarter of the twentieth century, so too did the matrix of national identity. It was not that Scots ceased to be British as that the meanings of these labels changed. As Jennifer Todd (2018: 75) has pointed out, classification is less important than the meaning of the identity categories – Scottish, Irish or British – understood within a slowly changing grammar. Jennifer Todd's metaphor of national identity as 'grammar' is an important one. It refers to the rules or codes of acceptable usage – how the elements associated with national identity (history, ancestry, state-belonging, place-belonging, cultural attributes, social practices) are understood and interrelated, to create closed and exclusivist or permeable and negotiable distinctions between national self and national other, or – most likely – a limited range of ways-of-being-national in each case (Todd, 2018: 76). In the Scottish case, then, it is the changing *grammar* of national identity, its prism-like quality, which is the key to unlocking our understanding of the process of social change, not simply as a term of vocabulary.

CONCLUSION

This chapter has painted a broad picture of social change in Scotland, with a view to exploring in subsequent chapters how the key factors played out in decades subsequent to the 'long' 1970s. The nub of the argument is that a constellation of social, economic and political forces changed Scotland in that crucial decade; from a society tied closely into the warfare/welfare nexus in the mid-twentieth century, to one in which Scotland was diverging in social and political terms from the rest of the UK, but in essence, England.

We can make a number of caveats. First, it was not simply that Scotland was moving away from England, but England was moving away from Scotland, notably in political terms (see Robinson et al., 2017). Behind that, there is an assumption of 'difference', especially in the scholarship of the 1970s, that one should try and identify the factors which Scotland did *not* share with the rest of the UK in order to explain that 'difference'. That took writers into unwarranted assumptions about Scotland's 'colonialist' relation to England, that its form of capitalism was 'complementary' rather than 'competitive', assumptions which have not withstood the test of time nor analysis.

Lying behind such assumptions was a failure to factor in institutional and cultural expressions of difference, that Scotland was not England, but more fundamentally that the UK was not a 'nation-state' but at best a 'state-nation'; or, in Michael Keating's words, worth repeating, that 'The UK is not a state, unitary or federal, but a union, and as such does not necessarily need a hard core or sovereignty or purpose' (Keating, 2021: 50). It was cobbled together by diverse territories into a political entity, above all imperial, for purposes of military and dynastic security, rather than the outcome of deliberate processes of nation-building (ibid. 22). It had a contradiction at its heart: it was 'unitary' in that it had a single and 'sovereign' parliament dominated demographically by England, but in essence the territory of the state was pluri-national. The departure of (most of) Ireland in 1922 was both the expression of multi-nationality but also its cover for English dominance. The nexus which bound Scotland into the UK ('Great Britain') was based on historic warfare with 'Others', notably France in the early nineteenth century, and Germany in the twentieth (Colley, 1992), reinforced by Protestantism, albeit in its various guises, but excluding most of Ireland. By the mid-twentieth century, and a vital part of the post-war settlement, welfare as well as warfare made the British state in its modern manifestation, in which the Labour Party was its post-war midwife. This settlement was a key part of *Les Trente Glorieuses* in these islands.

As Scotland departed from the assumptions upon which the British state was built, in the third quarter of the twentieth century we can see that similarities in industrial, occupational, demographic and even political structures could not explain different political and social outcomes. These were manifest through different prisms of understanding; that the relative autonomy of Scotland (more accurately, of Scottish *civil society*) refracted these structural changes which were impacting on virtually all modern, western, liberal capitalist societies.

Recall the metaphor of a wave of social change impacting upon different and distinct societies, and hence having different effects in terms of how these were managed. A society like Scotland which was relatively institutionally autonomous within an assumed unitary nation-state (but which clearly the UK was not) was most likely to react differently to similar social changes. Scotland, then, was transformed by much the same sets of economic, social and demographic factors as elsewhere, but domesticated and naturalised those differently – because its receptors, institutional and cultural, were distinct. In a British state which largely assumed homogeneity, that was always going to be problematic. This took a political expression, reflected in the divergence of Scottish/English voting habits; almost identical in the first two decades after 1945, and then strikingly divergent, such that Scotland increasingly got a government at Westminster it had not voted for. On the back of this democratic deficit, and the creation of a devolved parliament to assuage Scottish political (and cultural) differences, Scotland was transformed. Exactly how and why will be explained in the chapters which follow.

NOTES

1. Lewis Grassic Gibbon *Sunset Song*, 1971 [1932]: 193.
2. 'Social change' is used here as a composite for demographic and socio-economic change.
3. *Les Trente Glorieuses, ou la révolution invisible de 1946 à 1975* (Paris: Fayard, 1979).
4. Annie Ernaux *Les Années* (Paris: Gallimard, 2008) (translated into English in 2017).
5. Scotland is a Standard Economic Region of the UK for purposes of gathering such data.
6. This was not a contradiction, as we can see in Wales since devolution in 1999 where the Labour party has 'crowded out' the more overtly nationalist party, Plaid Cymru.
7. A remark attributed to the Labour politician, George Robertson, in 1995.
8. The term 'service class' refers to all higher-grade professionals, self-employed or salaried; higher grade administrators and officials in central and local government, and private and public enterprises; and managers in large industrial establishments.
9. That is, comparing one generation with another, mainly in terms of male occupations of fathers and sons.
10. Strathclyde and Heriot Watt had been technological institutes, and Dundee had been part of an association with St Andrews. Only Stirling was a 'new' university.
11. I am grateful to Lindsay Paterson for this reference.
12. Goldthorpe and Lockwood's *Affluent Worker* studies, published in the late 1960s, were classics of the genre.
13. Quoted in Tom Devine's *Independence or Union?* (London: Allen Lane, 2016), but attributed to James Naughtie's *The Rivals* (2001: 21). The late Michael Ancram was a scion of the Lothian family of landowners (the Kerrs), and later became the 13th Marquess of Lothian on the death of his father.

14. Mrs Thatcher's 'sermon on The Mound' given to the General Assembly of the Church of Scotland in May 1988 can be read as a reproach to the assembled congregation (<https://en.wikipedia.org/wiki/Sermon_on_the_Mound>.).
15. 'Metonymy' is a figure of speech where a symbol comes to stand for something; thus, 'the turf' for horse-racing, a 'dish' for a meal, a 'suit' for a man in authority, and so on.
16. J. Brand *The National Movement in Scotland* (London: Routledge, 1978).
17. The tables (Brand, 1978: 155–6) are percentaged by 'British' and 'Scottish' as regards vote, rather than the other way round, and therefore we cannot tell how Conservative, Labour, Liberal and SNP voters gave their national identification, as the sample sizes are not given.
18. Respondents could give multiple choices; hence, the figures do not add up to 100 per cent.
19. Figures are from the Scottish Social Attitudes survey, 2011. Using seven-point scales, one for 'Scottish' and one for 'British', 40 per cent of people in Scotland put themselves on the strongly Scottish (points 5, 6 or 7), and *also* strongly British (points 5, 6 or 7), end of the scales.

4

Demography

We are not the people we were ...

Let us begin our exploration of structural change in Scotland by looking at changing demography, shifts in populations and family forms. Why so? We might take the view that there is something individual and intimate about issues of reproduction which are made well away from public gaze, and are not the business of anyone else. They are, however, deeply social in that households and families imbibe social norms as a matter of course. How many children they have, where and how they live, may be considered as matters of purely personal choice, but they are made in a wider social context. To say they are 'determined' by society would be to put it too strongly, but what people do in their intimate lives is inherently social. Thus, patterns of health and illness are socially structured, as we confront the hazards of modern life, even though they are subject to choices which are themselves socially constructed and manipulated by product manufacture. Bear in mind, too, that while as a form of shorthand we refer to 'Scotland' as if it were a single homogeneous place, there are many 'Scotlands' as it were, both social and spatial, and that treating it singularly often masks considerable variation, notably in terms of population growth and decline.

BIOGRAPHY AND SOCIETY

In truth, the tensions between the highly social and the deeply personal – what in sociology is referred to as the 'structure-action' question – are embedded in our understanding of society.

In the 1950s, the American sociologist Dennis Wrong took issue with what he called the 'over-socialised conception of man' (he was writing at time when it was common to describe people as 'men', although we can assume he was using 'man' as short for 'mankind'), whereby people acted out the social roles allotted to them. In more recent years we have moved towards the view that social actors are free agents whose social identities are highly liquid; that we can be who we want to be by donning the appropriate values and demeanour. The rise of methodological individualism complements the *zeitgeist* of our age, and in the misunderstood words of Mrs Thatcher, 'there is no such thing as society'.[1] What we want as individuals is socially constructed and governed even though the *zeitgeist* presumes that wants are generated deep within the individual, and belong intimately to them.

Nevertheless, 'society' exists, and what we do and think is shaped by social forces. Emile Durkheim, often considered to be the sociologist of 'structuralism', had in fact a much more nuanced understanding of the relationship between social structure and social action:

> The characteristic attributes of human nature ... come to us through society. But on the other hand, society exists and lives only in and through individuals. Extinguish the idea of society in individual minds, let the beliefs, traditions, aspirations of the collectivity cease to be felt and shared by the people involved, and society will die... society has reality only to the extent that it has a place in human consciousness, and we make this place for it. (2001 [1912]: 258)

The point Durkheim was making was that juxtaposing social structure and social action in stark terms between 'society' and 'the individual' is a false dichotomy. There is a complex interaction between social structural influences and individual, personal, decisions, none more so than our intimate relations with others.

CHANGING PEOPLE

Populations at any point comprise three sets of elements: the numbers who are born, the numbers who die, and the numbers who migrate, in and out. The difference between births and deaths is the 'natural increase' (or 'decrease' if deaths outnumber births). The third element is net migration, the difference between those emigrating and those in-migrating. All told, the population level – call it a round 5.5 million in Scotland's case – conceals a considerable degree of churn below the surface, both past and present; shifts over time in both rates of natural increase coupled with the balance between in- and out-migration.

Consider the graph in Figure 4.1 of Scotland's population between 1861 and 2011, and in the context of what was happening in England and Wales by way of contrast.[2] What characterises Scotland is slow population growth in the *longue durée*.

Up until 1911 there were high levels of natural increase in Scotland as well as England and Wales; far more people were born than died. The next five decades, until the 1960s, show falling, but still high, rates of natural increase: births, by and large, exceeded deaths, and were broadly similar in the three British nations. Look now below the zero point, on the x-axis. For virtually the whole of the period, the century from the 1860s to the 1960s, Scotland (but not England and Wales) had high levels of out-migration which far exceeded in-migration, notably in the

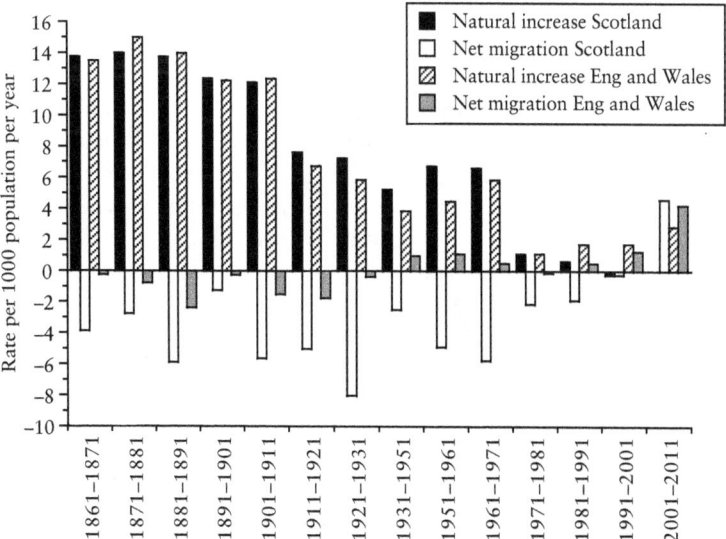

Figure 4.1 Natural increase and net migration per 1,000 population, Scotland and England and Wales, 1861–2011
Source: Based on M. Anderson, 2018: 118 (with kind permission of the author).

late nineteenth and early twentieth centuries, and most of all, in the 1920s. Clearly, in the fifty years from 1881 to 1931, large numbers of Scots left the country. Note too that emigration rates in Scotland were high post-1945, especially between 1951 and 1971, levelling off in the next two decades before turning to a surplus by the turn of the century. England and Wales, on the other hand, saw in-migration such that more people in-migrated than left, but not in Scotland.

And then something intriguing happened at the end of the century: there were more immigrants than emigrants, as measured by net migration. And from the 1970s the rate of natural increase plummeted. The baby boom of the post-war years ran out, at the same time as the death rate fell, set in the context of the National Health Service, founded in 1948. In truth, such changes were happening over a longer period, but from the late 1960s and into the 1970s Scotland was changing, even though many of the demographic changes did not manifest themselves until the turn of the century.

The graph showing the 150-year period from the mid-nineteenth century helps to make the point that, in the long run, the 1970s was the cusp of demographic change. It makes the point that a new kind of Scotland was emerging, one in which rates of natural increase were balancing out – birth and death rates were broadly comparable, and above all the long pattern of very high emigration from Scotland, at least in terms of out-numbering immigration, was diminishing. True, the numbers leaving were still greater, but they were on a par by the 1990s, and much more like England and Wales[3] which still saw immigrants outnumber emigrants.

What of the period after the turn of this century? Can we be sure that the post-1970s trend has continued?

While the cross-over of the rate of natural increase and the rate of net migration did not happen until the 1990s, the trend-lines (Figure 4.2) were converging in the decades previously. Not only had the rate of natural increase gone into reverse, but the rate of net migration balanced and then became positive. The point is made by the graphs in Figures 4.1 and 4.2: something quite fundamental was happening to Scotland's demography in the final decades of the twentieth century. We will seek to explain this later in this chapter, but first we need to explore the trends in some detail.

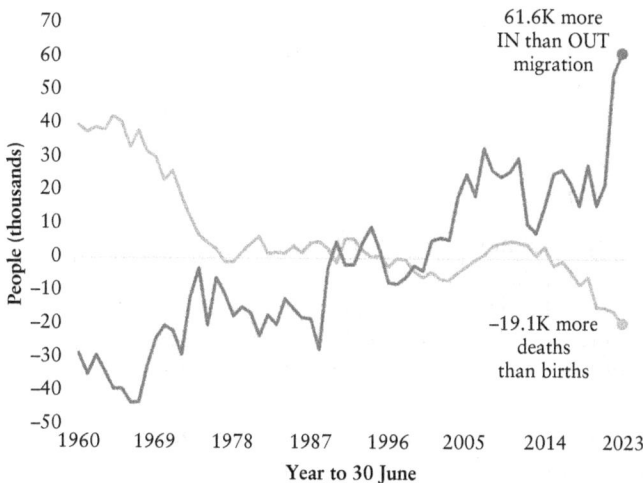

Figure 4.2 Natural change and net migration
Source: https://www.nrscotland.gov.uk/publications/mid-2023-population-estimates/#.

Population Parameters

By way of historical reprise, births in Scotland had been consistently at or about 100,000 births annually for the previous century, by the 1970s were down to 70,000 annual births, and by the beginning of the new century fell further to 56,000.[4] This was exactly *half* of what it had been between 1861 and 1871 when it was 112,000. In the final quarter of the twentieth century, births were beginning to flatline. The number of deaths, on the other hand, showed far less dramatic change, falling from 71,000 per annum between 1861 and 1871, to 55,000 between 2001 and 2011; and in the 1970s, stood at 64,000, a fall of around 10 per cent over the century. The effects of the differential falls in birth and death rates meant that 'natural increase' by the turn of the twenty-first century was zero. Michael Anderson observed that the annual average natural increase 'slumped dramatically from the 1970s to a point where, in 1976–8, 1989–90, 1995–6 and every year from 1997–8 to 2005–6, natural change was negative' (Anderson, 2018: 116). Thereafter, 'rising births and falling deaths meant … that it remained positive in each of the next ten years, another very significant change' (ibid. 116). Relative to England and Wales, as we saw in Figure 4.1 above, Scotland's natural growth from the 1970s fell almost to zero, whereas that for England and Wales was slightly higher. By 2023, deaths in Scotland outnumbered births, as they had for the previous nine years (see Figure 4.2).

Migration

The major demographic shift, however, relates to migration. Historically, far more Scots emigrated proportionately compared with England and Wales, never less than two and a half times greater than its southern neighbours. Migrants from Scotland, in any case, did not need to travel very far, and many simply crossed the border into England where jobs and opportunities were judged more plentiful. Figure 4.3 looks at trends in net migration (emigration minus immigration) as a whole.

Since the turn of the century, more people migrated into Scotland than left it. We can further disaggregate these data into (1) migration within the UK, and (2) in-migration from overseas, as follows (Figures 4.4 and 4.5).

The net flows of within-UK and from overseas are not identical, but in both cases there are net increases into Scotland after the turn of the century. By the first mid-decade of the

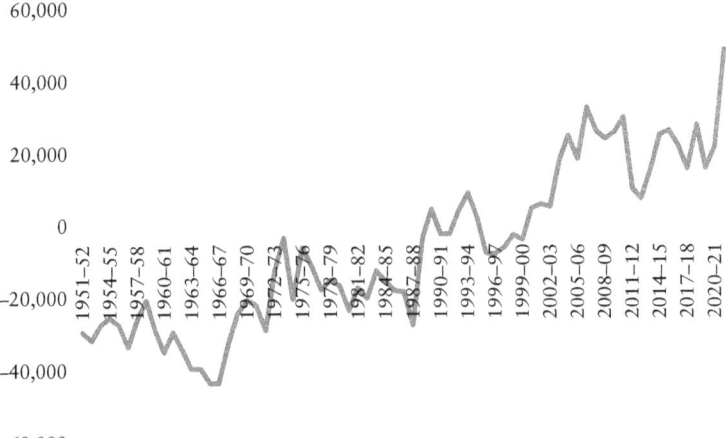

Figure 4.3 Net total migration, 1951–2021
Source: https://www.nrscotland.gov.uk/publications/migration-flows/ (author's graph based on excel data calculations).

Demography

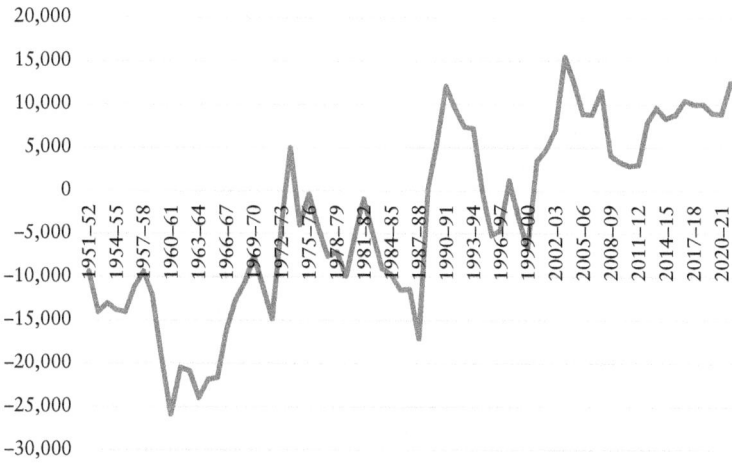

Figure 4.4 Net migration to and from the rest of the UK, 1951–2021
Source: https://www.nrscotland.gov.uk/publications/migration-flows/
(author's graph based on excel data calculations).

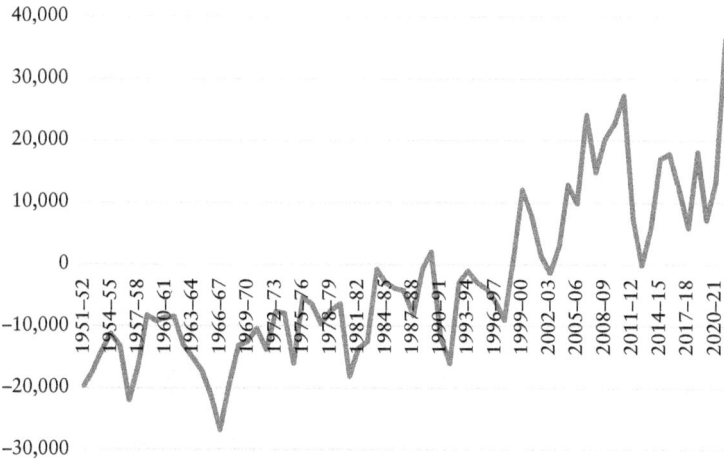

Figure 4.5 Net migration international, 1951–2021
Source: https://www.nrscotland.gov.uk/publications/migration-flows/
(author's graph based on excel data calculations).

twenty-first century, the net effect of migration is that in-migrants outnumber out-migrants, and within a symmetry of roughly the same proportion (about 40 per cent) coming from, or going to, destinations overseas. The majority migrated to the rest of the UK. While average net migration from other parts of the UK has been stable, most of the increase in total migration, especially in the 2020s, was due to higher levels of international migration.

In the long duration, however, Scotland's problem, if that's what it was, was not that it failed to attract immigrants; as Michael Anderson points out, Scotland had more people proportionately born outwith the country than England and Wales between 1851 and 2011. What made the difference was the historical rate of *out*-migration. And then this went into reverse (see Figure 4.1). 'Only from the 1980s ... did out-migration profiles in Scotland and in England and Wales begin to look much more similar' (Anderson, ibid. 135).

Furthermore, we cannot conclude that Scotland was an insular place from which people left, but few in-migrated such that there were few opportunities to refresh the population with incomers, demographically and culturally. Indeed, the Scottish population has long had proportionately *more* in-migrants compared with England and Wales, for at least a century and a half (see Figure 4.6).

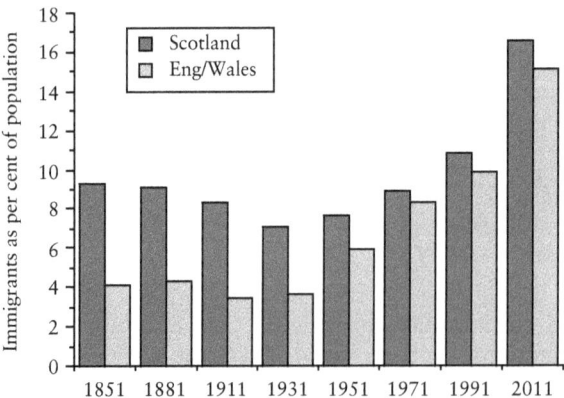

Figure 4.6 Immigrants as per cent of the population, Scotland, England and Wales, 1851–2011
Source: Based on census reports for relevant years (with kind permission of M. Anderson).

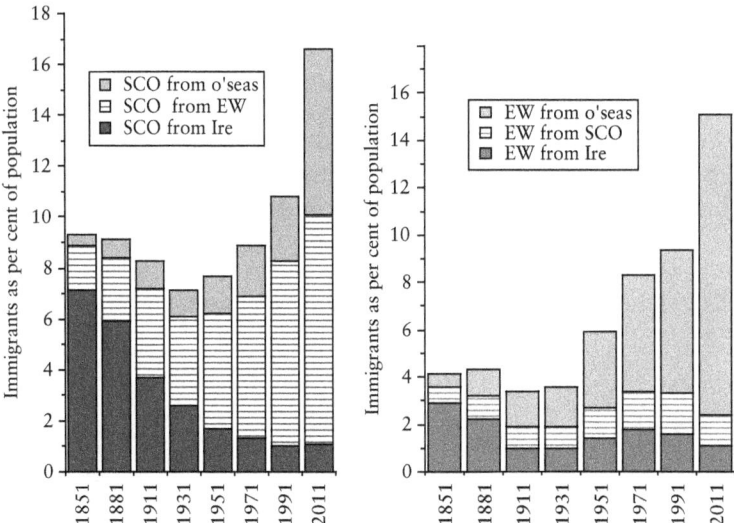

Figure 4.7 Immigrants as per cent of Scottish, English, and Welsh populations, 1851–2011
Source: Based on census reports for relevant years (with kind permission of M. Anderson).

The composition of those incomers to Scotland, compared with England and Wales, is also important (see Figure 4.7). Note the contrasting features:[5]

- Scotland, historically, had a much higher proportion of Irish incomers than England and Wales, but that differential has diminished over time;
- England and Wales had a much higher proportion of migrants from overseas than Scotland;
- A growing share of Scotland's migrants in recent decades have come from south of the border.

In the mid-nineteenth century, 'immigrants' were far more likely to be Irish, a flow which diminished in the twentieth century, to be replaced by people from England (and Wales) such that these were the majority by 1951, and remained so thereafter, while immigrants from overseas grow in proportion as well as in absolute terms.

The Changing Shape of Scotland's Population

So far, we have been looking at the broad parameters of population, but dramatic shifts have occurred in key elements. Consider, for example, these profiles (Figures 4.8 and 4.9), reflecting the age structures in the mid-twentieth century, and again, fifty years later at the beginning of the twenty-first century.

Looking at the shapes of the two graphs in Figures 4.8 and 4.9, we can see clearly what happened to the birth rate. In the 1951 figure, there are fluctuations for men and for women which

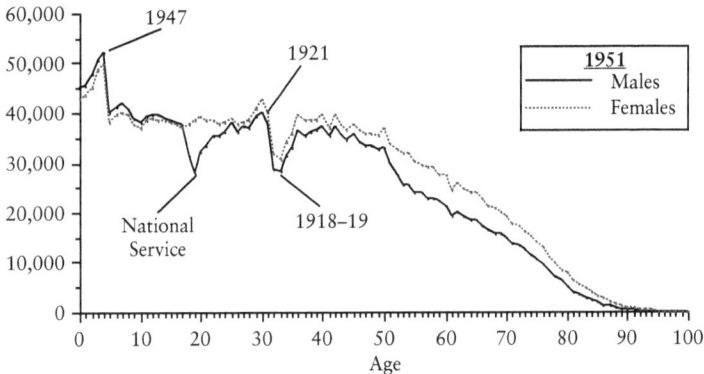

Figure 4.8 Scotland's population by age, 1951
Source: M. Anderson, 2018: 187.

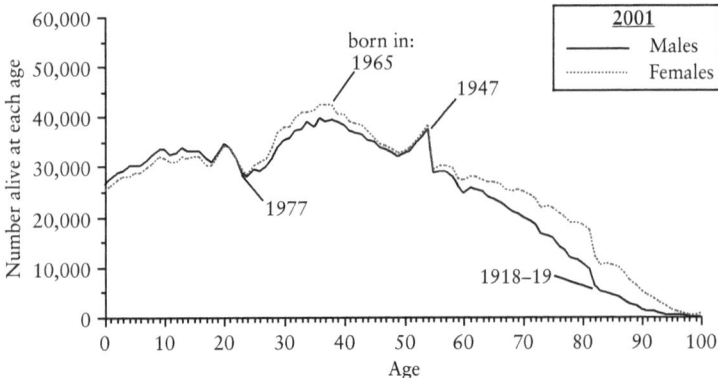

Figure 4.9 Scotland's population by age, 2001
Source: Anderson, 2018: 187.

Figure 4.10 Number of births in Scotland, 1866–2022
Source: National Records of Scotland, Time Series Data 2022, Table BT-01 (courtesy of M. Anderson).

reflect the two world wars, and especially the baby booms which followed them, in contrast to low birth rates during the wars. Fifty years later, we can see the 1947 baby boomers moving through the population, a modest boost in the mid-1960s, but in the younger age groups a proportionate fall in numbers such that there were fewer children aged 0 to 4 than people in any age group below the ages of 60 to 64. Note, too, the historic low in 1977, when fertility rates were virtually at their lowest.

Figure 4.10 shows the fall in the number of births in Scotland, such that by the 1970s, they were at historically low levels.

Fertility and Nuptiality

What we are seeing here is the aggregate of millions of micro-decisions by couples about having children, or not, how many, and when to have them; resulting generally in restrictions on family size. In contrast, at the beginning of the twentieth century there was a relatively high birth rate – 25.7 live births per 1,000 population – such that women marrying between the ages of 22 and 26 had on average as many as six children, unthinkable a century later. Furthermore, whereas in 1911 only one in twenty of the population was 65 or older, a hundred years later, that figure was one in six. By that date, women could expect to live until they were 81, and men to 76, which meant that babies at birth[6] could expect to live at least twenty-five years longer than our 1911 ancestors, reflecting particularly the fall in infant mortality. Thus was added another generation span to the population so that having *great*-grandparents still alive is no longer as unusual as it used to be.

Fewer children were being born; comparing the two graphs, 4.7 and 4.8, shows that. The total fertility rate which shows how many children on average women would have if current fertility remained the same was, by 2020, down to 1.28. Infant mortality rates were 4 deaths per 1,000, in contrast to 113 in 1911. Above all, there was a dramatic rise in the age at which people married, to 33 for men and 31 for women, up two years in only a decade; coupled with increasing rates of cohabitation between couples. In crude terms, births in 2001 were only 40 per cent of what they had been a century previously. Note too (Figure 4.11) how the age of mothers at births changed dramatically after the mid-1970s. Far fewer births were to younger women (in their twenties) in the years after 1975.

Shifts in fertility are related to patterns of *nuptiality*, the percentage of people in a given population who marry. Indeed, for a century before the Second World War fewer women in Scotland than in England got married, but when they did so, they tended to have more babies. Michael Anderson comments:

> The overall trend in fertility was markedly downward in the later twentieth century. However, this significantly reflected not a flight from childbearing altogether but the near disappearance of very large families, plus a general shift to later childbearing, which itself resulted in more very small families. As late as 1981–5 women's median age at childbearing was 25; by 2001–5 it was 29.3. In the same period, births to non-married mothers rose from 15 per cent to 45 per cent of all births ... Most of this rise was directly linked to the growth in cohabitation. (2012: 56)

In social trends, we are accustomed to relatively smooth increases and decreases; consider, however, the proportion of women at different time-points who were married. At the beginning of the twentieth century, less than one in ten women under 25 were married, rising to almost six in ten in 1971 before falling back to one in four in 1991.[7] The figures for women in the second half of their twenties also shows a peak in 1971,

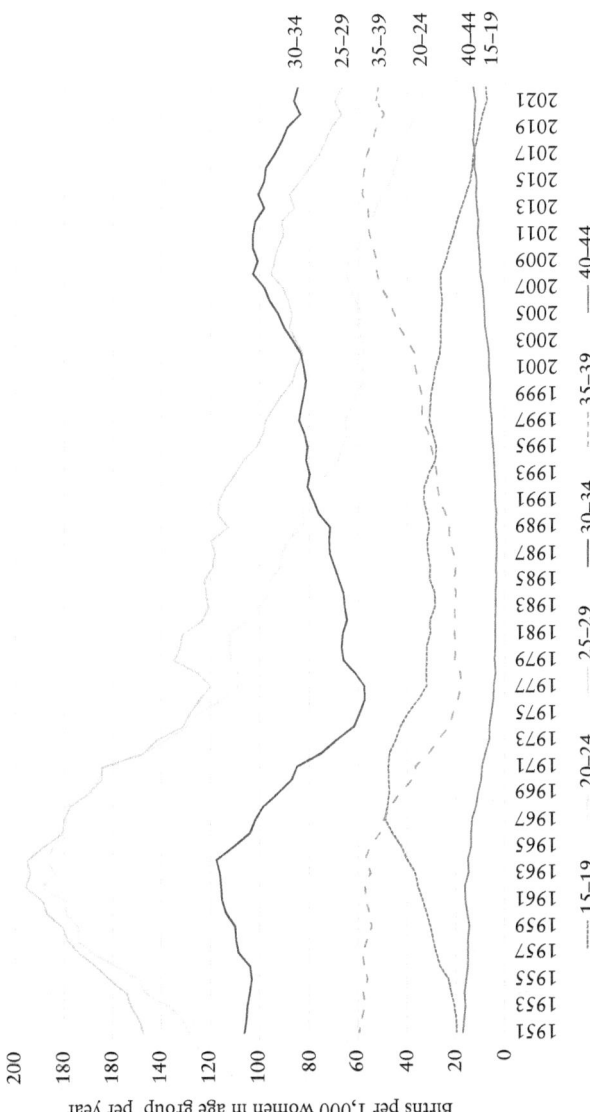

Figure 4.11 Births by age group, 1951–2022
Source: Data from National Records for Scotland, Vital Events Reference Tables 2022, Table 3.08 (courtesy of M. Anderson).

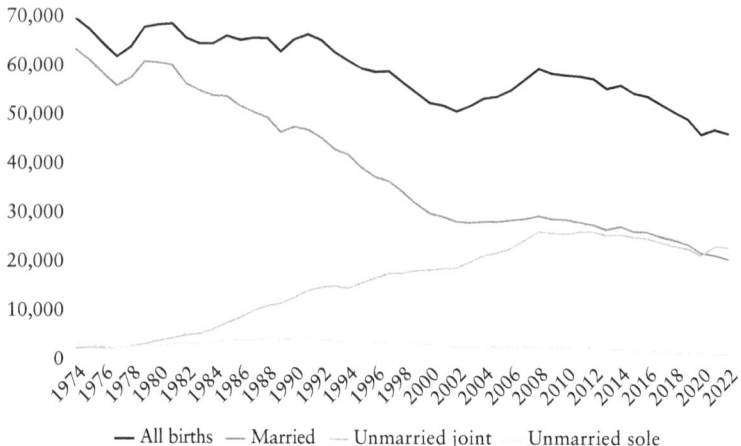

— All births   — Married   — Unmarried joint   Unmarried sole

Figure 4.12 Number of births, Scotland, 1974–2022, by marital status of parent(s) registering birth
Source: National Records of Scotland, Vital Events Reference Tables 2022, Table 3.02.

reinforcing the argument that the 1970s was one fulcrum of social change; the second fulcrum occurring in 2000. Note the falling number of births to married parents (Figure 4.12), such that by 2022 births to cohabiting couples was greater. Not only did the general fertility rate fall, but the late 2000s is the point at which births to non-married parents matched those to married parents. By 2016, births to unmarried parents made up the majority (51 per cent), and by 2021, that figure was 54 per cent of all births in Scotland.[8]

Shrinking Households

Reflecting demographic change, households were getting smaller if we compare the first two decades of the twenty-first century.[9] One-person households are now the most common (37 per cent), followed by two-person households (34 per cent), then larger households (3 persons or more), which constituted 29 per cent. These proportions show a substantial change compared with the turn of the century when they were more or less equally matched (a third in each category). Put another way, in 2001 the average household size was 2.27, while by 2022, it had fallen to 2.12. The change in household composition is even more dramatic if we consider that in 1961 only 14 per cent of households consisted of a single person, while 60 per cent were of three persons or more. Single-adult households are already common, projected to increase by half in the next twenty years, according to the Scottish Household Survey;[10] closely followed by two-adult households, likely to increase by a quarter, changes with obvious implications for housing-stock needs. Concomitant decreases in household forms are likely among larger households (especially containing two or more adults with children), as well as those with three or more adults, all likely to decrease by one-third.

Gender and Demographic Change

What, behind all that, has happened to relationships between men and women? The answer lies in increasing rates of cohabitation, reflected in Figure 4.12. Unmarried couples living together without formally registering their relationship as a marriage was uncommon as late as the mid-1970s. There has also been a sharp rise in the proportion of births to women who are not married but cohabiting. The turning-point was 2016, when more than half (51 per cent) of births were to unmarried parents, compared to 47 per cent ten years earlier, and 31 per cent in 1994 (*The Registrar General's Annual Review of Demographic Trends*, 2014: 21). At the same time, the proportion of births registered solely in the mother's name (historically, a sign of 'illegitimacy') has fallen since the late 1990s to just under 5 per cent (it was around 6 to 7 per cent in the 1980s and 1990s), suggesting that the increase in births to unmarried parents has been to cohabiting couples rather than to single mothers.

More people were cohabiting than ever before (among women aged 20–24, twice as many were cohabiting as were married), but more young people have chosen to remain unattached rather than enter formal (married) or informal (cohabiting) relationships. Marriage seems to have become a minority pursuit among young adults, while a quarter of adults over 16 have some experience of having been married, but are no longer, at least to their original partner.

The Impact of Education

Running alongside these shifts in demography, and arguably driving them, have come transformations in education. A far higher proportion of young adults (those aged 16 to 24) are in higher education: 34 per cent in 2019, compared with 24 per cent twenty years earlier. The transformations in education are especially true for women. Lindsay Paterson has observed that 'whereas among school leavers in 1951–4, 10% of boys but only 6% of girls gained the equivalent of three Highers, that proportion was equalized a quarter of a century later (at 18% in 1975) and was reversed before the end of the century (27% and 34% in 1997.)' (Paterson, 2017: 253). The interactions between social class and gender can be gauged by his finding that the proportions of girls passing at least one Higher rose to the male equivalent by the 1970s in social class I (professionals); it overtook boys in the early 1980s in social class III (skilled workers), and in the late 1980s among social class IV (unskilled workers) (Paterson, 2023a: 49).

As secondary education expanded, so too did higher education. School attainment was increasingly important in giving school leavers access to post-school education, and this applied to women as well as to working-class people. In 1980, 19 per cent of men and 16 per cent of women entered higher education; in 2000, the proportions respectively were 45 per cent and 56 per cent (Paterson, 2023a: 255). Likewise, adults with a degree or professional qualification are broadly one-third of the population, up from under a quarter in 2007. Those aged 25 to 34 were especially likely to have one: 4 out of 10 had a degree or professional qualification (Scottish Household Survey, 2019[11]). Concomitantly, those with no formal educational qualifications fell from 23 per cent in 2007 to 15 per cent in 2019.

We can, then, begin to see how and why the age of marriage, and the age at which people have children, have increased; as has remaining in education. Extending full-time education, especially for women, a preference for cohabitation rather than marriage – the former frequently leading to the latter – postponing the age of having children, all contributing to the relationship patterns we see in the second decade of the twenty-first century.

Transforming Gender

The transformations occurred especially among women, although social class differences continued to matter. Not only did far more women enter higher education, but a much higher proportion of women in general were in paid work. In 1951, about one-third of women over the age of 15 were economically active, and by 1971, it was still well under half (42 per cent).[12] By the turn of the century, it was well over half (57 per cent), and by 2019 had risen to over two-thirds (68 per cent); a much steeper gradient than for men over those twenty years (71 per cent, and 74 per cent respectively). Taken as a whole, then, we can see that the proportion of women in the labour force doubled from one-third in 1951 to two-thirds seventy years later, virtually a lifetime change. By the 2020s, there was virtual gender parity in the labour force.[13] While it is true that women were more likely to work part-time, this participation in the formal labour force has helped to transform gender relationships. What is striking about the distributions in Figure 4.13 is how similar women and men are in being economically active over their lifetimes.

Nevertheless, formal participation in the labour force does not generate gender equality. Earlier gender audits in Scotland

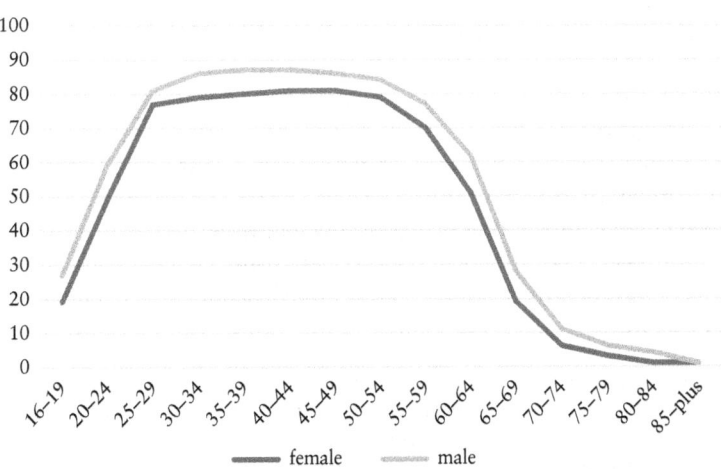

Figure 4.13 Economic activity by sex and age, 2022
Source: https://www.scotlandscensus.gov.uk/2022-results/scotland-s-census-2022-education-labour-market-and-travel-to-work.

in 2007 and 2014 showed a considerable gap between men's and women's earnings (Breitenbach and Wasoff, 2007; Engender, 2014). Working part-time and in personal services, administrative and secretarial occupations, as well as in sales and customer services, carry lower pay rates than for men. And far more women than men lack pension provisions. In 2004–05, for example, 60 per cent of women part-time workers had no pension provision at all. Women were also far more likely to be unpaid carers, and to rely on benefits and tax credits than men (Engender, 2014).

In 2020, the Scottish government published its Gender Equality Index for the first time, and repeated the exercise in 2023.[14] The index provides measures as to how close Scotland is to full equality between men and women in a number of 'domains', including paid employment ('work'). The report concluded:

> The domain of Work measures the extent to which women and men have equal access to employment and good working conditions. Within the work domain (score 79[15]), inequality was highest in 'labour market inactivity due to caring', with caring roles impacting far more women than men. Occupational segregation also contributed to inequality, with more women than men concentrated in the care industries. These findings corroborate the pattern described in the 2020 iteration of the Index.

In terms of the domestic division of labour, while there is a strong ideology of sharing household tasks between men and women, in practice women do most of the household work. While both men and women believed that they both *should* be responsible for housework (86 per cent in each case), 70 per cent of women, and 65 per cent of men, agreed that women actually did most of the housework (Scottish Social Attitudes survey, 2005). Ideology is one thing; practice another.

We need only to look back to see how far gender relations have come since our parents' and grandparents' days. The writer Ailsa McKay observed:

> The point being made is that women and men occupy very different spaces in advanced capitalist economies and these 'spaces' serve to influence their access, participation and voice in political life. However, whilst the space they occupy may restrict and limit their ability to participate, women remain resourceful in finding alternative spaces to organise, influence and ensure their voices are heard. (McKay, 2013[16])

WINNERS AND LOSERS

Thus far, the story is relatively positive: less out-migration, a growing population largely as a result, women making gains through education and employment. Consider, however, Figure 4.14. Scotland's people are falling short.

For men and for women, life is getting shorter, both relative to other countries, and in historic terms. Note, in particular, the tailing-off at the end of the second decade of the new century. There was a gradual improvement in life expectancy until 2012, and it stalls, thanks to Covid (see Figure 4.14). We might explain the downturn in terms of Covid-19, which has had its effects on life expectancy rates, but it was occurring before that, and was plain to see from around 2012. Between 2012–14 and 2015–17, for example, male life expectancy at birth (e_0) was getting lower by one week every year.[17] By 2020–22, life expectancy for men was 76.5 years, and for women, 80.7 years. National Records for Scotland estimate that it has decreased for three weeks for men, and 5.7 weeks for women since 2019–21,[18] bearing in mind that these were the Covid years.

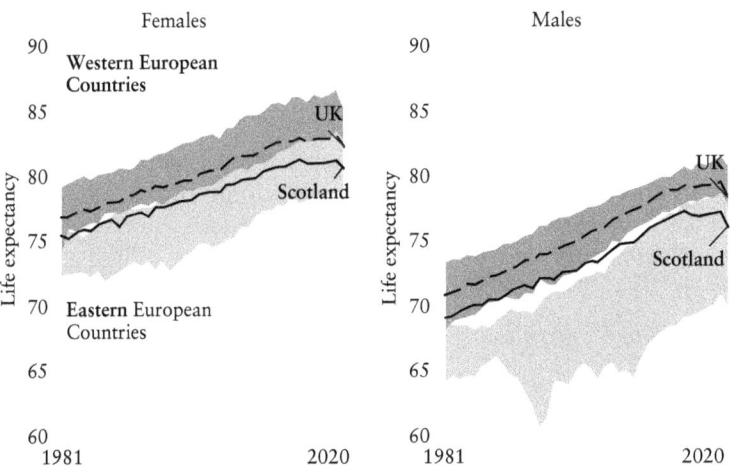

Figure 4.14 Life expectancy at birth in Scotland by sex compared to other countries, 1981 to 2020
Source: Life Expectancy in Scotland (NRS), Life expectancy at birth by sex (Eurostat) (The dotted lines in the figures represent the UK, and the solid line, Scotland).

It remains to be seen whether this is a blip or a longer-term trend. By 2021–23, life expectancy in Scotland had risen to 80.9 years for women, and 76.9 years for men, although still lower than before the Covid pandemic.[19]

Figure 4.15 shows some of the causes of death that changed most after 2012–14 for males (this pattern is similar for females).

The positive message is that improvements in deaths from heart disease have boosted life expectancy, but that the rate of progress has slowed since 2012. On the other hand, the rise in deaths from drug abuse, and from dementia, have reduced life expectancy for the population as a whole, although in the case of dementia this might well be compounded by an ageing population. Bear in mind that 'causes of death' is subject to changing definitions, and that the rise of deaths from dementia is partly the result of that.

All of this was occurring before Covid, which had its own dramatic effect, as we can see from Figures 4.16 and 4.17, for men and for women.

While there were gains in life expectancy after 2017–19 to be had from improvements in respiratory conditions, cancers and dementia, drug misuse and especially circulatory conditions, notably among men, showed a worsening. Above all, deaths from Covid, and the data only show up to 2021, were dramatic in their effect.

Nor can we take notional comfort from an assumption that intra-UK comparisons with regard to life expectancies up to and including Covid would be much the same (see Figure 4.18). In comparison with the other home nations, both for men and women, people in Scotland on average live two years less than their fellow citizens in the UK.

Multiple Scotlands

There are, as we might expect, considerable differences *within* Scotland.[20] Life expectancy was highest in East Renfrewshire for females and East Dunbartonshire for males and lowest in Glasgow city for both males and females in 2020–22. Most of Scotland's council areas have seen a fall in life expectancy over the last few years. Overall, people live longest in Orkney (80 for men, and 84 for women[21]), East Renfrewshire (79, 83), East Dunbartonshire (80, 83), Shetland (79, 83), Na h-Eilean Siar

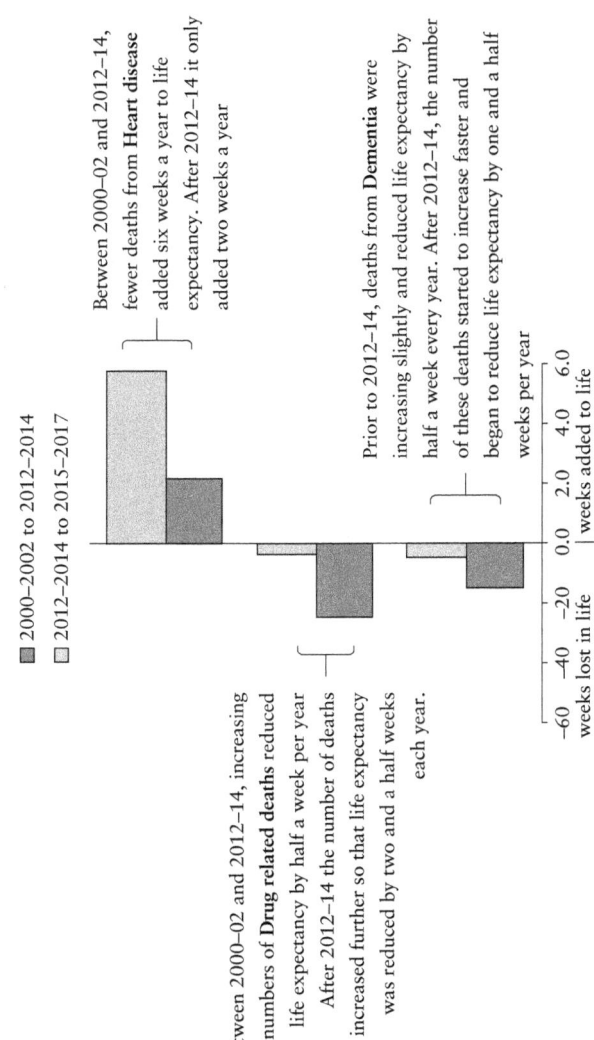

Figure 4.15 The changing causes of death and life expectancy
Source: https://blog.nrscotland.gov.uk/2019/07/18/why-is-life-expectancy-stalling-in-scotland/.

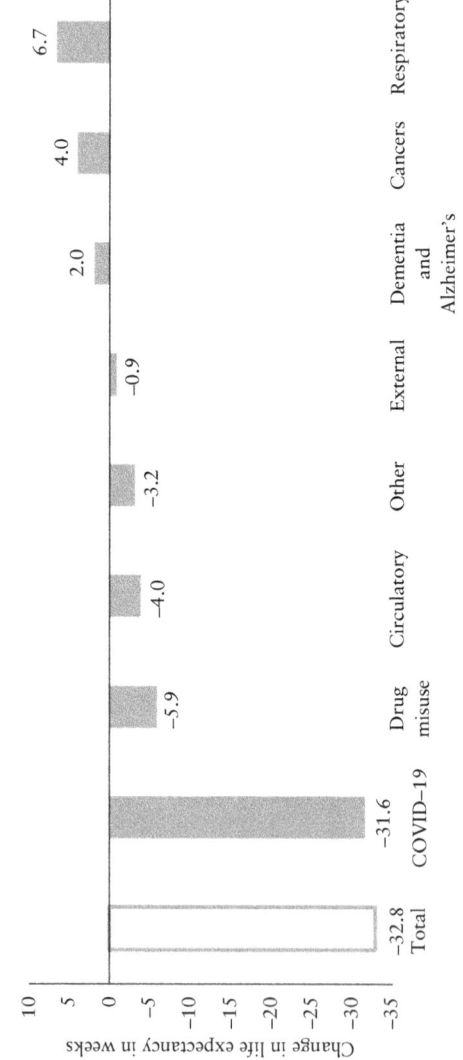

Figure 4.16 Life expectancy changes from 2017–19 to 2019–21 by cause, males
Source: https://www.nrscotland.gov.uk/publications/life-expectancy-in-scotland-2021-2023/ (with analysis carried out by the author).

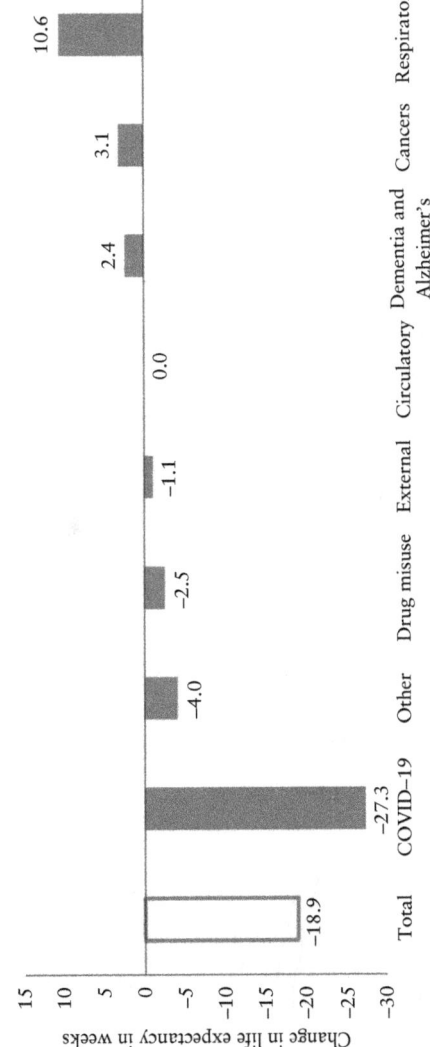

Figure 4.17 Life expectancy changes from 2017–19 to 2019–21 by cause, females
Source: https://www.nrscotland.gov.uk/publications/life-expectancy-in-scotland-2021-2023/ (with analysis carried out by the author).

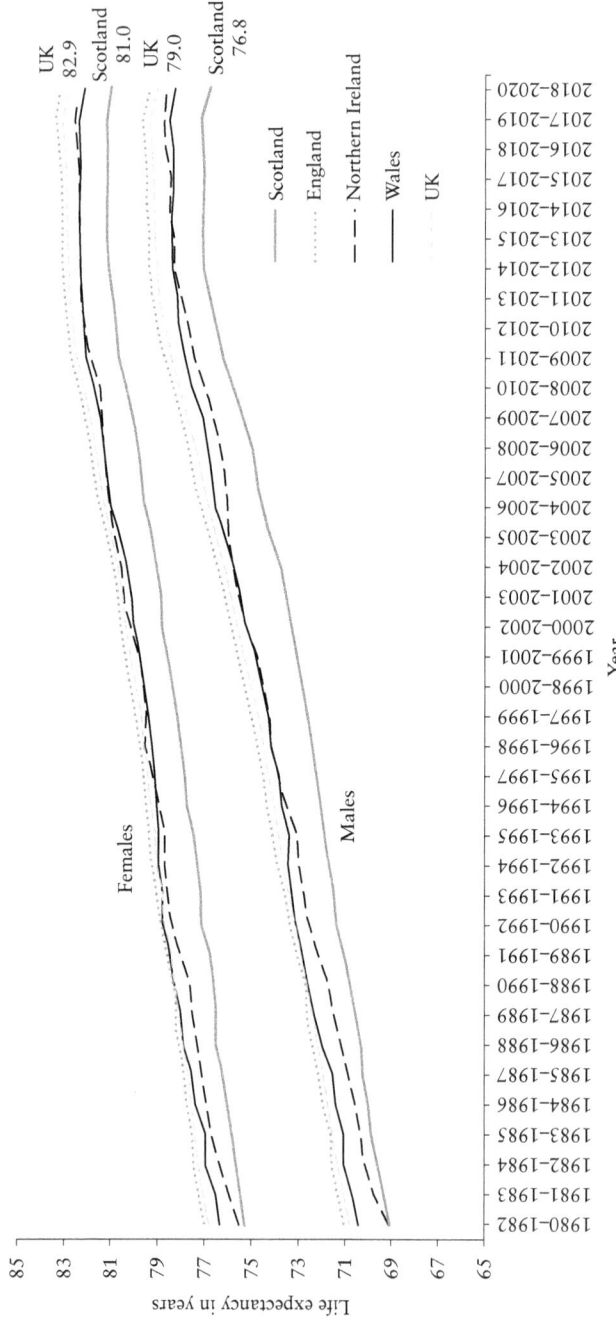

Figure 4.18 Life expectancies in Scotland and the UK
Source: https://www.nrscotland.gov.uk/publications/life-expectancy-in-scotland-2021-2023/ (with analysis carried out by the author).

(Western Isles) (77, 82) and East Lothian (79, 82). Lives are shorter in places like Glasgow (73, 78), West Dunbartonshire (73, 78), North Lanarkshire (74, 78), Inverclyde (74, 78), Dundee (74, 78), and East Ayrshire (74, 79).

Using life expectancy at birth figures (e_0), people can expect to live six or seven years longer if they live on Orkney than in Glasgow, and within the latter in particular, we know that there are considerable differences by neighbourhoods. For example, for men in 2015–19 it ranged from 65.4 years in Greater Govan to 83 years in Pollokshields West. For women it was 72.7 years in Ruchill and Possilpark, but 86 years in Anniesland, Jordanhill and Whiteinch.[22] Plainly, people's socio-economic conditions of life are highly relevant with regard to life expectancies. Thus, as regards measures of social deprivation (SIMDs), a man living in the least deprived areas could expect, on average, to live 13.7 years longer than a man in the most deprived areas (to 82.3 and 68.6 respectively); and for women, a difference of 10.5 years (85.5 and 75).[23] In other words, on average, men living in deprived areas barely live beyond retirement age.[24]

The Covid Pandemic

Covid-19 itself had its own special effects, frequently interacting with other health indicators of morbidity and mortality. Social deprivation is likely to be a significant compounding factor in what is known as 'long Covid'. Thus, one systematic study published in the journal *Nature* in 2022 used multivariate logistic regression to indicate that people living in the most deprived SIMDs are 40 per cent *more* likely than those in the least deprived to suffer from long Covid,[25] especially as research shows that organ damage, to lungs, kidneys and brains, is greater among long Covid cases.[26] Truth to tell, measuring the impact of Covid on Scottish health is compounded by the historic trajectory of ill-health in Scotland. The Scottish government was credited in social surveys with handling Covid-19 better than the UK government, at least in terms of public perceptions,[27] but rates and outcomes are, at the end of the day, not very different north and south of the border, especially given propensities to ill-health in Scotland.

Longer-term international comparisons pay too little attention to questions of historical life experiences, different epidemiological regimes, income and wealth configurations, and varying climatic conditions (compare living in wet, cold Scotland with living in southern Europe). Superficial contrasts of changes in mortality in many European countries relative to Scotland can provide only very limited understanding of why Scotland became the Western European country with the highest mortality by the 1980s. As Michael Anderson observed:

> it is clear that many [of the] countries which 'caught up with' Scotland's relatively lower mortality by the middle of the twentieth century had done so by eliminating problems which were of little relevance to our understanding of Scottish death rates over time. (Anderson, 2018: 333)

Nevertheless, Scotland continues to have one of the highest rates of mortality in Western Europe, in which the leading causes of death are (still) heart disease, lung cancer, cerebrovascular diseases, dementia and Alzheimers, and for younger people, drugs deaths, which on any measure, relative or absolute, is almost off the scale. And the Scottish mortality rate for chronic liver disease, for both men and women, which had been static between the 1950s and the 1970s, by the turn of the new century, for men, was six times what it had been in the 1950s, and for women, five times the rate.

Accounting for Variations in Morbidity and Mortality

Let us return to an issue raised at the beginning of this chapter: if we want to account for differential rates of morbidity and mortality, to what extent is it simply to be explained by changes in social structure? If Scotland (or Glasgow, for that matter) is more 'working-class', in that a higher proportion of the population are in manual work, or there are proportionately older people, and working-class people and the elderly have higher death rates, might this 'explain' the differentially high death rate?

Alastair Leyland and his colleagues in their study 'Inequalities in Mortality in Scotland, 1981–2001' (2007) compared age-standardised death rates by social class categories in the major cities of Scotland for the period 2000–02.[28] They showed that the four cities differed from each other and from the Scottish mean. As a ratio of the Scottish mean calibrated at 100, they found that Edinburgh's rate was 92 per cent, Aberdeen's rate was 100, Dundee's 118, and Glasgow's 163. Perhaps that is not so surprising: Edinburgh and Aberdeen have higher proportions of middle-class people, and Dundee and Glasgow more working-class people. It is, however, not the class composition of the different cities which makes the difference. The researchers found that age standardised death rates for lower managerial/professional workers were 30 per cent *higher* in Glasgow than in Edinburgh, and for 'routine' manual workers, they were 70 per cent higher.

If we compare Edinburgh and Glasgow in the early 2000s, death rates for *all* the social classes were higher in Glasgow; for example, higher managerial/professional workers in Glasgow have a rate 60 per cent higher than Edinburgh. In other words, there does seem to be a 'Glasgow effect' on mortality. Thus, the higher risk of death is a feature of the *populations* of Clydeside and Glasgow rather than the simpler explanation that a higher proportion of working-class people live there, coupled with the unknown effects of differential out-migration of the better-off and healthier.

So what *is* it about Clydeside or Glasgow which has this effect over and above social class differences, assuming that Leyland's findings for the turn of the century (1981–2001) still apply? Social class attaches to individuals and households, rather than to the areas in which they live. For most people their life chances are determined by what they work at, the usual source of income for most people. It characterises their life security, gives them access to housing, education, social capital and so on. Spatial differences, then, are not simply reflections of differences in people's social class. And in any case, how spatial units are defined points to significant differences between urban and rural areas.[29] One measure is not a substitute for the other – they tell us different social things.

Social class differences are endemic as regards morbidity. Once more, cancers of the lungs, bronchus and trachea have the most pronounced rate of difference in class terms (the rate for routine workers being five times that of higher managers and professionals). The occupational gradients are less pronounced for cancers of the colon and rectum (2 to 1) but four times greater with regard to stomach cancers (Leyland et al., 2007). The authors of that study concluded that, at the turn of the century, the male mortality rate in each social class was higher in Glasgow than in Clydeside as a whole, and was higher in Clydeside than in the whole of Scotland. Social class differences are not the only explanation for differential mortality rates; they also have to do with where people live, an area factor, regardless of the social class they belong to. That there is a connection between social class and causes of death is clear, but it is far from clear what the precise mechanisms are which connect them.

The Glasgow Effect

And then there is what became known as 'the Glasgow effect'. The city contains a disproportionate number of Scotland's areas of multiple deprivation. In 2012, the city had 36 per cent of the most deprived areas in Scotland, an improvement on 2004 when it contained almost half of them,[30] and within the city, almost half of the population live in the most deprived areas. Scottish government data for 2020[31] found that Glasgow city had the highest proportion of its citizens living in the most deprived areas (43 per cent), the same as Inverclyde, followed by North Ayrshire (41 per cent), West Dunbartonshire (40 per cent), Dundee (38 per cent) and North Lanarkshire (33 per cent).[32] Edinburgh (11 per cent) and Aberdeen (10 per cent) fared much better.

What has attracted particular interest in the 'Glasgow effect' is that, compared to English cities like Liverpool and Manchester, Glasgow has an appreciably higher mortality level. Just why Glasgow should have such concentrations of deprivation remains an open and interesting question, and furthermore, why it should have higher illness and death rates than similar British cities. There have been attempts to explain Glasgow's excess mortality in terms of broad political-economic causes such as 'neoliberalism' and the imposition of 'austerity' policies.[33] The difficulty with that explanation is that it is unclear why neoliberalism and austerity should have a *specific* impact on Glasgow, as opposed to Liverpool, Manchester and Belfast all of which were subject to similar economic policies from UK governments.

One possible explanation for higher mortality in Glasgow relates to differential out-migration. The city embarked on extensive programmes of population overspill from the late 1950s notably to New Towns such as East Kilbride, Cumbernauld and Livingston. Those who left the city were younger and more occupationally skilled, and if nothing else they had the material and social capital, leaving behind those less endowed. There is, then, the possibility that differential out-migration has left the city with a relatively unskilled population, and that people who remain are somehow more prone to disease than out-migrants. This still does not explain why higher rates of mortality attach to those in *higher* non-manual employment living in the city, whether this relates to lower in-migration rates of the 'healthy', or to features of the place itself.

Epigenetics

Then there are epigenetic differences.[34] These focus on possible ways in which environmental factors can affect how elements of the genetic code in DNA are switched on or off, thus altering how these genes function (McGuinness et al., 2012). This research showed that even taking into account age and sex, and the interaction effects between variables, those living in deprived conditions showed markedly *lower* levels of DNA methylation.[35] These low levels of methylation were linked to a number of predictors of poor health, notably those associated with enhanced levels of cardiovascular risk.

Studies of the aftermath of famine in general where parental food deprivation, coupled with extreme switches between periods of glut and starvation, produced physical and mental long-term effects not only on those who suffered these conditions but also on their children. Thus, the famines of the mid-nineteenth century in Ireland (as well as the Highlands), and the seasonal fluctuations of food supplies, had the potential to embed in subsequent generations 'epigenetic ageing' by accelerating factors which result in poor health especially from such conditions as cancers and heart disease.[36] Since this line of socio-medical research was reported in 2012, there does not appear to have been a systematic analytical attempt, medically or sociologically, to follow it through (see Michels, 2022, for an account of epigenetic epidemiology; and Lux Fatimathas' research note on early life factors and their impact on the genes of Glasgow's poorest, also 2022[37]).

For the time-being, epigenetic explanations for the Glasgow effect remain in the realms of plausibility, but it is amenable to testing and research, and ought to help us understand better why places such as Glasgow with its history of in-migration from Ireland and the Highlands is susceptible. The plausibility of such an explanation also rests upon the common-sense notion that all of us inherit the genetic make-up of our ancestors, which do not determine patterns of morbidity and mortality, but are certainly an influence on them, which is why we get asked by doctors about family propensities to diseases and causes of death. Our propensity to suffer (or avoid) certain medical conditions deriving from those of our parents and grandparents make this an interesting line of enquiry, bringing together as it does genetic and social factors. As Michael Anderson observed, it does seem plausible to argue that much of Glasgow's population will have had an unusually long and intense track record, going back several generations, of deprivation, disease, uncertainty and stress. If we add to this the fact of selective out-migration of skilled and healthy workers over several centuries, then we have interesting lines of research using new forms of long-term record linkage of health, census and vital registration data which is some way in the future.

Health Warning

In this chapter, we have moved almost seamlessly between characterising individuals, and characterising spatial areas. There is, however, a health warning attached to this shift, known as the ecological fallacy, that the characteristics of individuals and those of the areas in which they live are the same, and that we can infer one from the other. The fallacy arises when we deduce from aggregate data the characteristics of individual people who comprise the aggregates. We might find this puzzling because aggregates are composed of individuals. Strictly speaking, the ecological fallacy results from inferring that because there is a relationship between variables at the aggregate level it also holds for those between individual people.[38]

Thus, we may find a putative relationship between, say, people's health and levels of education if our datum is 'area', such as local authorities, or what the Scottish Index of Multiple Deprivation calls 'data zones' of which there are almost 7,000 such units in Scotland. The ecological fallacy results when we assume that our putative relationship between health and education which we find at aggregate level also applies at individual-level data. This is not so puzzling if we bear in mind that grouping areas together depends on what our purpose for doing so is, and that our 'data zones' are usually statistical constructions in any case; but then so are local authority areas, reflected in the periodic re-organisation of their boundaries. They are not set in stone. The answer to the fallacy is not to reject all aggregates as false, but to be aware of their artefactual nature. After all, they are only as good as the purpose in hand, and what it is we are trying to explain. Strictly speaking, *'data'* (the Latin for 'given') should be treated as *'capta'* ('taken'), for the purposes/hypotheses we are trying to test out.

What does this have to do with Scotland's demography? People's life chances (and indeed, their 'death' chances) are reflections of their characteristics dealt to them as individuals, but also of the areas they inhabit. A good example of that is how people of similar social class in Glasgow and Edinburgh have differential chances of mortality and morbidity. There must be something about *where* they live which impacts on their lives, even if we are unsure what it is at the aggregate level, epigenetics or not. When we think about 'place', then, we become sensitised to a further realm of understanding about the complex factors which determine our lives, and this is the point about pluralising 'Scotland', which in any case is simply a big – national – place.

Which Scotland?

At this point in our argument, we return to a basic point: *which* Scotland are we talking about, for, as Michael Anderson observed, there are different demographic *Scotlands*.

Beginning in the 1970s, a clear change began to occur such that from the 1990s, with a few exceptions,[39] the widespread pattern of population decline in mainland rural parishes became much more localised. Thus, the populations of the islands of Mull and Skye have grown, largely due to in-migration from retired people, many born in England, and from those seeking 'a better life', as well as the rising tide of tourism. The expansion of supermarkets many miles away, especially if they provide a home delivery service, can encourage such migration, as well as having deleterious impacts on local shops. All of this challenges us to think of local lives as taking place within 'activity spaces' which expand well beyond administrative and even physical geographies.[40]

The decennial census for 2022 affords us a broad sweep of population shifts at local authority level. Those showing greatest population growth from 2011 to 2022 are mainly in the east, and/or clustered around Edinburgh and Glasgow (see Table 4.1). All have seen population increases above the Scottish average of +2.7 per cent.[41]

Aberdeen and Dundee show stability, respectively, +0.5 per cent, and +0.6 per cent, although Aberdeenshire shows an increase of +4.3 per cent (suggesting a 'greater Aberdeen' effect, much like Edinburgh and Glasgow), while there is no such effect in Angus, the county around Dundee (−1.4 per cent).

Those showing the greatest population loss are either mainly rural areas such as Na-h-Eileanan Siar (−5.5 per cent), and Dumfries and Galloway (−3.6 per cent), or de-industrialising areas such as Inverclyde (−3.8 per cent) and North Ayrshire (−3.4 per cent). Such trends are evident in the longer-term, taking the thirty-year period from 1991 to 2020.[42] The biggest and most consistent population declines over that period were around the Clyde Basin, in Inverclyde (−16 per cent), West Dunbartonshire (−9 per cent), North Ayrshire (−3 per cent), as well as, in the east, Dundee (−4 per cent), though that city has shown signs of population recovery subsequently, as the 2022 census data indicate. It is, however, the suburban local authorities surrounding these cities which grow most: around Edinburgh, East Lothian, and West Lothian, and in the west, East Renfrewshire.

Most of this population drive comes from in-migration, with the highest net inflows between 2001 and 2018 to Edinburgh (+33 per cent), Glasgow (+19 per cent) and Aberdeen (+16 per cent). In contrast, the highest net outflows are in South Lanarkshire, Dumfries and Galloway, Ayrshire (North, East and

Table 4.1 Population changes in and around Edinburgh and Glasgow, 2011–22

Edinburgh (+7.6%)	Glasgow (+4.6%)
Midlothian (+16.1%)	East Renfrewshire (+6.9%)
East Lothian (+12.7%)	Renfrewshire (+5.1%)
West Lothian (+3.5%)	East Dunbartonshire (+3.7%)

Source: https://www.scotlandscensus.gov.uk/2022-results/scotlands-census-2022-rounded-population-estimates/.

South), East Dunbartonshire, and Argyll and Bute. Behind those flows lie age-related shifts, with the Scottish cities showing higher shares of young adults (most obviously, students in higher education), an influx comparable to London, and Manchester (and on a par with Bristol) in England. While post-industrial areas such as Inverclyde and West Dunbartonshire lose young people, they do not gain an influx of older, retired, people such as Argyll and Bute do, for example. Whether these are the 'right' kind of in-migrants, able to make an economic contribution to the labour force, while requiring health and social services needed by the elderly is another matter.

The Registrar General predicts that Scotland's population will peak in 2028 at 5.48 million, and thereafter decline to 5.39 million by 2045.[43] This will be driven by a further fall in the birth rate, a stabilising of the death rate, though the downturn in life expectancies might well continue with roughly equal numbers of people migrating in and out of Scotland. The population age composition is crucial in influencing the birth rate vis-à-vis the death rate.

Beneath those summary figures lies ongoing loss in population from outlying rural areas, and an ongoing process of de-industrialisation and its aftermath (see, for example, Phillips, Wright and Tomlinson, 2023). It is, however, not simply a divide between urban and rural Scotland. Indeed, there has been population growth in accessible rural areas within commuting distance of the Central Belt, other large cities and major towns. Take the case of Inverness. A Highland Council study of commuting into the town, based on 2011 travel-to-work data, showed that less than half of those employed in the city had homes in Inverness, whilst just over half travelled to work there, almost all (88 per cent) coming from the 'settlement zones' in Highland. At least one in seven travelled more than 30 kilometres in each direction. In 2011 (and 2022 census data should confirm this in due course), in more than one in eight of Scotland's parishes, over 20 per cent of the working population travelled at least 30 kilometres to work, and there were fourteen parishes, mostly but not exclusively in remotest Highland, where at least 10 per cent travelled more than 60 kilometres (Census of Scotland, 2011, Parish Data).

CONCLUSION

Why include a chapter on demography in a book on changing Scotland? It makes a number of key points. First, it deals with the most intimate and personal of decisions, over birth and death, and mobility, which are among the most basic to social life. Second, it shows that these myriad decisions are highly social, in that they are replicated and reproduced across the social structure. We may think of them as our personal, intimate, property, but so do millions of other people who act in quite similar ways without paying attention to them. Third, demographic change since 1945, but especially since the 1970s, has been dramatic and life-changing. We are not the people our parents and grandparents were. We live in smaller households; we live longer; we are susceptible to different diseases; and we die from conditions quite different to those of our forebears.

Looking at these data also makes us question old assumptions; that because historically Scotland was a place people migrated from, we failed to notice that it was also a place for incomers. In proportional terms, Scotland has long been a country with a higher proportion of in-migrants than England and Wales. This has a cultural effect; that it brings people with different experiences and values, that what it means to be Scottish changes and broadens as a result, as we shall see in Chapter 6. Changes in social structure also ramify more broadly. For example, because more women stay on in education and participate more than ever in paid employment, they have babies later in life, once they are established. Broadly speaking, there is now a bimodal pattern as regards fertility and nuptiality such that social class effects – but more precisely education effects – can be seen in the age at which women have children.

The lives of women (and girls) have been especially transformed. Educational advancement since 1945 has evened out many gender inequalities built into the schooling system (Paterson, 2023a). This is not to say that boys and girls, men and women, have equal life chances, but compared to our parents and grandparents they have been transformed. To be sure, there are still institutional as well as cultural barriers to be clambered over or got around, for Scotland is a significantly unequal society. Indeed, that is why we can talk about different Scotlands, plural. It is not simply a matter of our own personal resources, or lack of them, but of where we live. The spatial lottery of place helps to determine what we end up with, a point to be borne in mind throughout a book entitled *Changing Scotland*. The social and spatial aspects interact with each other to determine that. The decline of solidaristic communities known to our parents and grandparents has had a double-edged effect: far less social support and communal belonging; and much more freedom to be whom we choose to be. This is double-edged because with social support went communal discipline.

Broadly speaking, then, demographic change from the 1960s onwards is one of the key frameworks of changing Scotland. Individuals lived their lives and took their life chances within changing demographic frameworks which are reflected in new patterns of social and geographical mobility. Mapping Scotland lets us see how much has changed, notably the depopulation of post-industrial Scotland which has spatial as well as social implications.

These are matters of social structure, but also of culture. We grow up expecting our lives to be different, and by and large they are, but not predictably so. It matters what resources we have, material capital from the jobs we do, but also what we might inherit materially and culturally from our families, and what we might pass on to our children. Materiality matters, as we shall see in the next chapter, but our life chances are conditioned by what we have come from. Social inequality matters, and we inherit 'cultural capital' as well as the material sort, to say nothing of health inequalities, even healthy and unhealthy genes.

So this is a matter of culture as well as materiality. For example, as Michael Anderson observed:

> a fundamental shift in attitudes ... occurred in a world where individual consent replaced public morality, and where the search for personal fulfilment through relationships inside and outside marriage replaced marriage as an institution based on the achievement of limited extrinsic ends. (Anderson, 2018: 320–1)

The authorities built new housing schemes without thinking over-much about how people would manage to live there. Anderson again: '... the general lack of local employment and social amenities rapidly turned many of them in to areas of multiple social deprivation with dramatic long-term consequences for their long-term death rates' (Anderson, 2018: 36).

Sociologists observed that allocating public housing was deliberately selective. Tenants were judged as fit-and-proper people, and got what the authorities thought they 'deserved' (see Damer, 2020, for an excellent account of how judgements were made about who were 'fit and proper' people). This was, in essence, a moral economy, usually highly implicit and judgemental; people got allocated what the powers thought were 'suitable' for their station in life. As Phillips, Wright, and Tomlinson (2023) observed, the process of de-industrialisation was a deliberate affront to a moral economy which had sustained communities and social relationships through the hard times of the twentieth century. Bathgate, Linwood… no more.

The transformation of demographies which we have described in this chapter have been both cause and effect of social change. On the one hand, material circumstances, especially education and employment, as well as the availability of housing, changed in such a way that population demographics came into line. On the other hand, as people had fewer children, 'got on' – or not – through education and training, and were geographically mobile, moving to new places with greater amenities, they came to live a more privatised existence. The cultural sociologist Raymond Williams (1974) described this as 'mobile privatisation'. We may cavil at his use of the term 'privatisation', which within a decade had come to mean the selling-off of public assets notably council housing, but he was not to know what would become of it in the hands of Thatcherism and subsequent political-economic regimes.

Almost twenty-five years later, another cultural sociologist Paul du Gay talked about 'mobile privatised social relations' in his book *Doing Cultural Studies: The Story of the Sony Walkman.* The Walkman itself was neither here nor there; it was to become an outdated technology quite quickly, for by 2010 production had ceased, to be superseded by 'smart' devices. Du Gay observed that the Walkman was 'generally credited with making recorded music portable in a new way, allowing its users to immerse themselves in private worlds of entertainment in public – on the metro, in the bus, or on the beach, for instance' (duGay, 2013: 12). The point is not that these processes are inherent in the technology per se, but in the social meanings which encapsulate them. The Walkman was selected in preference to television, the mobile phone, the personal computer and many more because it epitomised a very

Demography

discrete (as well as discreet) object. It was not to be taken simply as an object, external to us, and in essence neutral, but the objectification of social and personal relations.

And so it matters not whether the demography preceded the 'materiality' of shifts in employment opportunities and social class – which we will deal with in the next chapter – or whether materiality drove demographic change. The interactive effects, one on the other, were such that to attribute causes and effects is to simplify social and economic processes inherently combined with each other. Suffice it to say that in this book, demography has set the scene for what comes next: how the material existence of the lives of people in Scotland changed utterly.

NOTES

1. Mrs Thatcher's words became famous despite being taken out of context. She used them, in an interview with the magazine *Woman's Own*, to excoriate appeals that 'society' should do something to ameliorate people's social condition, when the first appeal should be to 'individuals and their families'. All this considered, her statement that 'there is no such thing as society' became epigrammatic of her political regime. <https://www.margaretthatcher.org/document/106689>.
2. I am grateful to Michael Anderson for allowing me to use this graph from his book *Scotland's Populations from the 1850s to Today* (Oxford: Oxford University Press, 2018), p. 18, Figure 8.2.
3. Treating England and Wales together, a common feature of much official statistics, misleads us into thinking that Wales follows England's path, when that is unlikely to have been the case.
4. At the time of writing (2024), full analyses of the Scottish census for 2022 were not available, but are used where they are to hand. For details of publication programme, see <https://www.scotlandscensus.gov.uk/2022-results/>.
5. These are calculated proportions, not absolute figures, to make comparison possible.
6. Life expectancy at birth is expressed as e_0 hereafter.
7. The 1971 figure was unusually high, for between 1851 and 1931, the figure was never more than 25 per cent. See Anderson, 2012: 55.
8. National Records of Scotland, Vital Event Reference Tables 2012, T3.01b.
9. <https://www.nrscotland.gov.uk/publications/households-and-dwellings-in-scotland-2023/>.

10. Scottish Household Survey (SHS) carried out a useful survey comparing 1999, when SHS began, and 2019. For details, see <https://www.gov.scot/publications/scottish-household-survey-2019-twenty-years-scotlands-people-summary-report/>.
11. <https://www.gov.scot/publications/scottish-household-survey-2019-annual-report/>.
12. Figures are from Census of Scotland, 1951 (Vol. 4, Table C) and 1971 (Economic Activity Table 1).
13. <https://www.nomisweb.co.uk/reports/lmp/gor/2013265931/report.aspx>.
14. <https://data.gov.scot/genderindex/gender-equality-index-2023.html>.
15. In the 2020 report, the work index figure was 76.
16. Quoted in D. McCrone, *The New Sociology of Scotland* (London: Sage, 2017), p. 277.
17. See <https://blog.nrscotland.gov.uk/2019/07/18/why-is-life-expectancy-stalling-in-scotland/>.
18. <https://www.nrscotland.gov.uk/publications/life-expectancy-in-scotland-2021-2023/>.
19. <https://www.nrscotland.gov.uk/publications/life-expectancy-in-scotland-2021-2023/>.
20. <https://www.nrscotland.gov.uk/publications/life-expectancy-in-scotland-2021-2023/>.
21. These have been rounded to nearest whole numbers to aid comprehension.
22. <https://www.understandingglasgow.com/glasgow-indicators/health/life-expectancy>.
23. <https://www.understandingglasgow.com/glasgow-indicators/health/life-expectancy/deprivation>.
24. The current retirement age in the UK is 66, due to rise to 67 in 2026.
25. <https://www.nature.com/articles/s41467-022-33415-5>.
26. <https://www.nature.com/articles/s41579-022-00846-2>.
27. See, for example, <https://www.whatscotlandthinks.org/questions/do-you-think-scotland-would-have-responded-to-coronavirus-better-or-worse-as-an-independent-country/>.
28. To my knowledge, Leyland's valuable work has not been updated.
29. SIMD is less helpful at identifying the smaller pockets of deprivation found in more rural areas, compared to the larger pockets found in urban areas. SIMD domain indicators can still be useful in rural areas if analysed separately from urban data zones or combined with other data. (<https://www.gov.scot/collections/scottish-index-of-multiple-deprivation-2020/>).
30. See McCrone, 2017: 183.

Demography 109

31. <https://datamap-scotland.co.uk/2020/03/population-in-scotlands-deprived-zones/>.
32. As Michael Anderson observed, it does seem plausible to argue that much of the population will have had an unusually long and intense track record, going back several generations, of deprivation, disease, uncertainty and stress. If we add to this the fact of selective out-migration of skilled and healthy workers over several centuries, then we have an interesting line of research using new forms of long-term record linkage of health, census and vital registration data which is some way in the future.
33. <https://www.scotpho.org.uk/comparative-health/excess-mortality-in-scotland-and-glasgow>.
34. For an accessible account of epigenetics, see <https://www.cdc.gov/genomics-and-health/about/epigenetic-impacts-on-health.html>.
35. DNA methylation works by adding a chemical known as a methyl group to DNA, so that genes are turned off and on. The hypothesis is that gene expression in one generation can be passed on to subsequent generations.
36. See The Annual Report of the Chief Medical Officer for 2011: Health in Scotland 2011, transforming Scotland's health (NHS Scotland, 2012).
37. <https://www.progress.org.uk/newsletter_issue/bionews-642/>.
38. This is not to deny that people are social creatures, merely that we cannot confuse in methodological terms the characteristics of individuals and those of the areas in which they live.
39. These included large parts of Argyll, Wigtown and parts of Kirkcudbright.
40. I am grateful to Michael Anderson for these observations.
41. Other local authorities showing above-average population growth are South Lanarkshire (+4.3 per cent), Orkney (+3.0 per cent), and Perth and Kinross (+2.8 per cent).
42. <https://www.scotpho.org.uk/population-dynamics/population-estimates-and-projections/data/population-projections>.
43. Population projections can vary wildly. The National Records of Scotland projection estimates for 2047 are for a population of 5.8 million, the increase virtually all of which is explained by inward migration (<https://www.nrscotland.gov.uk/publications/projected-population-of-scotland-2022-based/>.)

5

Materiality

Once made in Scotland, from girders

What do you do for a living? That is such a common enough question that it seems banal. It contains, however, a fundamental truth, that in order to *live*, we need some means of financial support, so for the vast majority of people that means 'working for a living'. Indeed, some occupations, such as being a minister of religion, were simply called a 'Living'. The point is that the vast majority of people work in order to live. Their relations to the means of production, as Marx had it, broadly defines, and even determines, who they are.

In this chapter, I will explore this 'materiality' insofar as it determines social relations between people. There is an added twist to asking this question in Scotland because it raises some fundamental questions about what Scotland is existentially, an issue raised in Chapter 2. Put at its simplest, if working in Scotland is no different to working in England, that patterns and structures of industry and employment are virtually the same, what makes Scotland worth studying? In terms of these structures, that led, in the 1970s, to an assertion that Scotland was a colony of England; that its industrial and employment structures were set by the greater power, and a process of 'development by invitation' took place in the eighteenth and nineteenth centuries. This is not the place to delve deeply into this debate, which, by and large, has ceased to be, but to point out that behind it lay a quest to justify studying Scotland, indeed, whether in sociological terms it made any sense at all.

SCOTLAND AND SPECIALISATION

Between 1750 and 1850, Scotland became not simply an industrial society, but one of the world's foremost examples. In particular, as historian Christopher Smout pointed out:

> The central belt of Scotland became ... one of the most intensively industrialised regions on the face of the earth. By 1913, Glasgow, claiming for herself the title of 'Second City of the Empire', made, with her satellite towns immediately to the east and west, one-fifth of the steel, one-third of shipping tonnage, one-half of the marine-engine horsepower, one-third of the railway locomotives and rolling stock, and most of the sewing machines in the United Kingdom. (1987:85)

Given that prosperity (for a few) rested upon a small number of industries, it is tempting to conclude that Scotland's development depended on becoming regionally specialised. The dominant image of Scotland's industrial structure was, in the words of the historian Bruce Lenman, that 'by the 19th century, Scotland had developed a very specialised regional branch of the British economy, heavily oriented towards the manufacture and export of capital goods and coarse textiles'. (1977: 204)

We find this assumption of regional specialisation in Marxist and non-Marxist accounts alike. For example, one of the most influential and comprehensive histories of capitalism in Scotland (Dickson, 1980), underlined 'the commitment of Scottish industry to the production of a relatively narrow range of specialisms, like ships and other heavy engineering equipment, which were so essential to the growth of world trade' (ibid. 194). The author accounted for this specialisation in terms of the way capitalism developed in Scotland:

> In relation to Britain as a whole, what were to emerge in Scotland were complementary rather than competitive forms of capitalism, their interdependence being regularised under the political domination of Westminster. Such were the roots of the dependent or client status of the Scottish bourgeoisie. (Dickson, 1980: 90)

Insofar as capital would flow into those sectors where profits were to be made, that capitalists would invest in areas on strictly economic terms, the notion of 'complementarity', with its implication of explicit intervention in the workings of the market, does not ring true. If, for example, the structure of industrial employment in Scotland was significantly different from Britain as a whole, for example, we can conclude that it had a more specialised economy, nested within the broad parameters of the British economy. This argument was flagged in Chapter 3, which outlined the key features of 'transformation', and here we explore it in greater detail.

In the second half of the nineteenth century, between 1851 and 1911, while there were differences between Scotland and Britain, they were nowhere near as great as those between Wales and Britain. While 37 per cent of total employment in Wales in 1851 was in mining and quarrying, rising to a massive 52 per cent in 1911, the figures for Scotland were 9 per cent and 17 per cent, respectively, and Britain as a whole, 10 per cent and 15 per cent; which makes for a combined difference of only three percentage points. If the structures were identical, the index would be zero. If there were no overlap at all, the value would be 100. In 1851, the index of dissimilarity between Britain and Scotland was 12.3, and in 1911, 10.2. The comparable index for Britain and Wales, on the other hand, was 37.6 in 1851, and 41.9 in 1911. We can conclude, then, that Wales had a specialised economy, and Scotland plainly did not.

In fact, if we calculate the indices of dissimilarity between the industrial structures of the ten British Standard Regions, Scotland in both 1851 and 1911 appears closest to the overall British structure. In 1851, the mean value of the index between the regional structures and that of Britain as a whole was 25.4 compared with the figure for Scotland of 12.3, and in 1911 the mean was 25.7 compared with 10.2 for Scotland.

In the four decades in the middle of the twentieth century from 1931 to 1971, the industrial structure of Scotland was marginally more differentiated from that of Britain as a whole than was the case in the nineteenth century. Thus, the indices of dissimilarity between Scottish and British industrial employment structures were as follows: in 1931, 15.4; in 1951, 16.1; in 1961, 18.2; and in 1971, 14.6; in truth, a process of trendless fluctuation. In comparative terms, in 1931 and 1951 Scotland was the economic region with the industrial structure closest to the British mean, and in 1961 and 1971, only North-West England was closer. In general terms, the other British regions were converging with Scotland. Nevertheless, the general process of convergence in the industrial regions of Britain in the twentieth century is not mirrored (up to 1971) within Scotland.

On this evidence there are no grounds for saying that Scotland in the nineteenth century had an industrial structure which was particularly specialised with respect to the British economy. As such, it remained a country within the British state with a high degree of civil autonomy within the structure of that state, and was not reduced to a region of England (like the North of England, simply, and revealingly, called 'the North'). Furthermore, Scotland was able to take advantage of Britain's highly advantageous structural position within a world economy itself shaped around Britain's interests. When the international order collapsed, Scotland – locked firmly into it – suffered in the same way experienced by Britain as a whole.

In most respects, industrial differentiation *within* Scotland has been of a higher order of magnitude than the industrial differentiation of Scotland from the rest of Britain. Writing the economic history of Scotland from the standpoint of west-central Scotland reflects itself in the belief that all of Scotland is, accordingly, regionally specialised and heavily industrial. Far from being a specialised 'region' of Britain, however, Scotland throughout its industrial history has shared a very similar profile to Britain as a whole, while containing considerable internal specialisation, reflecting its position as a distinct country within the United Kingdom.

TRANSFORMING THE ECONOMY

By the end of the twentieth century the Scottish economy had been transformed. Between 1979 and 1994, employment in banking, finance, insurance and business services had increased by a massive 66 per cent, whereas employment in agriculture, fishing and forestry had declined by 46 per cent, as did manufacturing, by 41 per cent. This period also saw the transformation of employment in gender terms. Male employment had fallen by almost 20 per cent, and female employment had risen by over 10 per cent, with the effect that by the mid-1990s there were actually more women than men in Scotland's labour force, albeit that most women worked part-time. One of the effects of this transformation was that Scotland caught up with the rest of the UK in terms of differentials, such as gross domestic product per head and rates of unemployment. By 1996, its GDP per head stood at 98 per cent of the UK average, with only London and South-East England having larger shares per capita (*Regional Trends*, 1999: Table 2.3, p. 33). Taking the twentieth century as a whole, we can see that Scotland 'has occupied a position in the middle range of the United Kingdom per capita income distribution' (Lee, 1995: 54).

The increase in the share of jobs in the service sector – from 24 per cent in 1951 to 80 per cent by 2022 – is undoubtedly the greatest single shift in sectoral employment that Scotland has experienced in modern times. The growth of the service sector has been by far the greatest single driver of social change in Scotland since 1945. The changes in occupational structure, patterns of female employment and social mobility right through to household structure, demographic behaviour and political orientations can be traced back to this single transformation. By 2011, the index of dissimilarity between Scotland and the rest of the UK was 13.7, roughly the same as it was in the final quarter of the twentieth century. For Wales, the demise of mining and quarrying brought it into line with the rest of the UK, with a score of 16.2. De-industrialisation has had its effect.

By the middle of the second decade of the twenty-first century, fewer than one in ten in Scotland were employed in 'industry', compared with over four in ten in the mid-1950s (Phillips, Wright and Tomlinson, 2023: 41). However, as Phillips and his colleagues pointed out:

> 'industry' was never a neutral, descriptive term for a particular type of economic activity. It always carried connotations of progress, modernity and effective nationhood ... Scotland's economic history had embedded a widespread notion of the country as an 'industrial nation'. National identity strongly featured industry and industrial employment. (2023: 41)

In sociological terms, occupational distributions are more relevant than industrial orders, in that what people work *at*, rather than what they work *in*, tells us more about their social and economic relations. The index of dissimilarity for occupational distributions in 2011 was smaller than the one for industrial orders. The biggest difference[1] related to the proportion of managers and directors in Scotland (−2.4), followed a long way behind by skilled trades (+1.0), but the overall message was once more that Scotland was more similar to England and Wales than different. In summary, neither with regard to industrial orders nor occupational orders does Scotland in the twenty-first century differ very much from England and Wales, which is well in line with historic trends.

By the beginning of the 2020s, the shape of industrial orders in Scotland was clear.[2] Around 3 per cent worked in 'primary' industry (agriculture, farming and fishing; and mining and quarrying); 17 per cent in 'secondary' industry – manufacturing (8 per cent), construction (7 per cent), the rest in electricity, gas, water etc supply. A massive eight out of ten people worked in a variety of 'services', the largest proportions being in human health and social work (15 per cent), public administration and defence (9 per cent), and education (8 per cent). These proportions had changed little since 2011, a percentage point difference over the two censuses of only 11, with the largest changes occurring in wholesale and retail (down 4) and public administration and defence (up 2). Comparing Scotland, England and Wales[3] in 2023–4, we find the similarities in occupational structures far outweighing the differences between them. Scotland, and Wales, have marginally fewer employed as managers, directors and senior officials, but Scotland compensates with more professional workers.[4] However, the percentage point differences between Scotland and England, and Wales and England are 8 and 11 respectively. In other words, most of the major industrial transitions in Scotland had occurred decades before, that is, by the end of the twentieth century, helping to confirm our argument that the final decades of that century were the crucial ones for industrial and occupational change.

Comprehending De-industrialisation

Processes of *de*-industrialisation in Scotland, as in the rest of the UK, provide important challenges to economic and social identity. This plays out in a particular way in Scotland, for it does not fall naturally into conventional categories. It is not an independent state, neither is it an administrative 'region' of the British state, but, as we saw in Chapter 2, its economic identity is problematic. In other words, it is not the facticity of industry and occupational structures which matter so much as how they configure with representations of who we consider ourselves to be, and in this respect, being an 'industrial nation', the second, after England, to industrialise in the late eighteenth and early nineteenth centuries is an important part of that representation.

Such processes of representation are akin to 'cultural formations', described in the 1970s by Raymond Williams as 'those effective movements and tendencies, in intellectual and artistic life, which have significant and sometimes decisive influence on the active development of a culture, and which have a variable and often oblique relation to formal institutions' (1977: 117). Such cultural formations help to frame which issues are discussed, and how they are understood. They are, in essence, framing devices which set the parameters of how we see, and hence, explain social and cultural phenomena. We will discuss these in detail in Chapter 8, but they play an important part in our understanding of Scotland as an industrial 'imagined community'.

Clydesidism

In the early 1980s, and largely as a reaction to what were deemed dominant discourses of 'tartanry' and 'kailyard', a more progressive cultural formation was proposed – Clydesidism – 'extremely refreshing in the Scottish context', said Colin McArthur; it is not a 'pernicious discourse', as he observed in his edited collection, *Scotch Reels*. What Clydesidism had in its favour is that it is constructed from 'real' images of working-class life, from the discourse of class, and from naturalism. The term was coined by John Caughie in his essay in *Scotch Reels*, for the tradition 'based on working class experiences which, since the twenties, have seemed to offer the only real and consistent basis for *a Scottish national culture*' (my emphasis) (Caughie, 1982:121).

It was no coincidence that this argument about Scottish national culture was taking place in the 1970s and early 1980s. It reinforces the point of this book, that this was a key period of considerable sociological and cultural change in Scotland. It was the end of the old, and the beginning of something new – whose parameters were as yet unclear. The problem was that interpolating the cultural framework of Clydesidism into a comprehension of 'Scotland' was rapidly becoming obsolete even as it was being taken up. As Cairns Craig (1983) pointed out,

Clydesidism was becoming a historic discourse even in its heartland of west-central Scotland by the late twentieth century.

Its language evoked early twentieth-century Clydeside, with its appeal to the 'industrial masses' and to skilled masculine culture. And as Eleanor Gordon and Esther Breitenbach observed, 'skill' is a social construct which is 'saturated with male bias' (1990: 6). It is fine, said Cairns Craig, to break out of the mental traps of the historic myths of tartanry and kailyard, to imagine a future, even a revolutionary future, through which to overcome the static quality of the dominant myths, but we risk embracing another myth based on a fast-disappearing working-class culture. Craig observed: 'What is worrying in the contemporary situation [the early 1980s] is the way that the death throes of industrial West-Central Scotland have become the touchstone of authenticity for our culture.' And he continued: 'if we make the victims of that decline the carriers of our essential identity, we merely perpetuate the cultural alienation in which we negate the on-going struggle of our experience by freezing its real meaning in a particular defeat' (1983: 9).

To flag a debate we will return to in Chapter 8 when we examine Scottish culture, the search for a single, dominant, 'national culture' was itself something of a snark.[5] The point was not to find a new, pure, Scottish national culture fit for the twenty-first century, but to recognise that the relationship between cultural forms and political movements is never straightforward. It is, rather, driven by the classical nationalist formulation of the late eighteenth and nineteenth centuries, whereby 'a people', unique in their culture, reach for political self-determination as an expression of that culture.

Rather than there being a single people with a single culture, there were advantages in diversity and fragmentation, as Cairns Craig has observed:

> The fragmentation and division which made Scotland seem abnormal to an earlier part of the 20th century came to be the norm for much of the world's population. Bilingualism, biculturalism and the inheritance of a diversity of fragmented traditions were to be the source of creativity rather than its inhibition in the second half of the 20th, and Scotland ceased to have to measure itself against the false 'norm', psychological as well as cultural, of the unified national tradition. (1987: 7)

Scottish Tropes

These conceptions of Scottish national culture were tropes which emerged from film, screen and media; they were representations of 'Scotland' as it was imagined to be. Duncan Petrie, in his important book, *Screening Scotland* pointed to the filmic traditions which shaped that understanding, which was also the theme of Colin McArthur's book *Scotch Reels* (1982), described by Petrie as 'the most influential critical and cultural analysis' of Scottish cinema (Petrie, 2000: 2). Petrie credited McArthur with arguing that Clydesidism's version of Scotland,[6] associated as it was with working-class, masculine industrial labour, failed 'to escape the taint of regressive discourses, eschewing any political analysis of the realities of class conflict and industrial relations by seeking refuge in human drama' (ibid. 4).

Giving his assessment of the Scotch Myths tradition,[7] Cairns Craig observed:

> What the Scotch Myths theory wanted was to mock the Scottish past out of existence so that we could start over with a clean slate. It wanted Scotland to be in real history, not fake history, and real history, of course, was the one narrative of class operating everywhere the same; real history was the history of our incorporation into a modernity in which all advanced countries were identical with each other and all other places would eventually catch up and share the same identity. Real history, in other words, happened as though geography, and difference, and alternative pasts did not matter, as though we had become inheritors of one past (the development of capitalism; the development of socialism) which was everywhere the same and which was carrying us into the future of identically 'pluralist' societies. (Craig, 1996: 112, and cited in Petrie, 2000: 6)

And so a vibrant and contentious argument about Scotland and its culture(s) came to an end in the early 1980s; or did it?

De-industrialising the Old Scotland

In the second decade of the twenty-first century, a new genre of studies emerged around the theme of 'de-industrialisation' in Scotland, led by historians at Glasgow University, notably, Jim Phillips, Jim Tomlinson, Ewan Gibbs and Valerie Wright. Their books, *Deindustrialisation and the Moral Economy in Scotland since 1955* (2021 and 2023), and Gibbs' *Coal Country*

(2021) reflect its output. These are not simply economic historical accounts of the accelerated process of de-industrialisation since the 1970s, but are premised on the concept of 'moral economy' coined by E. P. Thompson in his classic *The Making of the English Working Class* (1963), but especially his later essay on the 'moral economy' of the English crowd in the eighteenth century (Thompson, 1971); and Karl Polanyi's exploration of the industrial revolution, *The Great Transformation* (1944).

Phillips and his colleagues documented the phases of de-industrialisation in Scotland in the post-war period: the first, from the mid-1950s to the mid-1960s saw the shrinkage of staple industries such as coal, metals, ships, textiles, and the growth of new manufacturing. The second phase, from the mid-1960s to the late 1970s, saw that new investment stagnating, such that the UK government stabilised employment in the staple industries. Latterly, this was the period of a minority Labour government and its battles to retain and reform coal and steel. Finally, the period from the late 1970s until the mid-1990s saw the accelerated loss across all industrial sectors, with no meaningful policy effort to protect working-class economic security. Although de-industrialisation in the public mind is associated with Thatcherism after 1979, the authors point out that Mrs Thatcher and her governments neither initiated de-industrialisation, nor even willed it to happen. It was an unintended consequence of policies pursued, though insofar as the process reconfigured class relations especially with regard to politics, it was not unwelcome for the Right.

The study 'Coal Country', by Ewan Gibbs, is a case-study of this focus on de-industrialisation. Gibbs's thesis can stand for a description of the approach as a whole:

> The closure of mines, steel mills and factories fundamentally altered livelihoods and associations by challenging a strongly held social order in towns and villages which had developed around coal mining. Colliery closures and the experience of labour market alterations have significantly contributed to the questioning of Scotland's position within the Union and the realignment of the politics of class and nationhood since the mid-twentieth century. (Gibbs, 2021: 1)

We can perceive in that comment that the approach is not simply a conventional 'economic history', but a claim that the process of de-industrialisation undermined political ties binding

Scotland into the Union, and, above all, the 'moral economy' of employment. Drawing upon the work of E. P. Thompson and Karl Polanyi, Phillips and his colleagues argued that industrialisation as a process had heightened the influence of market forces, thereby abstracting economic life from social obligations and cultural expectations. This, in turn, had generated resistance and sought to re-establish the social, and moral, basis of economic activity, and with it 'popular notions of justice and morality [which were] central to these movements and their demands' (Phillips, Wright and Tomlinson, 2023: 6). Thus, they argue, 'industry was never a neutral, descriptive term for a particular type of economic activity. It always carried connotations of progress, modernity and effective nationhood' (2023: 41).

Their work was based on a series of oral histories in and around industrial plants and associated communities: Fairfield shipyard in Glasgow Govan, the Linwood car plant in Renfrewshire, assembling Timex watches and electronics in Dundee; and Gibbs's study of Cardowan colliery in Lanarkshire, but extrapolated from these cases. The 'moral economy' thesis runs through all of these studies: 'the culture of autonomous and skilled labour was instrumental ... especially in Lanarkshire, where the Clydesider tradition had a compelling subjective influence on working-class identity and activism' (Phillips, Wright and Tomlinson, 2023: 84). Note the reference to 'Clydeside' such that the 'transgression of the moral economy was not forgotten in Lanarkshire' (2023: 79). The authors argue that until the late 1970s, notably the Thatcher government of 1979, there was a political-moral understanding between government, in particular in the Scottish Office, which acted as a medium between Westminster and the Scottish policy community, and the grassroots in west-central Scotland that de-industrialisation would be the *quid pro quo* for inward investment in new factories, mainly American branch-plants. The Thatcher government had undermined this understanding through its mantra of 'leaving it to the market', and at a time when North Sea oil was raising substantially the value of sterling as a petro-currency to uncompetitive levels on world markets.

The use of oral history material, however, is problematic as evidence for a 'de-moralised' economy (in both senses, with and without the hyphen) in that interviews are necessarily selective and particular. Interviewing key activists is open to objections that the process is self-selective. To say that 'both middle-class and working-class Scots were offended in *moral* [my emphasis] as well as material terms by Thatcherism' (Phillips, Wright and Tomlinson, 2023: 7) might seem to require firmer evidence that this was so. Gibbs's claim, for example, that the closure of coal mines, steel mills and factories not only altered livelihoods, but also Scotland's place in the Union requires the spelling out of the political and social mechanisms which actually brought this about. It is one thing to invoke E. P. Thompson's analysis of eighteenth century riots against the liberalisation of foodstuffs, and quite another to apply moral economy arguments, particularly in a coal industry which had a long history of pit closures as coal measures became exhausted and workers moved on to other pits, usually well away from adjacent pit villages. The author shows that between the 1940s and the 1970s the closure of mines was managed consensually, and that the coal industry was concentrated into larger 'depersonalised, "cosmopolitan" collieries less embedded in localised communities' (Gibbs, 2021: 122). The consequence was that 'younger miners increasingly engaged in "conspicuous consumption", while living more private family centred lifestyles' (ibid.).

All that rings true, as does Gibbs' analysis of ethnic, religious and political divisions in mining communities across the Scottish coalfield: 'sectarian trends were especially concentrated in Lanarkshire where different Irish ethnic backgrounds, Catholic and Ulster-Protestant, intersected with residence, work patterns, and political affiliations' (ibid. 110). And while 'sectarianism was a fading but present source of division in the Scottish coalfield into the 1980s' (ibid. 117), by this time the mining industry was facing its nemesis in the miners' strike in the middle of that decade. There emerged subsequently 'a form of critical nostalgia': 'coal mining is remembered for its costs in human lives and industrial diseases as well as the instilling of a socially conservative culture. Yet a strong sense of bereavement for lost cohesion and collective mobilisation are also emphasised' (ibid. 185). There was, as the saying goes, blood on the coal.

In the twenty-first century, we now regard coal as a dirty fossil fuel, but there is little sense of that conveyed in these studies. The tone is elegiac of a dying, essentially male, culture. This view has a wider remit. Robert Gildea's *Backbone of the Nation: mining communities and the great strike of 1984–85* (2024) is another such study, its title taken from the remembered comment of one Fife ex-miner that 'the miners are the backbone of the nation. Without them the country just could not go' (p. 1). Gildea observes: 'The miner was the quintessential *homo faber*, man as maker, whose Promethean work pitted him against the elements of earth, air, fire and water' (2024: 3). Perhaps no other industry or occupation would feel able to offer such a sentiment, and hence its demise is all the more plangent.

Coal production in Britain was at its peak in 1913, when 287 tons of coal were mined, and 1 million miners employed; in Scotland alone, 138,000. By the late 1960s, pits were closed in Ayrshire, Lanarkshire and Stirlingshire, with new pits in Midlothian and Fife. The 'super-pits' were relatively short-lived: Seafield in Fife lasted from 1966 to 1988; in Midlothian, Bilston Glen from 1963 to 1989; and Monktonhall, from 1967 to 1997 (though mothballed in 1987). Gildea observed the strict division of labour in mining families:

> The miner was expected to demonstrate his masculinity, whether as the breadwinner earing a 'family wage', as a fighter in the union and on picket lines or controlling the womenfolk in his home. The miner's wife was expected to give up paid work when she married, to stay at home, ensure that food was on the table for her husband when he came home from work, raise the children and ensure the family stayed solvent. (Gildea, 2024: 19)

This highly gendered division of labour was destroyed by the strike of 1984–5. 'Miners' wives, in particular, were transformed by the strike, took advantage of educational opportunities and began new careers' (ibid. 325); as Gildea comments 'something of a gender revolution' (ibid. 415). This is reinforced by Florence Sutcliffe-Braithwaite and Natalie Thomlinson in their study of miners' wives in England, Scotland and Wales (2014–20). Changing material circumstances helped bring about changed understandings of womanhood. They observed: 'Work was not inevitably "liberating" for women, but, crucially it came to be constructed in this period as a route to independence and a marker of "modern" womanhood' (Sutcliffe-Braithwaite and Thomlinson, 2022: 292).

There remains, however, a matter of the nature of evidence in studies of de-industrialisation which followed. Reliance on oral history testimonies from key players in this process highlights these issues.[8] While it is true that 'Scottish miners' collective self-image was shaped by a strong occupational identity and national allegiances' (Gibbs, 2021: 202) it is not possible to judge too well the views of the rank and file vis-à-vis the leadership. Scottish miners' leaders, stalwarts of the Communist Party of Great Britain (CPGB), such as Mick McGahey and George Bolton, were supporters of 'Home Rule' and a devolved Scottish parliament, working with other trade union leaders such as Alex Kitson, Jimmy Milne and the Scottish Trades Union Congress (STUC) more generally. McGahey was reported in minutes of the executive committee of the National Union of Mineworkers (Scottish Area) in 1977–8 as saying that 'we must never allow the Nationalists to appear to be the banner of the Scottish nation. That honour truly belongs to the Labour and trade union movement' (Gibbs, 2021: 213). There were, in any case, political tensions between Labour (and factions of Labour, notably Militant) and the Communist Party,[9] to which most of the leadership was affiliated. It was not that unionised workers defected to the Scottish National Party – if anything, it was non-unionised labour which was more likely to do that (see, for example, Frank Bealey and John Sewel's study of Peterhead, *The Politics of Independence*, 1981). The loss of the iconic parliamentary seat of Hamilton in Lanarkshire in a by-election in 1967, won by Winnie Ewing, was probably the result of abstentions and anti-Labour voting coalescing around the SNP, rather than of direct switching.[10]

The political import of the 1984–5 miners' strike is described by this comment made by the daughter of a prominent Fife miner interviewed by Gildea: 'if I got my way, when she [Mrs Thatcher] died, I would have put her down Solsgirth pit. She was a horrible, horrible woman. She was out to destroy Scotland, she was out to destroy Britain, but she was gunning for Scotland' (Gildea, 2024: 389). Such feelings were not confined to Scotland (or Wales). Consider Anthony Cartwright's tongue-in-cheek novel '*How I Killed Margaret Thatcher*', 2012, evoking de-industrialisation in the West Midlands of England. It was, however, the added 'English' identity of Mrs Thatcher and her project that heightened alienation north of the border, and west of Offa's dyke.

Taken as a whole, this seam of academic work conveys a strong sense of elegy; the end of an auld sang. The iconic nature of the coal mining industry, and, more widely, 'popular notions of justice and morality… central to these movements and demands' (Phillips, Wright and Tomlinson, 2023: 6) are credited with bringing about '…political divergence from the 1960s to the 1980s' (ibid. 247). The most that can be said, however, is that the demise of 'heavy industry' in central Scotland significantly eroded Labour's strength, and allowed other political forces, notably Nationalism, to emerge, often because the SNP provided the political alternative in a crude first-past-the-post system, where anti-voting against the dominant party became the norm. Furthermore, whether workers in heavy industry were imbued with a particular commitment to a distinctive moral economy is a moot point. Indeed, the notion of 'moral economy' is hard to pinpoint; whether it operates among rank-and-file workers (contrasted with others in other forms of work), or among the leadership cadre (easier to glean from their public statements), or whether notions of moral economy operated as a social and political imperative at a national (Scottish) level.

Whatever the case, this work on de-industrialisation conveys a powerful sense of elegiac and epochal change in the 1970s and early 1980s, and that is its strength. While it does not attempt to harness directly Clydesidism as a cultural formation, even in its widest form, it conveys an implicit sense of male, working-class, largely skilled labour in which women had, at best, walk-on and supportive parts in which, in Gibbs' words, there is a 'feminine private domestic space and masculine domination of the public realm' (Gibbs, 2021: 120). This was a post-war world in which the notion of the 'breadwinner wage' was paramount, to be swept away by the extension of work for women, in electronic plants as well as in the public sector. That world in which 'masculinity was produced out of a certain distance from femininity through the demarcation of places, spaces and social roles' (ibid. 125) came to an abrupt end. The culture and politics associated with this world was consigned to history by the mid-1980s. With hindsight, critics of Clydesidism were correct not to load it with social and cultural expectations for the future. With radical industrial change came changing class relations, notably absent from these studies in which the nature of social class is taken for granted. It is this aspect of materiality to which we now turn.

MANUFACTURING SOCIAL CLASS

In an address to the British Academy in 2021, Robert Gildea observed that the 1984–5 miners' strike '... was the last great battle of the organised working class, of which the miners were the heroic vanguard'.[11] This fits in with the common perception which miners had of themselves, as the 'heroic vanguard' of the working class, reflected in the studies by Gibbs, and by Phillips and his colleagues. That powerful myth, in the sense of a truth held to be self-evident, resonates still throughout the labour movement, and carries with it our conception of social class. Accounts of Scotland tie in with 'social class', but cut both ways: that Scotland is indubitably a class society, but also one in which social mobility is somehow less culturally fixed than in England. For example, in the 1970s, the nationalist Stephen Maxwell observed that

> the idea that Scottish society is egalitarian is central to the myth of Scottish Democracy. In its strong nationalist version, class division is held to be an alien import from England. In the weaker version, it describes the wider opportunity for social mobility in Scotland as illustrated in 'the lad o'pairts'. (Maxwell, 1976: 5)

This was a cultural trope which attributed to Scots a degree of cultural and social openness, often described as the 'Scottish myth' (for which, see McCrone, 2001: 93–100). This is not to be taken as an objective descriptor of Scotland, but as a founding belief akin to the American Dream around which swirls arguments about truth and evidence, but actually functions as a 'truth held to be self-evident', words famously used in the American Declaration of Independence. A man (or even a woman) maybe not be 'a man for a' that', in the words of Burns's song, but the trope retains a degree of cultural truth about Scottish culture which proves hard to shift.

Class Accounts

So is Scotland a class society? Surely, in that power is structured with reference to the economic realm, differentiating people in the marketplace according to the skills and resources they bring to it, as well as the rewards they derive from it, but that is where the interesting questions begin. It is necessary to separate out three dimensions of social class: *structure*, what people have in common, what Marx called their relationship to the means of production; *consciousness*, shared levels of culture and meaning which people share to account for their lot in life; and *action*, the degree to which common interests, both objective and subjective, stimulate social action to defend those interests. Social class can refer to one or more of these dimensions, and it is uncommon to find all three in alignment. We might expect that some occupations, such as coal mining, would align all three, making miners allegedly the 'vanguard of the working class', but that is the exception, not the rule. Marx's famous dismissal of the peasantry as a 'sack of potatoes' was based on their commonality in structural terms, but without any or much common awareness between peasants themselves. They were simply a 'homologous magnitude much as potatoes in a sack form a sack of potatoes' (from *18th Brumaire of Louis Bonaparte* (1852)).

All advanced industrial or capitalist societies share similar features; namely, the private ownership of economic resources coupled with the capacity to transmit such property by sale or by inheritance, and this determines the power structures within them. To reiterate the point made in summary in Chapter 3, most people's life chances are determined by what they do for a living in selling their labour, what they work at, because that is the overwhelming source of their income. The jobs people do thus characterise their life security, give them access to housing, education and social goods, not only in terms of levels of earnings, but in terms and conditions of employment. Modern market societies, in ideal-typical terms, tend to be characterised by three main classes – a dominant class whose power is based on the capital it owns; an intermediate class whose power derives from the educational or organisational skills it possesses; and a subordinate class whose power, such as it is, tends to be based on its physical or routine labour. It is this relationship to the labour market that determines which social class people belong to.

Re-shaping Social Class in Scotland

From the late-nineteenth century around three-quarters of Scotland's labour force were in manual jobs, and roughly one in seven in white-collar work, with the rest under- or unemployed.

Alistair Gray's image in his novel *Lanark* captured men going to work: 'Hundreds of thousands of men in dirty coats and heavy boots were tramping along grey streets to the gates of forges and machines shops.' (Gray, 1981: 223) Hence, the pyramidal shape of the Scottish class structure, with the bulk of the labour force in manual work, a much smaller group than today in white-collar work, and at the top, a small, self-contained elite, the so-called 'boss class'. There were crucial internal differences of skills, pay and status in all classes, not least among manual workers where status divisions between skilled 'labour aristocrats' and unskilled residual labour, even in coal mining, and usually cross-cut against religious and other cultural differences. Getting a job in a Clydeside shipyard, for example, depended far more on your religion.[12] By the mid-twentieth century in Scotland as a whole, manual workers were less than half the labour force, and the rise in white-collar work had grown significantly, reflecting the occupational transition to service employment.

By the twenty-first century, around three-quarters of people worked in services, although such 'services' had been transformed over the previous hundred years, from jobs in domestic service, to office work, whether as a state functionary or in the private sector such as banking and finance. The growing trend for women to participate in the labour force became a common feature. By 1981, 57 per cent of married women in Scotland aged under 60 were 'economically active', that is, in paid employment, while most worked part-time. The expansion of new occupations for women involved the feminisation of certain occupations such as clerical work, in which the percentage of clerks who were female rose from about half in 1961 to three-quarters by 1981. Female pay and conditions, however, remained consistently poorer than those for men. In any case, many 'white-collar' jobs, such as those in call centres, and in care work, remain poorly paid and badly provisioned, despite being labelled 'non-manual'. By 2022, women were proportionately represented in professional and associated professional employment (see Figure 5.1), less so among managers, while over-represented in administration and secretarial work, sales and in caring and leisure occupations, and under-represented in manual trades (skilled, processing and elementary occupations.[13]

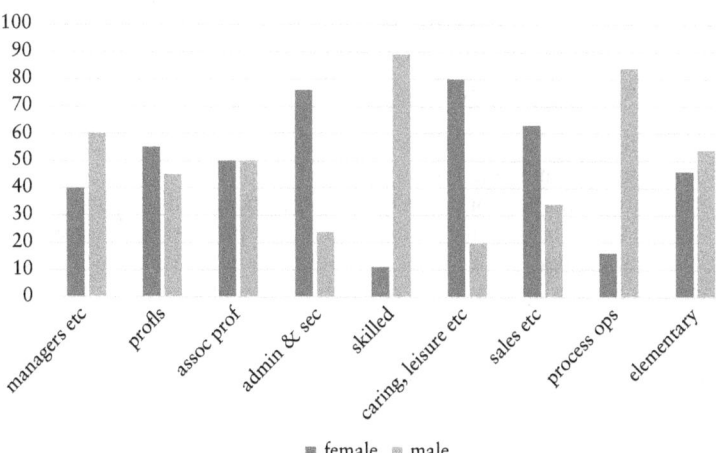

Figure 5.1 Percentage in work by occupation (SOC2020) by sex, 2022
Source: https://www.scotlandscensus.gov.uk/2022-results/scotland-s-census-2022-education-labour-market-and-travel-to-work/.

These patterns in Scotland are similar to those in England, and in Wales.[14] In each country, just under half of the labour force is female, and while proportionately more women in Scotland work in managerial and professional jobs compared with England,[15] it is the similarities, and not the differences, between the three countries which is striking. All three conform to the pattern shown in Figure 5.1.

However we choose to group these occupations will depend on what social class schema we have in mind and for which purposes, but nowadays around one-third of men and women are in 'professional' occupations, about one-third are in 'manual' jobs (routine or semi-routine) (roughly the same proportion of women), and one-third of both men and women are in lower-level white collar work. Whichever way we look at it, the pyramidal shape of the class structure has been transformed compared to the previous century.

What is it that has transformed the occupational, and hence the class structure? The process of de-industrialisation is an obvious candidate to explain the decline of the manual working class, historically understood. Even within the same industries, such as manufacturing, however, proportionately fewer are employed nowadays in manual trades. Thus, whereas in 1981,

41 per cent of the manufacturing labour force were skilled manual workers, twenty years later the proportion was down to 35 per cent and falling. Hence,

> the fall in the size of the working class, and the growth of professional and managerial employment, is due mainly to change in the nature of the work processes within nearly all sectors – more automation, more supervision and more professional autonomy. Sectoral change, such as the decline of manufacturing, has played a much less significant role. (Paterson, Bechhofer and McCrone, 2004: 87)

The proportion of professional and managerial workers in manufacturing more than doubled between 1981 and 2001, from just under 10 per cent, to 22 per cent. It is undoubtedly true that the decline in manufacturing has removed a tranche of manual jobs from the economy, but the transformation of the occupational – and hence, class – structure, is not simply driven by changes in industrial sectors. Even in coal mining, that iconic working-class manual occupation, there are now more technicians and managers, reflecting the automation and technical investment in coal mining machinery. The demise of deep mining in the UK, and its replacement with opencast mining, has not only reduced the scale of the industry, but has transformed the labour process within it.

So we can see, then, that changes in the work processes across all industrial sectors have been a more important cause of transformation than simply the rise and fall of such sectors. Thus, sectoral change *per se* is not the key factor leading to the growth of the professional and managerial classes, or to the decline of the manual working class. It is what happens to the labour process *within* these industrial sectors which makes the most difference to the class structure. Thus, the old image of the male manual worker as a metaphor for a particular kind of Scotland has plainly lost its potency, and partly for reasons of gender. Women occupy somewhat different niches in the labour market compared with men, and so their increasing participation in it has been another force reshaping the class structure. In only twenty years, between 1981 and 2000, the proportion of manual workers in Scotland fell from 39 per cent to 25 per cent; while the proportion of employers, professionals and managers rose from 12 per cent to 25 per cent (Paterson, Bechhofer and McCrone, 2004: 85). In terms of these structural changes, Scotland changed much as the rest of Britain did, because the underlying processes, notably early industrialisation (and later de-industrialisation) had a shared economic history across the island.[16] These were reinforced by a shared labour market. As we shall see later, however, the – cultural – belief that Scotland was more 'working class' than England largely remained. Thus:

> The second half of the twentieth century was a period of probably unprecedented openness in the class structure, in the sense that it became normal for people to move into a better kind of job than that of their parents. The main reason for this was that professional and semi-professional jobs were expanding their share, while manual jobs were contracting theirs. (ibid. 81).

Moving On Up

If we compare class structures in the same society at different time-points, we grasp that major changes have occurred such as we have described here: a higher proportion in non-manual jobs, and far fewer in manual ones. That, in itself, does not tell us the ease or difficulty of moving from one to the other. A crucial question is: how do people come to be in the class positions they are in? To what extent do people remain in the social class of their parents, or do they move into a different social class? In terms of their own biographies, do they remain, more or less, in the social stratum they started out in; that is, how much intra-generational mobility is there? And across the generations, to what degree do people move social class, upwards or downwards? How much social mobility takes place between social classes?

We can tell from studies of social mobility across the British nations conducted in the 1970s, and again in the 1990s. By and large, the patterns of social mobility in Scotland, England and Wales are quite similar, and that should not surprise us. They share common characteristics by virtue of early industrialisation and the demise of the peasantry, and hence provided a reserve army of labour formerly in agriculture as in much of continental Europe. In terms of comparative inflow rates, Scotland, as well as England and Wales, had high numbers in the top social classes who originated from manual working classes, and the lowest recruitment from farm origins. The picture of inter-generational social mobility in Scotland in the 1970s was of a society similar in many ways to England and Wales, with a substantial proportion of the service class drawn up from manual working-class backgrounds. As many as one-third of the top 'salariat' had fathers who had been in manual jobs, and for class II the figure was 43 per cent. The key point is that those in top jobs were drawn from diverse social origins.

On the other hand, the manual working classes (respectively skilled manual and semi-skilled manual workers, including those in agriculture) are much more homogeneous and self-recruiting. Thus, while there was considerable upward mobility into the social classes at the top, there was little corresponding downward mobility into social classes at the bottom. This lack of correspondence was due to the fact that, while the size of the manual working class had shrunk, that of the service class had grown, allowing those who were already in that class to remain, but permitting considerable upward social mobility from lower levels. The changing shape and size of social classes was allowing for class retention at the top and class mobility from the bottom.

We can see this more clearly in terms of respondents' 'origin class' (that of their father's[17]), in distinction to their 'destination class' (the one they themselves end up in).

Table 5.1 shows that those born in the later period (1967–76) were more than twice as likely to have fathers in the 'service class' (I & II) than those born in the earlier period (1937–46). Likewise, the pattern is reversed for those with fathers in unskilled or semi-skilled manual work, that is, virtually halved.

Table 5.1 Father's social class by birth cohort of respondent

% by column	Born between 1937 and 1946	Born between 1967 and 1976
Service class (I & II)	12.7%	27.2%
Routine non-manual (III)	4.9	4.3
Self-employed (IV)	11.9	14.7
Skilled manual (V & VI)	35.7	35.1
Semi & unskilled manual (VII)	34.9	18.6

Source: Adapted from Paterson, Bechhofer and McCrone, 2004: Table 6.3, p. 92. The intermediate birth cohorts (1947–56, and 1957–66) have been omitted in this table.

Table 5.2 Respondent's own class, men (women in brackets)

% by column	Born between 1937–46	Born between 1967 and 1976
Service class (I & II)	29.5% (36.0%)	38.0% (38.8%)
Routine non-manual (III)	7.4 (28.1)	12.2 (37.4)
Self-employed (IV)	20.5 (6.7)	6.6 (1.9)
Skilled manual (V & VI)	18.9 (2.2)	24.9 (9.7)
Semi & unskilled manual (VII)	23.8 (27.0)	18.3 (12.1)

Source: Adapted from Paterson, Bechhofer and McCrone, 2004: Table 6.4, p. 93. The intermediate birth cohorts (1947–56, and 1957–66) have been omitted in this table.

In terms of respondents' own social class (that is, their class *destination*, where they end up), and comparing the same birth cohorts, we can see in Table 5.2 the different patterns for men and women; the growth of professional employment for men, and the growth of routine non-manual employment for women, and the decline of semi- and unskilled manual employment for both sexes. Either way, the shift from manual to non-manual social classes is the dominant feature.

We observe from Tables 5.1 and 5.2, then, major changes in social mobility in Scotland, and elsewhere in Britain. Of those whose father was a semi- or unskilled manual worker when the respondent was aged 14,[18] 30 per cent ended up in the service class (I), and a further 20 per cent in routine non-manual work (II). Only 23 per cent were semi- or unskilled manual workers like their fathers, and 17 per cent were in skilled manual work. As many as half of the children of manual working-class fathers ended up in professional or semi-professional jobs; while 40 per cent remained in manual work similar to their fathers. By any account, this is major social mobility in that a significant proportion of 'working-class' people are upwardly mobile into professional work of one form or another. Think of these as 'outflows' – focusing on where the children of various social classes end up. If we look through the telescope the other way round – in terms of 'inflows', where people *originate* in class terms, we find that almost half (47 per cent) of people in social class I come from manual working class backgrounds (that is, they had fathers in skilled, semi- or unskilled manual work). Only a third of people in social class I originate in that class, so that professional classes draw upon very diverse social origins. The explanation is relatively straightforward, but significant nonetheless. The expansion of service class jobs in the last fifty years has drawn up a high proportion of people whose social origins were in lower social classes, while that expansion has allowed a significant amount of 'class retention' in the upper echelons. There is, then, little concomitant *downward* social mobility. We can conclude that 'inequality in opportunities for mobility associated with class of origin had remained fairly stable, but all classes had benefited from a higher level of overall opportunity' (Paterson, Bechhofer and McCrone, 2004: 95–6).

Much depends on whether openings for upward mobility continue into the future, and there are signs that the expansion of professional and service class jobs has slowed down. This could be because, by virtue of age, younger people still have to work their way through career mobility across their life spans; or it could be because of structural change where service class jobs no longer expand at the same rate (Bukodi et al., 2015). If openings for better paid professional jobs dry up, then we might expect different patterns of social mobility to emerge; but it is surely too soon to tell whether that will happen.

We need also to distinguish between 'absolute' social mobility whereby the expansion of such jobs gives working class people the opportunities to move out of their social class of origin, and 'relative' social mobility, inequalities of opportunity *between* different social classes. In the latter respect, there has been room at the top for both middle-class people to reproduce their social class, as well as for upward mobility from lower social classes, but inequalities *between* social class opportunities have remained much the same.

The children of the middle classes have not lost out in this game of snakes and ladders. And the key to that has been the expansion of educational opportunities as we saw in the previous chapter. These have been similar for men and women, particularly among younger people where education has mattered more as a ladder for mobility. While it is the case that educational opportunity is the main driver of social mobility, middle class children who do not reach the highest levels of educational qualifications have other forms of social and cultural capital (such as finance, and social networks) which help to keep them in their social class of origin.

The convergence between Scotland and England in terms of absolute mobility rates means that we can safely extrapolate the findings by John Goldthorpe and his colleagues (Bukodi et al., 2015) in their studies of England and Wales. They take issue with the assumption established within political circles that social mobility in Britain is in decline or has even 'ground to a halt – despite the evidence for such a view being slight and the evidence going contrary to it far more substantial' (ibid. 2). The processes they describe are far more subtle, namely, 'that among the members of successive cohorts, the experience of absolute upward mobility is becoming less common and that of absolute downward mobility more common; and class-linked inequalities in relative chance of mobility and immobility appear wider than previously thought.' (ibid. 1).

THE RISE OF CREDENTIALS: EDUCATION AND SOCIAL MOBILITY

It is self-evident that there are major interacting processes between patterns of social mobility and changes in class structure on the one hand, and the expansion of educational opportunities on the other. Lindsay Paterson (2023a) has pointed out that such opportunities have been transformed in Scotland, as elsewhere. The transformations are clear. In the early 1950s, only one in ten school leavers had acquired any publicly recognised certificate in education. By the end of the twentieth century, that had risen to 90 per cent, and by the second decade, 96 per cent, virtual saturation. Over the same period, the percentage staying on in education after the age of 16 rose from 14 per cent to 88 per cent; the proportion successfully completing any course in senior secondary school rose from one in ten to two-thirds; and the proportion reaching the threshold for university entry went from 6 per cent to 44 per cent. In terms of attainment at school, staying-on rates, satisfaction with schooling, and entry to higher education, had all improved immeasurably. By the late 1980s, sex differences as regards educational attainment had reversed completely. Furthermore, in terms of religious differences:

> Younger Scottish Catholics had attainment and patterns of social mobility that were indistinguishable from those of other Christians and people of no religion ... all this evidence shows the importance

of the Catholic schools in enabling Scottish Catholics to join the mainstream of social opportunity. (Paterson, 2023a: 193)

The point about the expansion of educational opportunities is that it reflects the demand for new sorts of education and training of the labour force, although it has wider social and moral ramifications throughout society.

Those opportunities were significant. Taking the longer view from the 1950s until the 2020s, the proportion in the top two social classes – those in professional and intermediate employment – doubled in the thirty years up to the early 1980s, and then doubled again in the following thirty years until 2016. Women in particular entered the new employment sectors in greater proportions than men (Paterson, 2023a: ch 9). Indeed, there was little systematic difference between Scotland, England and Wales, reflecting the fact that educational credentials were of similar value in the Britain-wide labour market. Furthermore, the extent and quality of Scottish education since at least the 1930s gave Scottish students a marginal competitive advantage in that labour market over their peers in England and Wales; and from the 1960s, the less advantaged in Scotland were ahead in such a way that they could compete in the pan-British labour market at rates corresponding to the relative advantage of secondary school credentials or a university degree, compared to their southern counterparts.

IS SCOTLAND DIFFERENT?

So how, in that case, can we conclude that Scotland is different? Recall E. P. Thompson's point about the nature of social class (Chapter 3), that it is a matter of 'culture' and not simply 'structure'. Class is embedded in cultural understandings and meanings generated in part by institutional differences – law, schooling, religion – but above all by myths and narratives including the 'lad o' pairts'; described by Robert Anderson and Stuart Wallace as:

> the boy from a relatively obscure background who rose through education to professional success. This was one of those powerful and enduring images which turn complex realities into national myths. The 'lad o' parts' (sic) was in part a literary construction, and the term itself did not appear until 1894 but the idea was an old

one. It was a very masculine ideal, and also a very Protestant one, seeing the Reformation as the source of modern Scotland's vigour and identity. (Anderson and Wallace, 2015: 267)

We might reply that Scotland is no longer that kind of society, but nevertheless conclude that much of the reason for the relative success of Scottish education lies in the fact that the progressive coalition of educators has held together better than in England. Believers in economic efficiency made sufficiently common cause with popular educators and humanists who argued for universal education, reinforced by a more widespread nationalistic belief that Scottish education was one of the defining characteristics of the nation. The role of the 'Scottish myth' has been to translate national distinctiveness into institutional characteristics, reinforced by relative success in improving access to cultural capital.

Neither does class structure straightforwardly determine how people see it; described earlier in this chapter as class *consciousness*. Asking a question such as 'Do you ever think of yourself as belonging to any particular class?' elicits quite systematic differences in Scotland and England. We find that employers, managers and professionals in Scotland are far *less* likely than in England to describe themselves as 'middle class' (a difference of 16 percentage points), or that they are *more* likely to say that they do not belong to any social class. While semi- and routine manual workers in Scotland and Britain differ little in class descriptions, almost half saying they do not belong to a social class, and four in ten saying they are working class. On the other hand, both intermediate and lower supervisory and technical workers are *more* likely to say they are working class in Scotland (respectively, percentage point differences of +9, and +12). And comparing those who say they are 'middle class' with those saying they are 'working class', we find there is parity among Scottish employers, managers and professionals (1:1), but a ratio of 1.76 to 1 among their British counterparts.

In all the other class categories, there is a greater propensity for Scottish workers to self-describe as 'working class'. The striking finding from surveys is how *few* people describe themselves as 'middle class' in Scotland, even among employers, managers and professionals, a majority of whom (56 per cent) deny that they are members of any class at all (compared with 40 per cent of their British equivalents). While those in non-professional jobs are equally likely to describe themselves as 'working class', those who are mobile out of the working class into the professional classes in Scotland are significantly *more* likely to describe themselves as 'working class' than similar people south of the border (+9), while even those who are professionals from professional origins are more likely than their counterparts in England to call themselves 'working class'. This means that the culture or meaning of class operates differently, that people in Scotland are much more likely to say they are working class, regardless either of their class of origin, or their class of destination. Asking why that is so makes the point that there is more to social class identity than what you do for a living.

Behind that lies a complex set of cultural and political meanings, which we shall elaborate in later chapters of the book, but it is important to flag that here. Suffice it to say at this point that matters of social identity and politics are key translators of social class. By the 1970s Scots were on the cusp of national identity change. Far fewer people voted Tory in Scotland compared with England from the mid-1960s. In 1974, 36 per cent of Scotland's professional and managerial classes voted Conservative, compared with 51 per cent of English equivalents. This held throughout the class structure such that semi- and unskilled manual workers were twice as likely to vote Tory in England than in Scotland. These were significant national differences, and held for every general election thereafter. By 1997, only 23 per cent of Scotland's professional and managerial classes voted Tory, compared with 37 per cent in England.

By the 2015 British general election, 38 per cent of the salariat – professionals, managers and employers – voted SNP, twice the proportion who voted Labour, and compared with only 17 per cent voting Conservative. In England, it was three times that figure – 51 per cent. In the 2014 referendum on Scottish independence, 37 per cent of the salariat had voted Yes. The salariat in Scotland had shifted to supporting a more powerful Scottish parliament, with one-third supporting one which would make *all* decisions about Scotland (that is, independence), and a further one-third who supported 'devolution-max', meaning that only defence and foreign affairs would be left with Westminster, and all other decisions made by the Scottish parliament.

Identity: Class or Nation?

Furthermore, there had been a turnaround in class identity in Scotland. Since the 1970s, surveys have asked people whether they identified most with 'same class English', rather than 'opposite class Scots'. In 1979, marginally more identified on *class* rather than nation lines (44 per cent to 38 per cent), but by 1992, it had switched around to 27 per cent to 45 per cent respectively; and that relationship has held ever since. By 1999, 41 per cent of Scotland's salariat identified with 'opposite class Scots', compared with 24 per cent with 'same class English' (among the manual working class the proportions were 47 per cent to 19 per cent). The conventional wisdom that 'class is the basis of British party politics: all else is embellishment and detail' (Pulzer, 1967: 102) no longer applies; we may wonder, indeed, if it ever did.

The movement for a Yes vote in the Scottish independence referendum of 2014 was led by left-leaning middle-class people, and this support was the result of interaction between political ideology and social class (Paterson, 2015). Lindsay Paterson has shown that the percentage intending to vote Yes was highest among people who identified as 'Scots', even those belonging to a different class, rather than those in England who shared the same class position; 46 per cent and 41 per cent respectively among such working class and middle class people, and significantly ahead of their respective classes as a whole (36 per cent, and 31 per cent). He concluded:

> not only may we conclude that the Yes intention was strong among left-leaning middle-class people; it was strongest among those left-leaning middle-class people who identified with working-class Scots, and among left-leaning working-class people who did not show much solidarity with working-class people across the border. (Paterson, 2015: 42–3)

CONCLUSION

Nothing quite makes the case for the transformation of Scotland than considering its materiality. Changes in the industrial and occupational structures, and out of those, the class structure, have been such as to shape and form a new Scotland, especially since the 1970s. The system of education, which historically carried so much expectation, values and culture to the point that national identity was bound up with schooling, has similarly been transformed. The elegies for an old industrial Scotland are symptomatic of the depth of social change, that a society defined and directed by masculine manual labour is no more. The abruptness and brutality of that change in the 1980s embedded new comprehensions of relations between different parts of the British state, most notably in Scotland and Wales, where traditional industries were swept away, and sets of political-cultural understandings emerged from the wreckage. It was not so much that labourist politics and culture took up the mantle of challenge to a Conservative-dominated England, as that it found itself adapting to new, nationalist, challenges. As E. P. Thompson pointed out in the 1960s,

> in the actual course of historical or sociological (as well as political) analysis it is of great importance to remember that social and cultural phenomena do not trail after the economic at some remote remove: they are, at their source, immersed in the same nexus of relationship. (1965: 356)

Furthermore:

> Classes do not exist as abstract, platonic categories, but only as men [sic] come to *act* in roles determined by class objectives, to feel themselves to *belong* to classes, to define their interests as between themselves and as against other classes. (1965: 356)

If people's notions of themselves in Scotland as 'working class' remained despite fundamental shifts in patterns of their employment, how did these play into other forms of social identity, notably national? We turn now to the key role in Scotland played by shifting forms of social identity. Have we become different people than our parents?

NOTES

1. A minus sign indicates fewer in Scotland are employed in the sector; a plus sign, that more are employed in proportional terms.
2. The data referred to are from Scotland's census 2022: scotland-s-census-2022-education-labour-market-and-travel-to-work-chart-data-for-publication, figure 5, <https://www.scotlandscensus.gov.uk/2022-results/scotland-s-census-2022-education-labour-market-and-travel-to-work/>.

3. England and Wales are properly disaggregated to allow a three-way comparison between the three 'mainland' countries.
4. In terms of the proportions in senior managerial and professional occupations taken together, Scotland has 34 per cent, England 38 per cent and Wales 32 per cent (<https://www.nomisweb.co.uk/reports/lmp/gor/2013265931/report.aspx#tabempocc>).
5. A snark is a fictitious animal invented by Lewis Carroll in his poem *The Hunting of the Snark* (1876).
6. Petrie had in mind films such as *Floodtide* (1949), on shipbuilding, and *The Brave Don't Cry* (1952), a film about the Knockshinnoch coal mine rescue in Ayrshire in 1950.
7. The film-makers Murray and Barbara Grigor had mounted an exhibition at the Edinburgh Festival and had written it up as a book called *Scotch Myths: An Exploration of Scotchness*, in 1981. In 1982 it was turned into a BFI film of the same name, with Robbie Coltrane, John Bett, Alex Norton and Bill Paterson, the last three starring in the 1973 production of *The Cheviot, The Stag and the Black, Black Oil*, produced by John McGrath.
8. Gildea's study is based on oral history interviews with more than 100 former miners across the British coalfields. The post-industrial landscape in Midlothian is well-described by Paul Gorman (<https://intothegyre.org/2018/11/23/king-coals-graveyard-a-walk-in-midlothian-mining-country/>).
9. CPGB had its own internal divisions, between 'Euro-Communists' and the more orthodox 'Tankies' who had stayed loyal to the Soviet Union.
10. The seat had been held by former miner Tom Fraser from 1943 until 1967 when he resigned on his appointment as chairman of the North of Scotland Hydro Board. The seat was regained by Labour in the following general election in 1970, but Winnie Ewing's victory marked a rise of nationalist voting in Scotland thereafter, and, as such, was iconic of the beginnings of the Nationalist surge that culminated fifty years later.
11. <https://www.thebritishacademy.ac.uk/podcasts/10-minute-talks-miners-strike-1984-85/>.
12. See Joan Smith's book on and with Harry McShane, *Harry McShane: no mean fighter* (1978).
13. Occupational categories used in the 2022 census are: managing directors and senior officials; professionals; associated professionals; administration and secretarial; skilled trades; caring, leisure and other services; sales and customer services; process, plant and machine operatives; and elementary occupations. Full SOC2020 codes are given at <https://www.ons.gov.uk/methodology/classificationsandstandards/standardoccupationalclassificationsoc/soc2020>.

14. <https://www.nomisweb.co.uk/datasets/aps218/reports/employment-by-occupation>.
15. For example, 39 per cent of senior managers and directors in Scotland are female, compared with 36 per cent in England and in Wales. The comparable figures for professional workers are, respectively, 52 per cent, 48 per cent and 52 per cent.
16. Northern Ireland, on the other hand, had a higher proportion working in agriculture, and was an outlier as a British region.
17. Far fewer women were in paid employment in the early years, so there would have been many missing cases. As a result, the convention has been to focus on fathers' employment over time.
18. Standardising on age when the respondent left school (here, 14, or later, 16) allows for more direct comparison.

6

National Identity: Who Have We Become?

> Oh would some power the giftie gie us
> To see oorselves as ithers see us.
> It would frae mony a blunder free us
> And foolish notion
> (Robert Burns, 1785)

There are few more assumed transformations in Scotland than those relating to national identity; and yet few which are more misunderstood. In this chapter, I explore whether people in Scotland have ceased to be British and become more Scottish, in which respects, indeed if at all. It might seem obvious that Scotland has changed since the 1970s in terms of national identity; from being British, to being Scottish. But all is not what it seems. In any case, 'being British' is not straightforward, any more than being Scottish is. The warfare/welfare nexus which shaped the British state after 1945, and which led to the British Nationality Act of 1948, created the legal status of 'Citizen of the United Kingdom and Colonies'. In full, it was 'an Act to make provision for British nationality and for citizenship of the United Kingdom and Colonies and for purposes connected with the matters aforesaid'. Previous to that, people were 'British subjects' of the Crown. So there are questions about what 'British' means, let alone 'Scottish'.

I will argue that national identity changes are nuanced and complex, and depend on the social and cultural meanings attaching to national identity rather than simply treating it as a badge, a straightforward system of cultural classification. I will also explore how 'national' identity relates not only to 'state' identity (being British) but to other forms of social identity such as social class, gender, ethnicity, age and religion, and how these change through time, and crucially from the 1970s onwards. The key point is that who we consider ourselves to be is a reflection of the kinds of social changes we have examined in previous chapters; our identities are not, however, determined by them.

NATIONALITY AND CITIZENSHIP

Broadly speaking, issues of 'nationality' are bound up with who has the right to be a British citizen, a legal status reluctantly entered into by the post-imperial British state in the late 1940s because former Dominions like Ireland and India were doing so. That is why in our discussion of 'national identity', the concept of 'nationality' is extraneous, because it belongs to the legal-political realm of rights of abode, and to formal citizenship.

Nothing is straightforward when it comes to 'national identity' in these islands. Take this example: at the time of the 2014 referendum on Scottish independence, the political scientist Vernon Bogdanor observed that 'those choosing the separatist option ... would be proclaiming that the two identities [Scottish and British] are incompatible, just as, when Ireland became independent in 1921, it signified that the identity of being Irish was incompatible with a British identity' (*The Guardian*, letters, 8 April 2013). Thus, Bogdanor judged that 'Scots will decide whether they want to remain British'. He was wrong. The 2014 referendum was not a choice between these two national identities, just as choosing to be Irish in 1921 did not rule out rights of abode in the UK for Irish citizens, reciprocity being formally enacted later in the twentieth century under the rubric of the Common Travel Area (CTA).[1] For Bogdanor, being British was a marker of citizenship, and by voting to secede from the UK, Scots would have been giving that up *de jure*. The problem was that being British in Scotland would have been likely to survive the break-up of Britain because there is far more to it than citizenship narrowly defined, notably of a cultural and historical nature.

In the light of the outcome of the 2014 referendum vote, this was not put to the legal test, but it reinforces the point that 'nationality' is not a synonym for national identity. In any case, both Scottish and British governments at the time of the referendum took a latitudinarian view of putative citizenship. The Scottish government indicated that all British citizens habitually resident in Scotland, as well as Scottish-born British citizens currently living outwith Scotland would be considered Scottish citizens. The UK government of the time issued a position paper stating that: 'The UK has historically been tolerant of plural nationalities, and therefore it is likely that it would be possible for an individual to hold both British and Scottish citizenship.' (see McCrone and Bechhofer, 2015: 170).[2] Being British, then, has what Robin Cohen called 'fuzzy frontiers':

> British identity shows a general pattern of fragmentation. Multiple axes of identification have meant that Irish, Scots, Welsh and English people, those from the white, black and brown Commonwealth, Americans, English-speakers, Europeans and even 'aliens' have had their lives intersect one with another in overlapping and complex circles of identity construction and rejection. The shape and edges of British identity are thus historically changing, often vague and, to a degree, malleable – an aspect of the British identity I have called 'a fuzzy frontier'. (R. Cohen, 1994: 35)

WHAT IS NATIONAL IDENTITY?

Before we can judge whether Scots have become more Scottish, and less British, we need to sort out what we mean by national identity; if not 'nationality', what is it? Consider this observation from the political philosopher, Margaret Moore, herself a Canadian:

> It would not be devastatingly dislocational, in a cultural sense, to leave Canada and live in the United States, or to leave Scotland to live in England, and would not involve the traditional costs involved in learning a new language or new symbolic repertoires. But it may be profoundly difficult for the Scot to think of herself as an Englishwoman, or the Canadian to think of himself as an American. (Moore, 2006: 98).

The essence of that comment is that national identity is about choice, how people construe who they are. What Moore is doing is pinpointing the personal nature of national identity, that even though we can fit into recognisable repertoires, and quite quickly, such that we become adept at reading the signs on how to behave, we do not necessarily 'become' someone else.

Most people think that where you are born is the common-sense criterion for national identity, but none of us get to choose where we are born. Birthplace, then, is an ascribed, not an achieved, characteristic, not something we have any control over. Better to think of national identity as fluid and constantly made and re-made. The social psychologist Margie Wetherall observed that 'identity needs to be "done" over and over. What "it" is and who "we" are escapes, is ineffable, and needs narrating, re-working, and must continually be brought "to life" again and again' (Wetherall, 2009: 4).

For migrants, national identity is especially problematic. By and large, people born in Scotland who are living in England almost never claim to be 'English', however long they have lived there; whereas English people in Scotland usually say they had never thought of themselves as 'English' until they came to live in Scotland, because that is how the 'natives' addressed them, much to their surprise; they had assumed that 'being British' was sufficient. As we saw in Chapter 4, the proportions of people born in England who have come to live in Scotland has grown substantially since 1945. Migrants are faced with challenges even if they move within the UK; that is why Margaret Moore's observation rings true. One could adapt quite quickly to the rubrics of a new life, while never becoming a different national person. Sharing a common language of 'English' can also be seen as a deterrent to a separate national identity, and strengthens the argument that Scots are 'no different' from people in England.

There is another angle to this, expressed by the writer Willie McIlvanney in a comment which captures both the ubiquity of national identity, as well as its fuzziness:

> Having a national identity is a bit like having an old insurance policy. You know you've got one somewhere but often you're not entirely sure where it is. And if you're honest, you would have to admit you're pretty vague about what the small print means. (*The Glasgow Herald*, 6 March 1999)

McIlvanney made this point at the time of the 1999 referendum on Scottish devolution, and while it implies that no explicit action is needed, like insurance policies it has to be explicitly renewed, and we might consider events like voting in the referendum as a confirmatory device as to who this 'we' is.[3] If 'natives', those born, brought up and living in a country struggle to work out 'what the small print means', then those confronted with not being 'one of us' because they were migrants are especially interesting.

Furthermore, the British state – the United Kingdom of Great Britain and Northern Ireland – is itself something of an anomaly. On the one hand, it is a unitary state with a dominant legislature at Westminster – the UK Supreme Court has reaffirmed in a ruling of November 2022 that 'devolution' is in the gift of that legislature, and has no legal autonomy except with its explicit permission (https://www.supremecourt.uk/cases/uksc-2022-0098.html). On the other hand, the UK is plainly a pluri-national state in cultural and political terms, and the Scots, the Welsh and the (Northern) Irish are not English, nor consider themselves as such. Put at its simplest, being British is a matter of citizenship; being Scottish/Welsh/Northern Irish, as well as English, is a matter of *national* identity, of nation-ness. Thus, theoretically, you can be Scottish and British, Welsh and British, even English and British; while Northern Irish and British has a different meaning altogether, given the unionist/nationalist divide in the province (for a perceptive account of national identity on the island of Ireland, see Jennifer Todd's book *Identity Change after Conflict* (2018)). This cognitive split between 'state' and 'nation' in these islands creates sufficient ambiguity for social scientists to explore people's sense of who they are. There are alternative ways of doing national identification other than citizenship or nationality, because of ambiguities about which nation one belongs to.

At this point, the argument gets more complicated, because we are faced with two pieces of conventional wisdom about national identity. On the one hand, there are those who aver that it is virtually impossible to get at national identity, expressed by the political philosopher David Miller that 'the attitudes and beliefs that constitute nationality [his term] are very often hidden away in the deeper recesses of the mind, brought to full consciousness only by some dramatic event' (D. Miller, 1995: 18). This has echoes of McIlvanney's insurance policy metaphor. Others, such as Sinisa Malešević describe national identity as 'a conceptual chimera, not worthy of serious analytical pursuit. It is a concept that is theoretically vapid while also lacking clear empirical referents' (Malešević, 2011: 272). It is hard to believe that they are mistaken to do so. It also seems a strange thing to say, in that people in these islands have no difficulty articulating their national identity and talking coherently about it (McCrone and Bechhofer, 2015). Either way, whether it is unknowable or even chimerical, national identity has become a contested concept, even though research in the real world indicates that people in Scotland and in England are well able to recognise and talk about it, often at inordinate length.

More generally, in the literature on nations and nationalism one is struck by how little research there is on national identity. Think of it as the puny offspring of muscular parents, these being the concepts of nation and nationalism. Primacy is usually given to sorting out what a 'nation' is – captured by David Miller's comment that 'to understand what we mean when we talk of someone having a national identity, we must *first* [my emphasis] get clear about what nations are' (D. Miller, 1995: 17); and linked to nationalism as its ideology. National identity is conventionally treated as an after-thought, or a by-product connecting nation and nationalism together. However, as Thomas Eriksen observed: '*Nation* is the metaphysical space in which people locate their personal histories, and thereby their identities' (in A. Cohen, 2000: 152).

In the late 1970s, the political scientist Bill Mackenzie published a book with the title *Political Identity*, describing it as a 'murder mystery': 'the victim was the word "identity", an ancient word, which once had a certain dignity. It was first harnessed to a dangerous topic in social science, that of national character, and was driven out of its wits by over-use' (Mackenzie, 1978: 11). Sociologists, notably Richard Jenkins whose work on social identity (his book *Social Identity* ran to three editions up to 2008), have helped to reinstate our understanding of social identity more generally. In retrospect, we would be better to deal in verbs ('to identify') rather than in nouns ('identity'), in order to get away from the notion of identity as a badge which is affixed to people, describing who they are, and whether they like it or not; but 'national identity' is in the public domain and in everyday use whether social scientists like it or not. Better to think of it as process – as identi*fication* – implying a more active process of *doing* identity, varying according to context. Treating people as agents, as manufacturers of identity (and not simply having a badge called 'national identity' affixed to their person) rather than as passive recipients, gets us closer to how they mobilise identity, for which purposes and in which contexts.

What are the implications of thinking of national identities in this way? They are the litmus tests of key changes in social, political and cultural relationships; what Jennifer Todd describes as the 'grammar' of national identity, involving the rules and codes of usage, and connecting elements associated with national identity – history, ancestry, culture, politics – how these are understood and interrelated. These meanings are shifting, not illusory, and in any case, in the classic 'definition of the situation', people act on the basis of what they *believe* to be the case, regardless of truth status however that is defined (Thomas, 1921). Anthony Cohen, captured the essence in his discussion of the related concept of 'nation':

> something which simply does not require to be well-defined, first, because people presume that they know what they are talking about when they refer to it; and second, because the lack of definition allows them scope for interpretive manoeuvre in formulating or inventing or imagining the nation in terms of their selves for the purposes of national identity. (A. Cohen, 2000: 166)

That idea of 'interpretive manoeuvre' is what matters here in discussing national identity; it requires to be decoded according to particular contexts. Processes of identification, especially relating to national identity, can be thought of as prisms which refract social change; we do not experience social change directly and passively, but envelope it into our lives as we go about them. We can imagine that people in Scotland might – or might not – construe who they are differently over time. One issue, of course, is that we simply do not know how people did national identity historically; that the data are simply not available to us. Indeed, only when national identity becomes problematic are we able to assess how and why it has changed.

Who Are the Scots?

What might we expect of changing national identity in Scotland, especially from the 1970s? We might assume that the dominant warfare/welfare nexus from the mid-twentieth century imposed a singular sense of being British on the citizens – who, as they formally became in 1948, were members of the United Kingdom of Great Britain and Northern Ireland.[4] After all, as we shall see in the next chapter, there was very little to separate political behaviours in Scotland and England in the decades immediately after the Second World War. To say that is to make an assumption that we can read off national identity from how people engage in politics. In the decade after 1945, there was little to distinguish Scotland and England in their propensity to vote Labour or Conservative; indeed, the proportions were virtually identical.[5] We surmise, because no systematic evidence was otherwise available, that people north and south of the border at the time shared a common sense of being British, reinforced by shared war experiences, and expressed in support for the new welfare state.

A more subtle understanding might have been that people in Scotland after the war saw little contradiction between being Scottish and being British, the one being nested in the other. Truth to tell and with hindsight, it is highly likely that people *could* tell the difference between the former and the latter. Being English and being British is, on the face of it, another matter. Claims that people south of the border could not tell the difference was arguably reinforced by the warfare/welfare nexus. It was a commonplace to claim that people in England could not tell the difference, and in any case, 'England' and 'Britain' were often used as synonyms.[6] The political campaigner Anthony Barnett asserted in the late 1990s that:

> The English ... are more often baffled when asked how they relate their Englishness and Britishness to each other. They often fail to understand how the two can be contrasted at all. It seems like one of those puzzles that others can undo but you can't: Englishness and Britishness seem inseparable. They might prefer to be called one thing rather than the other – and today young people increasingly prefer English to British – but, like two sides of a coin, neither term has an independent existence from the other. (Barnett, 1997: 292–3)

Later and systematic research by Susan Condor and her colleagues showed that this was an unwarranted assumption, and that people in England are well able to tell the difference (Condor, Gibson and Abell, 2006); the rise of an English nationalism since the 1990s making that more plausible (see McCrone, 2023). Still, Barnett's assertion can be taken as a working assumption of the conventional wisdom in the half-century since 1945.

And Scotland? We lack direct evidence as to how people construed their national identity in the immediate post-war period.

Not until the mid-to-late 1970s did surveys begin to explore systematically how people talked about national identity north of the border, and that was because it was evidently becoming problematic and contested. In the early 1990s, the historian Christopher Smout had argued that 'belonging' operated in concentric territorial rings, as follows: 'the inhabitants of Scotland can be imagined as having concentric rings of territorial identity in responding to the question every human being must ask of themselves: "who do I think I am?"' (Smout, 1994:102). Smout offered these concentric rings: home and family, 'kin, clan or surname', identity with locality, 'nationality' (by which he meant Scottish, English etc), statehood ('British'), 'loyalty to Empire', as well as 'hypothetical loyalties' (for example, to the EEC/EU, the UN, the English-speaking union). As regards being Scottish and/or British, he observed:

> a Scottish identity, is embedded in a group of other identities between the family and the supra-national, which include a *British identity that does not conflict with but rather co-exists with the Scottish identity* [my italics]; and that many other identities intersect with the territorially-based concentric loyalties, some of which (gender, class, occupation) have little effect on them, others of which (language, religion, sport, military tradition) have a substantial effect, usually along the lines of emphasising that loyalty to ring four [nation] is different from loyalty to ring five [state] - that to be Scottish is indeed different from being British, that the nation and the state are not the same, but can co-exist. (Smout, 1994: 107)

Smout is not denying the tensions between 'Scottish' and 'British', at least as these had developed in the last few decades of the twentieth century:

> both those who seek this end [to finish the Union] and those who resist it should realise how long and how valid is the history of concentric loyalties, that a powerful sense of being Scottish has gone hand in hand with a powerful sense of being British for centuries. It is neither good nor bad. It does not demonstrate some particular moral failing on the part of the Scots if they seem to be reluctant to carry their nationalism further than the football field, as Jim Sillars thinks. (Smout, 1994: 112)[7]

Smout was alluding to Scottish–English differences with regards to systems of loyalty; that 'any modern prime minister' including Winston Churchill or Margaret Thatcher would not make the case that 'loyalty to a smaller England was distinguishable from that to a larger Britain', nor that an English population would not consider the Union Jack as the national flag, while 'every Scot habitually distinguishes between a smaller Scotland and a larger Britain, and knows that the national flags are the saltire and the Lion rampant.' (ibid. 102).[8]

The importance of Smout's essay is that it conveys the nuances and complexities of national identities as they were being articulated in the early 1990s, in the context of political-cultural change and prior to the creation of a devolved Scottish parliament, as well as the SNP's electoral success from the mid-2000s. We can, however, take his account of national identity as a scholarly reflection on the *status quo ante*. As a historian, Smout was reviewing what would have been the case, and with an eye to how territorial identities had evolved in the two countries. It is his discussion of the relationship between 'national identity' (being Scottish) and 'state identity' (being British) which is relevant;[9] assumed complementarity rather than antithesis, which became much more of a conventional wisdom after the turn of the century. In any case, distinguishing Scottish and British identities in this way is not to deny that being British can also be considered a *national* identity, in that Britain is also a cultural expression as a 'nation', an 'imagined community' to use Benedict Anderson's felicitous term, rather than simply a state/citizen form. Nation/state in this chapter, however, is simply used as a convenient and non-repetitious shorthand.

Does National Identity Matter?

But does national identity really matter to people, especially vis-à-vis other social identities they may have? We tested that out in the 2001 Scottish Social Attitudes survey, with a preamble to the survey question: 'Some people say that whether they feel Scottish or British is not as important as other things about them. Other people say their national identity is the key to who they are.' We listed over twenty social identities including social class, gender, age, religion, parental and marital status, employment status, and ethnicity. Recognising that people had multiple identities we asked respondents to give their first, second and third choices. The question was also asked in the British Social Attitudes survey, and so covered England, and Wales, so we can see (Table 6.1) the relative importance of national identity in the context of other identities.

What is clear from those figures is that national identity in Scotland has a higher salience than it has in England, with Wales somewhere in between, and that 'being Scottish' is second only to being a parent. Our findings were challenged at the time of publication on the grounds that we had mentioned 'national identity' explicitly in the question preamble ('Other people say their national identity is the key to who they are.'), so we asked a similar question in the 2003 survey, this time omitting mention of national identity.[10] We found very similar responses, just as we did when we repeated the question in 2006, this time leaving 'national identity' out of the list entirely, and then asking a supplementary question whether, if it *had* been available to respondents, they would have chosen national identity. When we did that we found that almost half of Scots, and one-third of English people would have chosen their national identity. Both sets of nationals were quite similar in terms of choosing other social identities (such as being a parent, a partner and so on), but whereas for the English, slightly more chose English than chose British, for Scots the ratio was eight to one, Scottish over British. Furthermore, male and female Scots were *equally* likely to choose being Scottish (40 per cent and 41 per cent respectively); marginally higher levels of working-class people (47 per cent) than the middle classes (40 per cent), but still highly significant; and young people were more likely to do so than older people, but with higher levels for both age categories in Scotland compared with England.[11] The result of this systematic survey research was that we could be certain that being Scottish mattered to people

Table 6.1 Identity choices in Scotland, England and Wales, 2001

% choosing identity as 1st, 2nd or 3rd choices	Scotland	England	Wales
Mother/father	49	48	50
Wife/husband/partner	27	27	27
Woman/man	25	30	22
Scottish/English/Welsh	45	20	33
British	11	27	23
Working class	24	19	23
Working person	29	32	26

Source: British and Scottish Social Attitudes surveys, 2001; Welsh election study, 2001.

across a broad range of social categories (for further details, see Bechhofer and McCrone, 2009). Not only was national identity meaningful to people, but they felt able to rank it – highly – in the context of other social identities they had. We felt sure, then, that we were not chasing a chimera.

Comprehending National Identity

By the beginning of the twenty-first century there was a considerable body of empirical evidence which examined assumptions about territorial identities more closely. Consider these figures. When asked for their 'best choice' national identity in 1979, 56 per cent of respondents in Scotland replied 'Scottish', and 38 per cent, 'British'. By 1990, these figures, respectively, were 72 per cent and 25 per cent, and by 2000, 80 per cent and 13 per cent. Plainly, these can be read as indicating that being British was straightforwardly diminishing over time. 'Best choice' national identity has the merit of juxtaposing being Scottish and being British in a clear-cut way, as well as having the oldest pedigree of survey measures beginning in the late 1970s. Lindsay Paterson in his analysis of changes in Scottish education (2023d) has shown that it is not chronological age which matters so much as birth cohorts,[12] and has helpfully reconstructed the data as it relates to expressions of national identity. The table (6.2) gives the ratio of best-choice Scottish to British identities in successive surveys beginning in 1979, such that parity would be 1.00.

Cast an eye over the marginals in Table 6.2, that is, the summary columns and rows labelled 'all' – for they convey a complex picture. People born in the years before the Second World War have lower ratios of Scottish to British than those born between the 1950s and the 1970s (the vertical summary 'all') but the ratio diminishes in the final quarter of the twentieth century among younger cohorts. The horizontal summary 'all' shows that people surveyed from the late 1990s and into the first decade of this century have higher Scottish to British ratios than their predecessors, or indeed their successors. In other words, those coming to political adulthood during the rapid emergence of the SNP from the mid-1970s appear most likely to shift their national identity to 'Scottish' and away from 'British', in contrast to older cohorts whose political socialisation as adults

Table 6.2 Ratio of 'best choice' Scottish to British identities

	1979, 1992	1997–2003	2004–10	2011–14	2015–19	all
To 1926	1.83	3.20	3.05			2.69
1927–36	1.72	4.19	3.95	3.19	2.74	3.49
1937–46	2.26	4.24	3.93	2.90	2.53	3.45
1947–56	2.21	4.18	4.24	3.03	3.11	3.62
1957–66	3.00	5.46	4.77	3.88	2.93	4.33
1967–76		4.57	5.03	3.55	3.25	4.22
1977–86			4.46	3.20	4.16	3.80
1987–96				2.32	2.74	2.64
all	2.10	4.36	4.35	3.27	3.11	3.73

Source: Paterson, 2023d. The missing cells are where Ns are too small to produce meaningful percentages.

took place in the 1950s and 1960s before political nationalism occurred. It remains to be seen how and why the generation born from the late 1980s onwards have lower ratios, with higher proportions of 'other' identities (not shown in this table). We can see more clearly the fluctuations if we express these in graph form as in Figure 6.1.

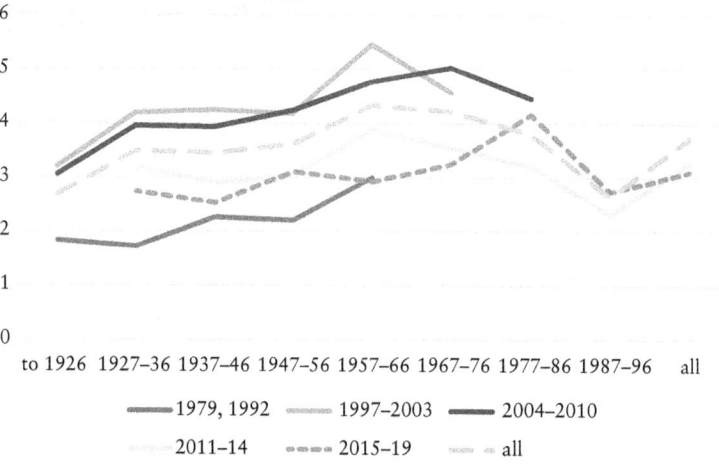

Figure 6.1 'Best choice' identity: Scottish to British ratios by cohorts over time
Source: The data are derived from Scottish Social Attitudes surveys and British and Scottish Election Surveys over the period, with analysis carried out by the author.

These data derive from the oldest form of survey question about national identity in the form of multiple choice: 'which words on this card[13] describes the way you think of yourself?' Options included 'British', 'Scottish', 'English', 'European' and so on, allowing for multiple choices to be made. And a follow-up question, usually called 'forced choice', asked: 'and which one best describes the way you think of yourself?', which are analysed and discussed above. Thus, taking the 2019 Scottish Social Attitudes survey as an example, 49 per cent answered 'British' on the first question, and 76 per cent 'Scottish', so that many respondents, about one in four, clearly felt they were both. Forced to choose ('which one *best* describes the way you think of yourself?'), 22 per cent said 'British', and 66 per cent 'Scottish', a neat ratio of 1 to 3.

It was plain from these figures that a significant proportion of people in Scotland thought of themselves as both British *and* Scottish, and so, in the late 1980s, Scottish Social Attitudes surveys began to ask an additional question about national identities in the form of a five-point Likert scale. Adapted by political scientist Juan Linz in the late 1970s in post-Franco Spain in order to measure the relationship between 'being Spanish' (state identity) and 'being Catalan' (national identity), it was applied to Scotland by Luis Moreno in 1986 for similar purposes, and became known as the Linz-Moreno question.[14] It was extended to surveys in England in 1997, and to Wales in 2001. Its value was that it was a more subtle and sociologically sophisticated measure, allowing respondents to relate 'national' to 'state' identities, without forcing them to choose between one or the other; in the form of a five-point scale ranging from 'Scottish not British', 'more Scottish than British', 'equally Scottish and British', 'more British than Scottish' and 'British not Scottish'. In essence, the scale was designed to be relational, that is, measuring national vis-à-vis state identity.

To anticipate, successive surveys – which were cross-sectional, that is, sampling different respondents at different times – showed that about two-thirds of people in Scotland gave priority to being Scottish (either 'not British', or 'more than British'), and about one in ten 'British' (either 'British not Scottish', or 'more British than Scottish'). The only piece of longitudinal research to date[15] used data from a cohort surveyed in 1997 and again in 1999 (that is, surveying the *same* respondents at two different time-points). This indicated that people in Scotland were fairly consistent over time; around seven in ten giving the same category response at both times, and thus very few shifting identity categories. The exceptions were those who thought of themselves in 1997 as 'more Scottish than British', for only 35 per cent of them gave the same response in 1999; 30 per cent said they were 'equally Scottish and British', and 29 per cent 'Scottish not British'. In other words, there was considerable leakage among those who described themselves as 'more Scottish than British'. Why so?

The late 1990s was a period in which a devolved Scottish parliament was mooted, and established in 1999 by an incoming Labour government in the UK, following a referendum in late 1997 in which there was a heightened debate about self-government. Those who thought themselves 'more Scottish than British' were attracted to the constitutional option known as 'devolution-max', control over all matters apart from foreign affairs and defence, but falling short of outright 'independence'. The dividing line in terms of the relationship between constitutional preferences and national identity fell somewhere between 'more Scottish than British', and 'equally Scottish and British', the latter significantly more 'unionist' than the two more 'Scottish' categories.

The Linz-Moreno measure as used in Scotland, however, can be criticised on the grounds that it is a measure of the *relationship* between national and state identities, and not of the *strength* of feeling about either. Consider: two people might opt for the same identity category, say, 'more Scottish than British', but one person might feel strongly about being both, but opt for the former over the latter; while the other person might not care much either way, but opt for the same response. In other words, we cannot tell from their response how strongly, or weakly, each feel. That is an argument for disaggregating the scales such that we measure the strength or weakness of each (for example, on feeling Scottish (and separately, feeling British) on a scale where '1' indicates a very weak sense, and '7' a very strong sense. The value of doing that can be seen in concluding from Linz-Moreno that, because only one in ten are at the 'British' end of the scale, it is weak, and weakening.

Using separate scales, for Scottish and British, however, shows that while being Scottish is unsurprisingly strong (points

6 or 7 on the seven-point scale) so too is being British, albeit not as strong as being Scottish. Thus, in 2011, among those saying they are Scottish *not* British almost half (46 per cent) score at the mid-point or above on the separate British seven-point scale. Plainly, they are using the 'not British' in Linz-Moreno to indicate strength of feeling, because in strict logic, they should be scoring zero on the seven-point Britishness scale. They are not wrong in their answer, however, nor have they misunderstood the question. They are simply emphasising strength of feeling about their 'Scottish' claim.[16] The largest proportion, 40 per cent, were on points 5, 6 or 7 on both scales, Scottish and British separately, whom we can call 'dualists', those who have strong Scottish as well as strong British identities. About 30 per cent were strongly Scottish but weakly British, whom we can label 'nationalists'.

Identity politics in Scotland, then, takes place across these two groups – both strongly Scottish, but with differential commitments to being British. Thus, measuring territorial identities separately avoids the temptation to assume that, because only around 10 per cent of people on the Linz-Moreno scale say they are more British than Scottish – or even not Scottish at all – that being British is not important, plainly an unwarranted assumption now that we have better evidence.

How we choose to measure has substantive consequences. Thus, 'dualists' were less likely than 'nationalists' in our terms, to vote SNP and to be in favour of independence. Hence, debate about constitutional futures hinges around identity choices, rather than any straightforward support for, or denial of, being Scottish. Indeed, when it comes to political-constitutional outcomes, the relative weakness of 'being Scottish' in statistical terms is only such because Scottish national identity is spread across the population despite, and not because of, constitutional views. To give an example: as regards voting Remain in the EU referendum of 2016, 'being Scottish' had no strong *discriminating* effect on voting choices because most people thought of themselves as Scottish. Voting Leave in England, on the other hand, in the 2016 referendum was strongly associated in statistical terms with 'being English', Remainers south of the border opting, by and large, to say they were 'British'. The point is a simple but important one: claims to national identity have to be read in the contexts in which they are made.

BEING SCOTTISH

We have now reached the point of being able to examine systematically the extent to which people in Scotland have changed their national identity – if indeed they have. Consider the graph in Figure 6.2, which shows responses to the Linz-Moreno identity scale between 1986 and 2021, a period of thirty-five years.

The most obvious feature of the graph is how constant the responses are over time, bearing in mind that these are derived from cross-sectional surveys, that is, of different people surveyed at different time-points. Overall, around two-thirds describe themselves as only or mainly Scottish, and this does not vary much over time. Rather, we encounter something of a 'ceiling effect' in that once a certain proportion is reached, there is little likelihood of it rising further. And in any case, the political fault-line as regards how national identity related to constitutional preferences, comes at the point where people describe themselves as 'equally Scottish and British', and not those who are mainly or only British who are few in proportion throughout. To flag a feature we will discuss in the next chapter, those describing themselves as 'mainly Scottish' are far more likely

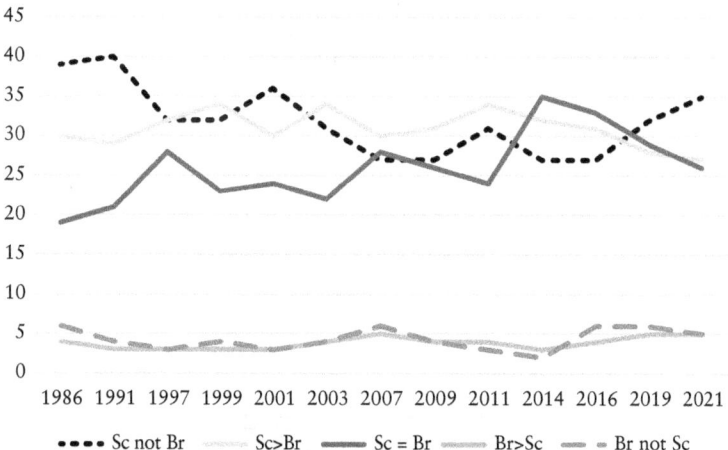

Figure 6.2 Linz-Moreno national identity, 1986–2021
Source: The data are derived from Scottish Social Attitudes surveys and British and Scottish Election Surveys over the period, with analysis carried out by the author.

to be in favour of further constitutional change compared with those who think of themselves as equally Scottish and British, or mainly British. This may not surprise us – once, of course, we know it – but it is significant to note that most 'unionists' are far more likely to say they are equally Scottish and British, than to say they are only or mainly British. Saying you are Scottish, then, runs quite far down the identity scale in terms of constitutional politics. So we can conclude that unionists do not give up on being Scottish, but do draw the line at prioritising 'national' over 'state' identity, preferring to treat them equally.

We have seen that about one-third of people say they are 'Scottish not British', about the same proportion are 'more Scottish than British', about a quarter are 'equally Scottish and British', and only one in ten say they are either more 'British than Scottish' or 'British not Scottish', taken together. People who opt for 'mainly Scottish' (that is, 'Scottish not British', or 'more Scottish than British') far outnumber the 'mainly British' ('British more than Scottish', or 'British not Scottish') by around 8 to 1, with peaks at the time of the 2014 independence referendum, the 1997 devolution referendum, and in the years shortly after the Scottish parliament was established, as shown in Figure 6.3.

The obvious, but interesting, point is that there is trendless fluctuation, and not a neatly increasing proportion of Scottish to British. These ratios show considerable movement over time,

Figure 6.3 Ratio of 'mainly Scottish' to 'mainly British', 1986–2021
Source: The data are derived from Scottish Social Attitudes surveys and British and Scottish Election Surveys over the period, with analysis carried out by the author.

as the proportions within the categories vary. Thus, the high of 11.8 occurred in 2014, accounted for largely by the fact that the 'mainly British' element was a mere 5 per cent, the lowest in the series. The 2007 low of 5.2 in the ratio is because the 'mainly British' were 11 per cent. Those who opt to say 'equally Scottish and British' range from a low of 19 per cent (in 1986) to a high of 35 per cent (in 2014) and 33 per cent (in 2016) when, as we shall see, there was considerable public debate, at the times of the Scottish independence referendum in 2014, and the Brexit referendum in 2016. We can better understand how commentators wrote off 'being British' when the Linz-Moreno scale was read as signifying such. However, behind those figures lies a more interesting, and more accurate, story which we now explore.

Consider the relationship between national identity, shown in Table 6.3, as measured by Linz-Moreno, and support for independence.

We can see that while there has been growing support for independence among the two polar groups, 'Scottish not British', and the 'mainly or only British', it is greater among the first group, as measured by the growing difference between them (from +37 to +54).

We can also see the changing relationship between national identity and constitutional reference by focusing on the increasing proportion of those who say they are 'Scottish not British' who are in favour of independence as shown in Figure 6.4.

In the first decade of the century, only around half of the 'Scottish not British' group were in favour of independence; while after 2010, it is well above that figure. In particular, it is what happens after 2014, the Scottish independence referendum, as well as the 2016 referendum on Brexit, which shows the steepest gradient; in other words, the tightening up of the relationship

Table 6.3 National identity and support for independence

	2010	2011	2012	2013	2014	2015	2016	2017	2019
Scottish not British	44	53	46	51	59	66	69	72	77
More Br than Sc, or Br not Sc	7	10	8	7	15	13	13	12	23
difference	+37	+43	+38	+44	+44	+53	+56	+60	+54

Source: Scholes and Curtice, 2020.

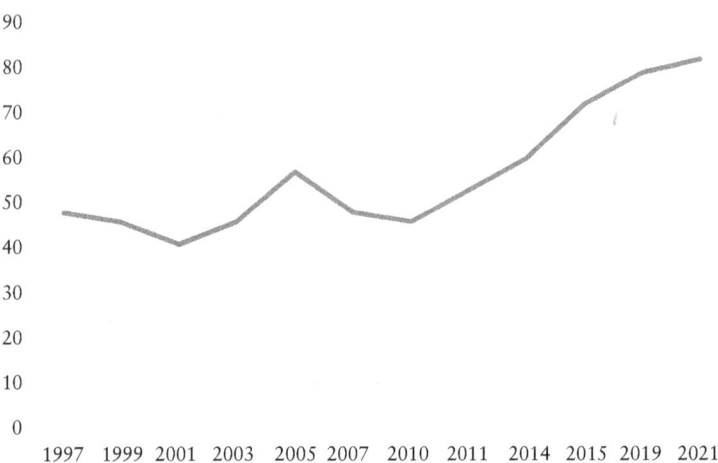

Figure 6.4 Percentage of 'Scottish not British' in favour of independence
Source: The data are derived from Scottish Social Attitudes surveys and British and Scottish Election Surveys over the period, with analysis carried out by the author.

between national identity and support for independence. So it is not simply how people construe their national identity which matters, but the *meanings*, especially political ones, with which they invest it. By 2021, the association between national identity and 'politics', widely defined, was clear-cut: asked how they would vote if there were an independence referendum tomorrow, a majority of both 'Scottish not British' identifiers (85 per cent) and 'more Scottish than British' identifiers (64 per cent) said they would vote Yes. On the other hand, an overwhelming majority of those saying they were equally Scottish and British would vote No (78 per cent), as would even more of the 'mainly British' (83 per cent).[17] So we can conclude that the tipping-point comes when people say they are equally Scottish and British.

Over a thirty-year period, since the late 1980s, there has been a tightening-up of the association between national identity and constitutional preferences such that it appears longstanding, even though we know it is of relatively recent vintage. Furthermore, the point is that this is neither set in stone, nor a simple matter of cause and effect. Rather, it is better to see national identity as 'a meaning-saturated prism of perception and practice that refracts social, political and cultural processes. National identity is neither cause nor effect of these processes, but the grammar through which they are accounted for' (McCrone and Todd, 2025). Still, only about a quarter (27 per cent) would score on all three explicitly 'nationalist' measures: being Scottish not British, voting SNP and being in favour of independence. Furthermore, this figure is much higher than in the 1990s when it was only around one in ten. It is, then, worth bearing in mind that most people, including those who say they are Scottish and *not* British, do not align their political and constitutional preferences with their national identity in anything like a straightforward manner.

We saw earlier in this chapter that the Linz-Moreno scale tends to imply a weak sense of being British, because 'being Scottish' is so dominant, but in fact not at the expense of being British. To reiterate the point: a claim to be 'Scottish not British' does not necessarily imply a weak British identity as strict logic would lead us to expect, for about half of 'strong Scots' score at the mid-point of a seven point 'British' scale or above. So there is no neat correspondence between where people place themselves on a Linz-Moreno scale, and how strongly British they are. It is possible to be both 'strongly Scottish' and 'strongly British', and that is where most Scots placed themselves in 2011.

The Referendum Decade: 2011–21

We might assume, over the decade until 2021, which includes the two referendums, on Scottish independence in 2014, and on Brexit in 2016, that there was a firming up of Scottish national identity. Consider different measures of national identity between 2011 and 2021. First of all, the oldest and most basic measure: the proportions describing themselves as 'Scottish', and 'British', which shows how many are both, and which *best* describes who they are (if they had to choose), as shown in Table 6.4.

Broadly speaking, we can treat such change in the figures as survey statistical 'noise', both indicating the strength of feeling 'Scottish' (around eight out of ten), but almost half with a sense of being British.

A similar pattern (Table 6.5) shows in data for the same two years using the Linz-Moreno scale.

Once more, the distributions between the two years are more similar than different, with 'mainly Scottish' (categories one and

Table 6.4 Preferred national identity

	2011	2021
'Scottish'	84% *(75%)*	79% *(68%)*
'British'	53% *(15%)*	47% *(20%)*

Source: Scholes and Curtice, 2020.

Table 6.5 Linz-Moreno five-point scale

	2011	2021
Scottish not British	29%	33%
More Scottish than British	33	26
Equally Scottish & British	23	25
More British than Scottish	5	5
British not Scottish	5	5

Source: Scottish Social Attitudes surveys, 2011. Author's calculations.

two) being 62 per cent and 59 per cent respectively, and the 'mainly British' identical on one in ten. We cannot, therefore, conclude that there has been a major shift in national identity over the decade if we rely simply on those figures.

If, however, we use the seven-point scales for 'Scottish' and 'British', with a score of '1' for low identification, and '7' for high, on both scales, we do find a significant shift, bearing in mind that the scales are designed explicitly to measure *strength* of identification. Previously, we described 'nationalists' on these scales as respondents who were 'strongly Scottish' (points 5, 6 or 7) and low on 'being British' (1, 2 or 3). In 2011, these comprised 28 per cent of the sample. By 2021, they were 26 per cent of that year's sample, signifying little change in the overall proportion. Turning to those we termed 'dualists' – those who scored highly (5, 6 or 7) on both Scottish and British scales separately; they were 40 per cent of the 2011 sample, but by 2021, only 15 per cent. Thus, there has been a significant decline in the proportion of 'dualists' over the decade, suggesting that the terms 'Scottish' and 'British' have become much more politicised. There is one further twist. If we simply consider the most extreme responses, those scoring '7' for high, and '1' for low, we find a polarisation such that among the 'not at all British' (those who score '1'), as many as 77 per cent describe themselves as 'very strongly Scottish' (that is, '7'). The obverse of that, among the 'very strongly British' ('7'), over half – 56 per cent – also describe themselves as 'very strongly Scottish' ('7'), so 'dualists' have not disappeared, the difference from 2011 reflecting a shift to extreme positions, in the context of the political-constitutional debate possibly framed by the two referendums in 2014 and 2016.

Why the Referendums Mattered

Referendums in the UK are relatively rare constitutional devices. There was the UK EEC membership (continuing) referendum in 1975 (67 per cent voted to remain in the EEC); the Alternative Vote (AV) referendum in 2011 (68 per cent voting No); the EU membership ('Brexit') referendum in 2016 (52 per cent across the UK voted Leave). By and large, referendums are devices to get governments off political-constitutional hooks. They have been more common in Scotland, where there is no shortage of such hooks. The 1979 referendum on a Scottish Assembly actually produced a Yes vote of 52 per cent, but insufficient to stymie the '40 per cent' of the electorate threshold, gerrymandered by opponents of constitutional change. The 1997 Scottish devolution referendum produced a 75 per cent vote in favour of the principle, and 63 per cent in favour of the parliament having tax-varying powers. The 2014 Scottish independence referendum saw 55 per cent voting No, but in its aftermath, the losers won and the winners lost in that the issue encouraged a re-alignment of Yes voters to boost support for the SNP, a significant number of erstwhile Labour voters making the switch.[18] The 2016 EU referendum also had a galvanising effect in that 62 per cent of Scottish voters elected to vote Remain (as did Northern Ireland where 56 per cent did likewise), in contrast to England where 53 per cent voted Leave (as in Wales, 52 per cent). Refusal by the UK government to permit another Scottish independence referendum on the grounds that Scotland had not voted to Leave the UK fell on deaf ears, fearing that a Yes vote for independence was more likely than in 2014.

National identity was at the crux. As Alex Scholes and John Curtice observed on the 'What Scotland Thinks' website:[19]

> The difference between these two groups ['Scottish not British', and the 'mainly British'] and in their level of support for independence is

markedly greater now [they were writing in 2022] than it was prior to the independence referendum. Although support for leaving the UK increased among those identifying as 'More British than Scottish' or 'British not Scottish' from just 7% in 2010 to 23% in 2019 – an increase of 16 percentage points – the equivalent increase among those identifying as 'Scottish, not British' has been 33 percentage points – from 44% in 2010 to 77% in 2019.

and they concluded:

> Scotland's political parties are addressing an electorate whose sense of Scottish identity has become more entwined with support for Scottish independence, a link that has seemingly been galvanised by both the 2014 independence referendum and the outcome of the 2016 EU referendum. Meanwhile, Brexit has ensured that support for independence is now more common among those with a liberal outlook. Between them these two developments have resulted in a sharper division between those who support independence and those who do not in terms of both identity and ideology. (ibid. 11–12)

Being European

A further twist in the national identity tale relates to 'being European' (see McCrone, 2019b). All forms of territorial identity have the capacity to take on political-constitutional meanings, and being European is no exception. After all, 'Independence in Europe' carries cultural and political significance, especially in the context of a strong and abiding association between voting for Brexit and being English. In that regard, being Scottish and European is no political contradiction in terms. The key point is that people in Scotland are much more inclined to say they are 'European' than people in England (see Table 6.6): 45 per cent of Scots, but only one-third of the English. Consider, further, these data, relating strength of European identity in Scotland and England, and the propensity to vote Leave/Remain in the 2016 EU referendum.

We can see that among 'weak' Europeans voting Leave in Scotland and England, the differential is as much as 16 percentage points (51 minus 35), whereas there is virtually no difference among 'strong Europeans' in the two countries (88 per cent and 83 per cent). This holds true across the spectrum of socio-demographic and political variables. Being strongly 'European' produced comparably high proportions of Remain voting in

Table 6.6 Being European and Brexit vote, 2016

%	Scotland		England	
	Remain voters	Leave voters	Remain voters	Leave voters
'weak European'[a]	51%	49	35%	65
'strong European'[a]	88%	12	83%	17

Source: McCrone, 2017.
[a] A 'weak European' is someone scoring 1, 2 or 3 on the seven-point scale where 1 is weak and 7 is strong; and a 'strong European' scores 5, 6 or 7.

both countries in 2016, while 'weak' Europeans in England were significantly more likely to vote Leave than their counterparts in Scotland. Similarly, the 'strongly British' in Scotland were far more likely to describe themselves as 'strongly European' than similar people in England. While 'national identity' in Scotland has little discriminating effect on 'being European' (people describing themselves as 'mainly Scottish' are just as likely to say they are 'weak Europeans' as 'strong'), being 'English' has a major effect in that the 'more English' people say they are, the more likely they are to be 'weak Europeans'. Leave voters in England were most likely to be people over 65, working class, Tory-supporting, with low levels of educational qualifications, holding authoritarian values, and being 'English' in terms of national identity. In Scotland, Leave voters tended to be men, with few educational qualifications, having authoritarian values, but there were no significant national identity differences compared with Remainers, reinforcing the point that 'being Scottish' is ubiquitous.

The strong Remain vote in Scotland in 2016, however, was not simply the result of people asserting their personal 'Scottishness'. Mobilising the 'Scottish interest' was effected by the Scottish government as a matter of institutional identity. Arguably, the strong Remain vote in Scotland in 2016 was the result of the assertion of institutional Scottishness along with being British, hence, strongly European. The unintended consequences of political action, in this case holding a referendum to get off a tricky political hook by Prime Minister David Cameron in 2016, mobilised and channelled territorial identities – Scottish/English, British and European – into outcomes which were unexpected as well as eventful. I will return to this important point in the final chapter and set it in the context of the argument of the book.

CONCLUSION

We began this chapter by addressing the conventional wisdom that in the last fifty years people in Scotland have shifted from saying they were British to saying they were Scottish. We now know that this was far too simple a conclusion. There was no straightforward shift from state to national identity in Scotland (nor, indeed, in England, despite 'being English' becoming a determining factor in explaining votes for Leave in the 2016 Brexit referendum). Rather, what mattered was what national identity terms like Scottish, British, and English came to signify.

Recall Anthony Cohen's useful term 'interpretive manoeuvres'. Armed with an array of identity possibilities, people are adept at mobilising and manoeuvring such terms around social, cultural and political issues of the day. There is much truth in Michael Kenny's observation that Englishness is 'an "empty signifier" which has been painted in various cultural and political colours and corralled in the service of a surprisingly wide range of arguments and ideas' (Kenny, 2014: 203). Kenny was writing that in the context of the association of 'being English' with voting Leave in 2016, a powerful trope mobilised by Boris Johnson's Conservatives in the 2019 British general election. National identity, then, is not a passive badge attached to people by their place of birth, but a manoeuvring device used to make sense of the situations people find themselves in. In other words, national identity is to be understood in the context of the grammar and syntax of 'politics' in the widest sense.

We have seen that the challenge of charting shifts in national identification is how we choose to measure it; how we do so is fundamental to what we find out. Social scientists only began to chart and explain these shifts once they became problematic, and it was not until the late 1980s and into the 1990s that we had systematic studies. The Linz-Moreno measure was an improvement on what had gone before, but it was only as good as its purpose, which was to *relate* national and state identities. It had the unintended consequence of implying that 'being British' no longer mattered, if only one in ten people ostensibly gave it priority. The measure, however, was explicitly relational, having been developed in post-dictatorship Spain to examine how being Catalan related to being Spanish. Importing and adapting the measure to Scotland made sense, given the national/state relationships between territories. Nevertheless, taken in aggregate over a period of more than thirty years from the late 1980s did not show dramatic shifts in how Scots 'did' national identity as our data show.

And what of being Scottish in this context? We have noted the strength and consistency of 'being Scottish' north of the border in that it resembles, in Clifford Geertz's term, 'thick description', an important form of social identity set in the context of other forms, of gender, age, social class and so on. It is, nevertheless, frequently implicit, hence Willie McIlvanney's likening it to an 'insurance policy', important, but not in everyday use.

The conventional assumption in the post-war period was that being Scottish and being British were complementary rather than antithetical: the UK was, after all, *de facto* if not *de jure* a pluri-national state. This belief in complementarity lasted until the final few decades of the twentieth century, an assumption that only became problematic when social, economic and political changes began to work their way through the social structures, and aided, but not created, by the rise of an explicit nationalist party, the SNP. In any case, substantial proportions of Scots, as many as two-thirds excluding those who say they are Scottish not British, describe themselves as British in some shape or form. As many as one-third are at least equally or mainly British in terms of the Linz-Moreno scale.

Furthermore, the easy, but misleading, explanation for any apparent strengthening of 'being Scottish' is that this is a political move. We now know that this is not so in any simple terms. Not only has 'being British' lasted much longer than we assumed, but more importantly, terms like 'Scottish' and 'British' have changed their meanings in subtle but radical ways. A large part of the change relates to generational replacement (Paterson, 2023a), in that the oldest birth cohorts, that is, those born just after the Second World War had their views and values shaped by the warfare/welfare nexus. As Lindsay Paterson has shown, 'these were the cohorts who experienced the British solidarity of the war mostly as adolescents or adults, and who, as voters and workers contributed to creating the welfare state' (Paterson, 2023d: 538). Their replacement by a generation, more highly educated and considering themselves more Scottish, gave rise to a population more sympathetic to independence. Hence, by the 2014 Scottish independence referendum, 'the percentage of independence supporters who were graduates with a Scottish identity was up from 23 per cent a decade earlier, 12 per cent in 1997, and a mere 7 per cent in 1979' (Paterson, 2023d: 536).

Only when we examine the meanings being given to national identity terms do we begin to appreciate what 'being Scottish' has come to signify. Above all, the political-constitutional events of 2014 and 2016 – the referendums – were the catalysts for change, imbuing new meanings and significance to old labels. Thus, what 'being Scottish' came to mean in the 2020s was quite different to what it meant in the 1970s and 1980s; a reasonable surmise, if only because we did not have the survey evidence which we later had, but not an unreasonable assumption to make in the circumstances.

Meanwhile, the Brexit referendum in 2016 in England was the catalyst for changing the meaning of 'being English'– ironically, given that conventional wisdom of those times asserted that people were unable to tell the difference between English and British; that it was, in Anthony Barnett's phrase, a puzzle they could not solve. We now know they are well able to solve it, and with far more political significance than 'being Scottish' in that 2016 referendum. Indeed, binary choices, such as referendums have that capacity to force people into being one thing or another, and while that rides roughshod over nuanced options (this was as true of what people felt about British membership of the EU, as it was about the range of options relating to Scottish Home Rule), it had an effect of manoeuvring identity shifts in new and unforeseen ways, and laid down new tracks on which it could travel. If much of that relates to 'politics', then we should not be surprised, though the message of the current chapter is that there is more to national identification than simply 'politics', which I explore systematically in the next chapter as we trace social changes through their political behaviour and attitudes.

NOTES

1. Under the CTA, British and Irish citizens can move freely and reside in either jurisdiction and enjoy associated rights and privileges, including the right to work, study and vote in certain elections, as well as to access social welfare benefits and health services.
2. In the 2003 Scottish Social Attitudes survey, two-thirds of respondents would choose a Scottish passport, and 25 per cent a British one.

3. I am grateful to Lindsay Paterson for making the point that just as insurance policies have to be renewed annually in order to still be valid, opportunities for validating national identity are necessary.
4. Even 'citizenship' is problematic and subject to political reconstruction. Since September 2021, taking a car abroad requires a 'UK' sticker unless it has a Union Jack on the number plate. While the old 'GB' sticker became redundant and was in any case inaccurate (Northern Ireland is not in GB but is in the UK), this arguably had more to do with post-Brexit assertion of 'British identity'. Scots, in any case, have long been in the habit of using 'Ecosse' or SCO stickers.
5. We can construct an index of Scotland–England differences by adding together Labour's proportional advantage, and Conservative shortfall, in Scotland (compared with England). The 'combined gap' in the elections of the 1945–55 decade was as follows: 1945, 1.8; 1950, 1.0; 1951, 1.1; and 1955, 0.4. Compared with later years, these are very small differences between the two countries.
6. Something which famously irked the poet Hugh MacDiarmid who complained of '... *the use o' England whaur the UK's meent'*. See Crawford, 1992: 2). The habit continues. To claim that 'England' won the war makes one wonder what the rest of us were up to.
7. Smout's allusion to Jim Sillars relates to Sillars's complaint that Scots were happy to cheer for Scotland on the football field (hence, they were 'ninety-minute patriots'), but not vote for independence at the ballot box. 'Ninety-minute nationalists' became something of a jibe aimed at others.
8. Inconsistencies still abound. Even today when England teams play rugby or football, the 'national' anthem played is God Save the King/Queen, which is the British, that is, state, anthem. Confusing England and Britain is thereby given official recognition.
9. Distinguishing between 'national' and 'state' identities does not imply that being 'British' cannot be 'national'. It simply takes cognisance of the fact that the UK is a pluri-national state comprising four territories.
10. The preamble read: '*People differ in how they think or describe themselves. If you had to pick just one thing from this list to describe yourself, something that is very important to you when you think of yourself, what would it be?*' The list of over twenty items was the same, and respondents were asked for their first, second and third choices.
11. In Scotland, 68 per cent of young men and 40 per cent of older men mentioned their national identity; compared with, respectively, 48 per cent and 28 per cent in England.

12. The distinction between chronological age and age cohort is important; two people, for example, aged 30, say, one in the 1960s, and the other in the 2020s will have been subject to different social, economic and cultural processes of socialisation which they will have carried into their later years. Hence, knowing *when* people were born is more meaningful than simply knowing their chronological age.
13. The question was asked in this way to avoid using the term 'national identity' explicitly.
14. For a technical assessment, see Guinjoan and Rodon, 2015.
15. Reported in McCrone and Bechhofer, 2015: 34.
16. We found a very similar effect when we applied our measures to Gaelic speakers in the Scottish *Gaidhealtachd*. Many of those who said they were 'Gaels not Scots' also said they were Scottish on a separate Scottish/British scale, often 'Scottish not British', or 'more than British'. They were using the different scales to emphasise strength of feeling about being Gaels. In other words, context is the key.
17. The data come from Scottish Social Attitudes survey, 2021, the latest at the time of writing.
18. Labour's vote in the subsequent British election of 2015 fell to 24 per cent, and it lost forty seats to the SNP, who won 56 seats on 50 per cent of the vote.
19. Scholes and Curtice, <https://whatscotlandthinks.org/wp-content/uploads/2021/04/WST_The-Changing-Role-of-Identity-and-Values-in-Scotlands-Politics_v2.pdf>.

7

Politics in a Cold Country

We say yes, and we are the people
(Kenyon Wright, 1989)

In this chapter, I will examine how and why politics changed in Scotland, especially from the 1970s. To what extent did politics reflect the social changes we have described in the earlier chapters of the book? That a transformation happened seems obvious. In the 1970 British general election, Labour and the Conservatives took four of every five votes between them: Labour, 44 per cent, and the Tories, 38 per cent. By 2019, half-a-century later, the respective figures were 19 per cent and 25 per cent; less than half of the popular vote, rising marginally in 2024 to 48 per cent. The difference, of course, is accounted for by the rise of the SNP to a position of dominance, both at the British election level, taking 45 per cent in the general election of 2019, and at the constituency level[1] in the Scottish parliamentary elections in 2021, where it took 48 per cent of votes; falling back to 30 per cent in the British general election of 2024. In first-past-the-post elections, as for Westminster, the number of seats is only loosely related to share of the vote, quite starkly in the 2024 election, so in this chapter we will focus mainly on vote share as a more accurate reflection of political trends in Scotland.

The starting point is 1945, the iconic post-war election, and in Scotland, as in the rest of Britain, Labour and Conservatives took 90 per cent of the votes. This fitted the conventional wisdom that Britain's politics were those of social class, and that all parts of the British mainland shared this dimension.[2] In Michael Keating's words: 'political perspectives on the United Kingdom in the middle years of the twentieth century were underpinned by the homogenization thesis' (Keating, 2020: 2). Furthermore, political homogeneity was constructed on the ostensible centrality of social class as the almost unique stratifying dimension in politics. Recall the motif of Peter Pulzer in 1967: 'Class is the basis of British party politics; all else is embellishment and detail.' If so, we would expect the differences between Scotland and England to be minimal on the grounds that their social class structures have grown more alike. Are they?

CHARTING POLITICAL CHANGE IN SCOTLAND

Much depends on what we take as our benchmark. If the 1970 British general election in Scotland is our starting point, in terms of vote share there appears to be little subsequent change, with Labour the most popular party getting at or around 40 per cent of the vote, dipping below 30 per cent thereafter and recovering to 35 per cent in 2024. It was not until the second decade of the new century that change became obvious, as we can see from Figure 7.1.

Taking the longer view allows us to see how the share of the vote in Scotland diverged markedly compared with the rest of Britain around the 1970s, the fulcrum of political change, but Scotland was diverging from British political patterns long before that, as Figure 7.2 shows.

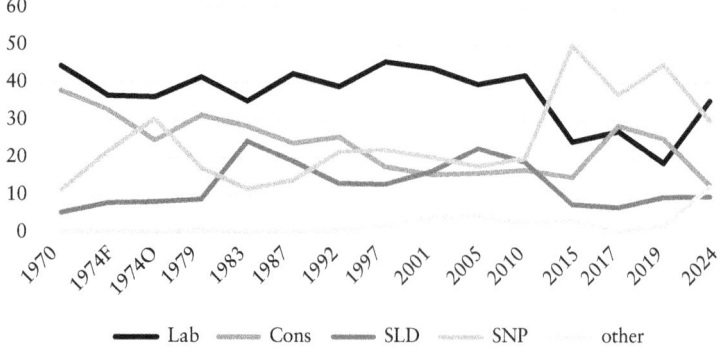

Figure 7.1 British general elections in Scotland: % share of the vote, 1970–2024
Source: British Election Surveys, 1970–2024, with analysis by the author.

Politics in a Cold Country   175

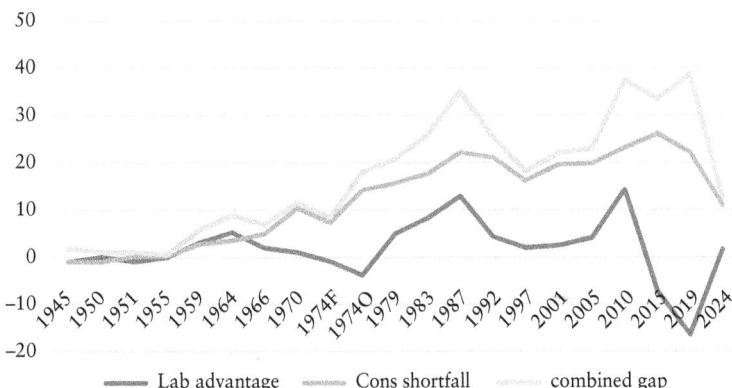

Figure 7.2 Labour–Conservative gap comparing Scotland and Britain, general elections, 1945–2024
Source: British Election Surveys, 1945–2024, with analysis by the author.

There are differences between Scottish and British vote share patterns in terms of (1) Labour's 'advantage' in Scotland, and (2) the Conservative 'shortfall' in Scotland. In 1945, for example, there is little difference to speak of, reflected in the 'combined gap' being close to zero.[3] That pattern, reflected in the top line of the graph, remained below a 10 per cent gap until the 1970 election (when it was 11.4 per cent), falling below that, to 8.3 per cent, in February 1974. Thereafter, starting with the British general election of October 1974, the combined gap was well into double figures (18 percentage points in that election), and more than double that (38.7) in 2019. The other interesting feature of the graph is that much of the combined gap between Scotland and the rest of Britain is the result of the shortfall in the Conservative vote share (the middle line in the graph) rather than Labour having a differential advantage north of the border. We can conclude, then, that it is an aversion to the Tories in Scotland, rather than love of Labour which made the difference.

Plainly, much of this divergence between Scottish and British politics had to do with the electoral success of the SNP. This was also reflected in its constituency vote share in Scottish parliamentary elections, where 2007 is the cross-over point in terms of electoral success (Figure 7.3). That year, the SNP got a marginally higher share of the vote (32.9 per cent) than Labour

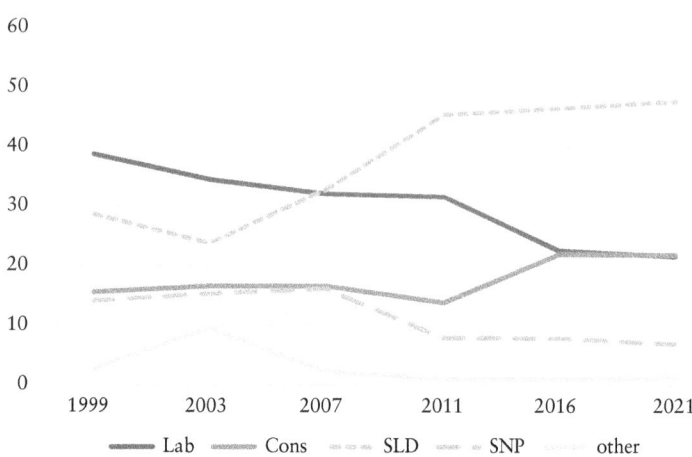

Figure 7.3 Scottish parliament elections constituency vote share %, 1999–2021
Source: British Election Surveys, 1999–2021, with analysis by the author.

(32.1 per cent), and, overall, one seat more, thus allowing them to form a minority government at Holyrood.

Union State

How do we explain the change in share of the vote? Chapter 3 gave a preliminary sketch of the political, economic and social transformations which underpinned it. Such transformations were common to almost all advanced industrial societies, but their impact was differential, according to the socio-cultural landscape on to which they were imprinted. For Scotland, Graeme Morton's term 'unionist-nationalism' (1999) captures this landscape well. The Treaty of Union of 1707 was a negotiated compromise, in Michael Keating's words:

> an 'incorporating union' in which the parliaments both of England and of Scotland were abolished in favour of a new Parliament of Great Britain but there was not even an election for the new Parliament, which carried on as though it were the continuation of the English parliament with Scottish members added. (Keating, 2020: 3)

Nevertheless, due attention had to be paid to the maintenance and independence of Scotland's governing institutions, notably legal, educational and ecclesiastical, the last being taken care of by the Act of Settlement of 1690, which formally recognised the reformed church as Presbyterian, and ratified in the grandiloquently titled 'Protestant Religion and Presbyterian Church Act' of 1707. This ensured that Presbyterianism would not be affected by the Act of Union with England in the same year: and so a key source of conflict was removed.

The 1707 Union protected the institutional autonomy of Scotland, and as Michael Keating observed, 'Scotland has long constituted a political space, strengthened by devolution, within which issues are defined and debated, albeit nested within a wider UK political space' (Keating, 2020: 14). In many ways, the Union was about having your cake and eating it, for, as Lindsay Paterson pointed out:

> The Scots could believe that they had won a great bargain because their culture could flourish and their economy could grow. This was their conception of liberty. It is not ours, nor that of nationalism: there was no mass franchise, nor even the nineteenth century icon, a national parliament. (Paterson, 1994: 45)

In principle, Union meant that Scots had the national right to be treated as equals. The historian Colin Kidd (2008) made the point that, in the ensuing centuries, unionists asserted the theoretical independence of Scotland, while nationalists argued for equal treatment with England in the Union. In this way, much of unionism was tinged with nationalism, and nationalism with unionism. Nationalists and unionists alike insisted on the constitutional equality of Scotland with England.

This was a difficult balance to maintain, given the dominance, both demographic and political, of England in the British state. It required careful and sensitive footwork, and the maintenance of the 'union-state' rather than a unitary state with a single legislature. We can assume that the more voting habits resembled each other on both sides of the Border, the more likely the state was to hold. Scotland and England had diverged politically in the nineteenth century when Scotland was a Liberal fiefdom, so what happened in the final decades of the twentieth century was not unique. Between 1832 and 1918, support for the Liberals in Scotland did not fall below 50 per cent at Westminster elections. The Scottish Unionist Party was a confection made by Conservatives and Liberal Unionists in 1912 which lasted until

1965, when it was incorporated into the Conservative and Unionist Party. Liberal-Unionists acted as 'a bridge over which middle class man could pass from Liberalism to Toryism without suffering any sense of betrayal' (Checkland and Checkland, 1984: 85).

After 1945, the Tories in Scotland were doing much better than they could have expected in terms of the social base. The political scientist Bill Miller (1981) calculated that they were doing as much as 8 per cent better than their notional class base allowed. This was because: (1) they had a social base in municipal politics in the guise of so-called Moderates and Progressives, their localised manifestations, for much of the twentieth century; (2) they had differential appeal to the Protestant working-class. As late as 1986, 45 per cent of members of the Church of Scotland claimed to vote Tory (Brown, 1990: 82); and (3) they were in command of the nexus which connected Protestantism, unionism and militarism; potent, given the recency of the Second World War and the generations involved in it. This ideological complex underpinned a focus on civic duty and social responsibility operating through different levels of Scottish society, all the way up to the Scottish Office at St Andrews House; personified by Walter Elliot, Scottish Secretary between 1938 and 1940, a member of parliament between 1918 and 1958, and cabinet minister. Elliot epitomised the Tory politician embedded in Scottish civil society; a member of parliament in turn for the seats of Lanark, Glasgow Kelvingrove and the combined Scottish universities, a Lord High Commissioner of the Church of Scotland, Rector of both Glasgow and Aberdeen universities, and with a strong war record, having won the Military Cross twice in the Great War.

Conservatives, in whatever guise, were happy to play the 'freedom' card in the post-war period, but they were no Thatcherite neo-liberals. Malcolm Petrie, in his book *Politics and The People, 1945–79* notes that Labour's programme in 1945 was seen by some opposition parties as a threat to Scottish institutional autonomy: '… after 1945 Unionists embraced these complaints, and posed as the protectors of Scottish distinctiveness, critical of Labour's alleged efforts to impose socialist homogeneity' (Petrie, 2022: 14). Sharing that critique for the Scottish National Party were Douglas Young and Robert McIntyre. Petrie argues that the fundamental contest in Scottish politics post-1945 was between collectivism and individualism, in which 'constitutional questions occupied a subordinate position' (ibid. 38), with the SNP ostensibly on the side of individualism. More to the point: given a Labour government at Westminster nationalising the governing apparatus, and eschewing Home Rule for Scotland, 'individualism' did not have the meaning it took on with the emergence of Thatcherite neo-liberalism thirty years later.

Whatever the ideological position of the SNP in the post-war period, all that was to change from the late 1960s and early 1970s. The cusp year for the SNP was 1974. In the February election they won seven seats (up six from 1970) on 21.9 per cent of the vote. In October they won eleven seats on 30.4 per cent of the vote, its highest share ever, until it won 50 per cent in the British general election of 2015, but that was almost forty years into the future. Given the exigencies of the first-past-the-post electoral system, major victories (and losses) can be stacked up on small shifts in the popular vote; exemplified by the outcome of the 2024 British general election in Scotland, when Labour won 37 seats on 35 per cent of the vote, and the SNP, nine seats on 30 per cent.[4] Underneath that, however, are shifts in social structure such that changes in social and geographical mobility along with secular changes eroded or amplified political changes. Thus, the Conservatives found that they had a shrinking social base – recall Miller's 8 per cent value-added over and above its notional class base – and the SNP were able to benefit from disillusion with the two main parties. Meantime, a generational as well as an ideological shift occurred in the SNP, with the emergence of the 79-Group led by Alex Salmond. Expelled from the party in 1982, it went on to dominate, and established the SNP as a left-of-centre party.

Labour, the beneficiary of the state project to modernise the economy after 1945, found itself under pressure to deliver Home Rule, without properly understanding the rationale, but seeing it mainly as a device to counter the rising SNP. And so, at the tail-end of a Labour government in the late 1970s, it introduced a hobbled referendum on devolution, with a 40 per cent rule wished upon it by its opponents within and outwith the party. In the event, the referendum achieved a 52/48 vote for Yes,[5] but insufficient to meet the gerrymandered 40 per cent rule whereby that proportion of the electorate had to vote Yes for the measure to pass. This meant, by default, that the dead and those abstaining were counted as No voters whether they liked it or not. That failure, coupled with the advent of a Thatcherite government, changed Scottish, and British, politics in a way unforeseen.

The Cusp of Change

The late 1970s proved to be the key moment of political change. Labour had run out of a majority at Westminster – it only had a three-seat majority when elected in October 1974, and the Winter of Discontent in 1978–79 had convinced the Prime Minister James Callaghan that there would be a sea-change in British politics.[6] The devolution referendum in Scotland, and in Wales, in March 1979 saw a small majority in favour in Scotland, and a massive majority against (four to one) in Wales. The SNP, who had supported setting up a Scottish Assembly, voted against the Labour government, which lost a vote of confidence in March 1979.

The election of Mrs Thatcher ushered in a different order of things. Her kind of Conservatism spoke with a southern English voice. The populist and nationalist anti-state appeal which sustained her government in England during the 1980s had negative resonances in Scotland. Despite the Conservative majority at Westminster of forty-four in 1979, in Scotland Labour had twice the number of seats (forty-four, on 41 per cent) as the Tories (twenty-two, on 31 per cent), and the SNP was reduced to only two seats, on 17 per cent of the vote. The incoming Conservative government rescinded the Scotland Act of 1978, and the Thatcherite strategy of cutting down the state and asserting the primacy of the market ran hard up against the policy communities in Scotland, thus alienating the middle-classes who helped to run them. By 1997, the Conservative share of the vote in Scotland was half (17 per cent) what it was in England. Among the professional and managerial classes in Scotland in that year, only 23 per cent voted Tory, compared with 37 per cent in the rest of Britain, a differential which had existed at least since 1974, and was to grow in years to come.

Labour, meanwhile, had inherited, almost by default, the nationalist mantle, and in any case had been responsible for putting in place the Scottish frame of reference in the 1960s, as we saw in Chapter 5. Labour played the card with relish.

Its vote share in Scotland at British general elections held up at or around 40 per cent (see Figure 7.1 above), and its long period out of power encouraged the party to consider and adopt 'devolution' of powers as a half-way house between the status quo and independence. This it could safely do, given the electoral weakness of the SNP, especially as the latter had stood aside from the Scottish Constitutional Convention on the grounds that devolution was a half-way house it did not support, and some in the party considered it a 'unionist trap'. This allowed Labour and its Liberal Democrat allies to promote a 'Scottish Assembly' and a 'Scottish Executive' (not called a 'government' until 2007).

Recasting Scottish Politics

Breaking into British party politics has long been difficult for small parties, because the first-past-the-post system is a device to keep them out. The SNP breakthrough did not come until the mid-1970s, but there were signs of it happening long before then. In 1955, for example, the party got 14.5 per cent of the vote in the two seats they contested, and by 1959, they fought five seats, in which they got an average of 11.4 per cent. By 1964, they were fighting fifteen seats, with 10.7 per cent, and in 1966, twenty-three seats, for 14.1 per cent. By-elections were far more important for smaller parties, given the publicity they afforded. In the West Lothian by-election in June 1962, won by Labour, the SNP came second with 23 per cent, while in Glasgow Pollok in March 1967, they got 28 per cent of the vote, coming third, only 3 percentage points behind Labour, who lost the seat to the Tories. A few months later, in November 1967, the breakthrough came with Winnie Ewing's victory in the Hamilton by-election. Margo MacDonald's win in Glasgow Govan in November 1973 helped to raise the profile of the SNP. The following year, 1974, in which there were two general elections, one in February and one in October, the party prospered, winning seven seats on 21.9 per cent in the former, and eleven seats on 30.4 per cent eight months later.

The SNP's strength, as well as its weakness, was its cross-class appeal, from 27 per cent among employers and managers, 40 per cent among intermediate workers and 35 per cent among skilled manual workers. It did best among the 'new' working class, such as technicians and craftsmen, rather than the traditional unionised manual working class like miners and steelworkers (Davis, 1969). Outwith the Central Belt, notably in small towns in north-east Scotland, the SNP appealed to non-unionised workers in particular. In Peterhead, for example, in a seat won later by Alex Salmond, 'the SNP was most successful in winning affiliations from the upwardly aspirant who were renouncing the class of their homes while not yet entering the middle class' (Bealey and Sewel, 1981: 160). This was its strength as well as its weakness, because after the debacle of 1979, the failure of the devolution referendum to meet the 40 per cent target, and the election of a right-wing government, it had few places to go but down; especially as there was an alternative 'nationalist' party available in Labour which took on the task of speaking for Scotland, and thus was better placed to take on its historic class enemy.

PARTY WARS

In this section I will look at the changing fortunes of the main political players in Scotland: the Tories, Labour, SNP, and Liberals/Liberal Democrats, who had influence well beyond their vote share. Furthermore, as Liberals, they are the political party in Scotland with the longest-standing commitment to Home Rule, tracing that back to Gladstone's attempts to create 'Home Rule All Round', starting with Ireland in 1886. This failed for various reasons, not least the division among Liberals, and the breakaway of 'Liberal Unionists' in Scotland, which helped to scupper Home Rule.

Liberals and Home Rule

Between 1945 and 1960, Liberals barely had a presence in Scotland, winning only one seat, for Orkney and Shetland, held by Jo Grimond[7] from 1950 until 1983, when he stood down. Their fortunes improved after 1964 when they were winning between three and five seats, but their vote share did not rise above 10 per cent. The period from the 1980s until 2010 saw them win between eight and eleven seats in Scotland, and their vote share was comfortably in double figures. The Liberals joined with the newly formed Social Democrats to form the

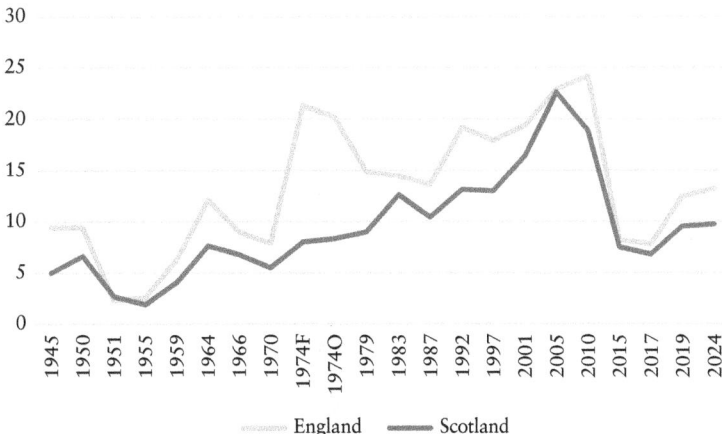

Figure 7.4 Liberal/Lib-Dem vote share at British general elections, 1945–2024: Scotland and England
Source: British Election Surveys, 1945–2024, with analysis by the author.

Social and Liberal Democrats in 1988, becoming the 'Liberal Democrats' a year later. Coalition with the Conservatives after the 2010 British general election saw their vote share in Scotland fall back into single figures, reverting to where they had been in the 1960s and 1970s.

Their influence, however, was channelled through the Scottish parliament where they formed a coalition with Labour until the 2007 Scottish parliamentary election, when the SNP formed a minority government. In broad terms, the Liberal/Liberal Democrat vote share in Scotland was not very different from that in England (see Figure 7.4), with the exceptions of the two 1974 elections when the SNP made their breakthrough. With the exception of 1951, and only by less than one percentage point, the trend lines in Liberal voting in Scotland and England are very similar; and, if anything, their share of the vote was higher south of the border.

Conservatives and the Union

Let us now look at each of the other main political players in Scotland in turn. The Conservative and Unionist Party prides itself on that title, even though the 'Union' referred to is the one with Ireland, and reflected the politics of Home Rule on

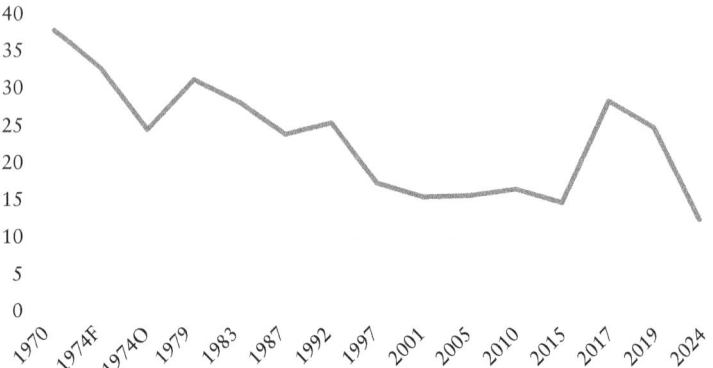

Figure 7.5 Conservative vote share in Scotland at British general elections, 1970–2024
Source: British Election Surveys, 1970–2024, with analysis by the author.

the other island. We know that it punched above its weight in Scotland in the first half of the twentieth century, but once it lost its social and cultural base by the 1970s, it was on the way down. Indeed, its fall was dramatic, as we can see from Figure 7.5, made more stark by the electoral system which left them with no seats in Scotland whatsoever in 1997 even on 17 per cent of the vote.

The gradient is steeply down, but it recovers dramatically in 2017 and 2019 for reasons we will discuss later. The election of Mrs Thatcher had a lot to do with the decline, even though this trend had begun before she became party leader. Nevertheless, she seemed to antagonise Scots, for reasons spelled out by Andrew Gamble:

> Thatcherism has reinvigorated it [the old Tory state-authority], and restored the confidence of the party in its basic appeal to the English. This is not Unionism. The Scots, Welsh and Irish are increasingly detached, but then so too are the former colonies of Greater Britain. There can be no return to the dream of Empire (Gamble, 1988: 172)

Rescinding the Scotland Act of 1978, her party had little need of Scottish seats and votes in a state where England was over 80 per cent of the demographic. Almost ten years into her 'reign', she delivered what became known as the Sermon on the Mound to the General Assembly of the Church of Scotland in May 1988. There was respectful attention at the event, but little evident support. The Rev Stuart McQuarrie, among several dissenters, announced: 'I am the Minister of a place called Toryglen, and I wish to record my dissent.' Her 'sermon'[8] did not, however, include any reference to the Good Samaritan, an assumption often made thereafter by commentators, but she had used the reference before, in 1968 and 1980, to make her point that the Samaritan was able to carry out his good deed because he had adequate means (https://en.wikipedia.org/wiki/Sermon_on_the_Mound). Mrs Thatcher was fond of religious quotations, giving on the steps of 10 Downing Street on her election in 1979 a version of a prayer apocryphally attributed to St Francis of Assisi which began 'where there is discord, let me bring union…'. She is remembered for her supposed observation that 'there is no such thing as society', uttered in an interview in the magazine *Woman's Own* in 1987, but usually misquoted. Her point was that people's immediate family were the first court of appeal in times of need, not something as amorphous as 'society'. Nevertheless, 'no such thing as society' became her lasting epitaph, like it or not. The year 1988 was a good year for anti-Thatcher protests in Scotland. The STUC had orchestrated one at the Cup Final in May between Dundee United and Celtic at Hampden Park at which fans waved red cards as a symbol of sending her off.

Her party was deeply unpopular in Scotland; the 1990 Poll Tax, imposed on Scotland first, at the request of her Scottish party conference in 1989 as a replacement for Council Rates is misremembered as being wished on Scotland as an 'experiment'. The travails of the Conservative Party north of the border were not, in essence, the fault of Mrs Thatcher, but she became a lightning conductor for political ills, and an icon to friends and foes alike. The collapse of heavy industry, notably of deep mining, left a legacy of blame which was long remembered (and misremembered), as we saw in Chapter 5. There was irony that the party with Union in its title appeared to do most to undermine it, which is in large part a reflection of its increasingly English political base. It took a quirk of political fate in 2015 to revive its fortunes, and that owed much to two referendums: one on Scottish independence in 2014, and reinforced by the other, the EU referendum, two years later. We will deal with that revival later in this chapter.

Labour and Devolution

The real party of Union, the party which had support throughout most of the post-war years in Scotland, Wales and England,[9] was Labour. Its hegemony north of the border can be gauged from Figure 7.6.

Labour's vote share in Scotland was remarkably stable for much of the forty-year period from 1970, a period of considerable political turbulence. It had painfully (re)converted to believing in Home Rule, devolution, having ditched it in the period after 1945, despite the pressure from the Scottish Covenant of 1949 when 2 million signatories signed up to it. Labour was split between centralists and home rulers, and the latter were further divided into true believers and those who saw it simply as a tactical device for seeing off the SNP. The Scottish Executive of the Labour Party had its moments of political farce. It met one Saturday afternoon in June 1974 at an office in Glasgow's Dalintober Street to consider a paper from the UK National Executive advocating Home Rule, and voted it down by six votes to five (it had twenty-nine members, but Scotland were playing Yugoslavia at football that afternoon, and there were unavoidable absences). The Scottish Executive was forced to

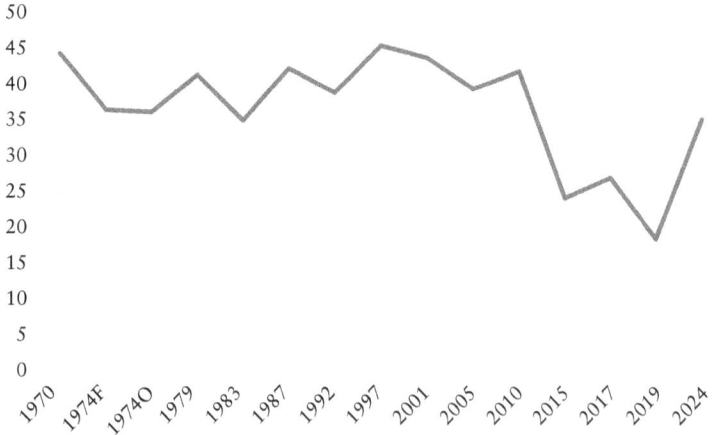

Figure 7.6 Labour vote share in Scotland at British general elections, 1970–2024
Source: British Election Surveys, 1970–2024, with analysis by the author.

re-convene in August 1974 to put matters right, and this it did, voting through its support for a Scottish Assembly. It took pressure groups like CSA, the Campaign for a Scottish Assembly (later, the Campaign for a Scottish parliament) and Scottish Labour Action (SLA) as well as from civic Scotland to re-convert the party to devolution (see Hearn, 2000). Agitation against the Poll Tax, and the 'democratic deficit', that Scotland got a Conservative government whether it liked it or not, broadened the campaign beyond party politics. CSA pushed for a constitutional convention to include political parties and civic bodies, which argued for proportional representation (but only for the Scottish Assembly, not Westminster), and under pressure from the STUC women's committee pressed for a 50:50 gender balance. In the words of Pat Kelly, a Labour member of CSA,[10] 'the overwhelming feeling within the Labour party drifted towards home rule'. Some were true believers (such as Donald Dewar, who became First Minister of the Scottish parliament in 1999) while others, like George Robertson, saw it as a device for 'dishing the Nats'.

Nevertheless, a Scottish Claim of Right was issued in 1988 by the Scottish Constitutional Convention, declaring that Scotland had the right of self-determination, and all but one Labour MP, Tam Dalyell, signed it, along with the Liberal Democrats, who chivvied Labour into supporting Home Rule. Together they would form the first Scottish Executive (government) in 1999, and again in 2003. Arguably, a version of proportional representation (the Alternative Member System – AMS) came about at the behest of the Liberal Democrats as their price for participation, as well as a counter to the 'elective dictatorship' of the first-past-the-post system, and the election of Tory governments at Westminster on a minority of electoral votes. After the false dawn of the 1992 British general election which Labour failed to win, many took to the streets in the guise of new campaigning groups such as Scotland United, Common Cause, and Democracy for Scotland, judging that the conventional political process had failed to deliver Home Rule. This brought into play civic activists who never went away, and who were re-activated in support of another referendum, in 2014, this time on Scottish independence.

Labour surfed the wave of political activism, and to no-one's surprise formed the majority party in the first and second Scottish governments, in 1999, and again 2003. Labour's re-conversion to Home Rule was helped, in retrospect, by the refusal of the SNP to participate in the Scottish Constitutional Convention on the grounds that outright independence had been ruled out *a priori*. Meanwhile, the Conservative and Unionist Party, unsurprisingly, was having nothing to do with Home Rule in whatever guise, and was steadfast for its version of the Union, *sans* devolution. Not all Tories at the grassroots were opposed to some version of Home Rule; around 30 per cent of their voters in 1997 were in favour of Scottish devolution.[11] Their party, under the Westminster electoral system, had no seats at all in Scotland despite getting 17 per cent of the vote. However, proportionately, they would have had eighteen seats in the new parliament, all on the basis of the list system, devised to correct proportional imbalances in the constituency vote. Both the main Westminster parties, Labour and Tories, found themselves in a new political arrangement twenty years after the failure of the 1979 referendum.

The SNP and the National Question

Even when not doing well electorally, the SNP has made the political weather in Scotland. They put pressure on Labour in the 1970s, forcing them to convert to Home Rule, in an attempt to see them off. Their electoral fortunes were highly variable, as we can see in Figure 7.7.

The October 1974 election result was a false dawn for the SNP, for they were not to regain that share of the vote for another forty years; by 2024, they were back down to their 1974 figure, 30 per cent. The doldrum years, however, were not wasted; during this time, the party worked out where it stood ideologically. The younger cadre of leaders led by Alex Salmond and the 79-Group saw off the old leadership under Gordon Wilson, and it became a left-of-centre party, but in reality 'social market centrist' when it came to power in the Scottish parliament in 2007. The SNP opting out of the Constitutional Convention did Labour a favour by recovering its commitment to Home Rule. Labour and the Liberal-Democrats joined in common cause for the 1997 devolution referendum, wished on Scotland by Tony Blair's incoming government, but in the event, it gave validation to both the institution and its tax-varying powers, although the latter were never used. The nationalists did not do especially

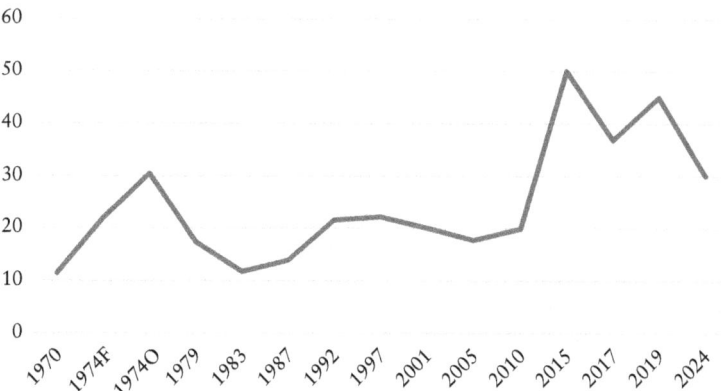

Figure 7.7 SNP vote share in Scotland at British general elections, 1970–2024
Source: British Election Surveys, 1970–2024, with analysis by the author.

well in the first two Scottish parliament elections (28.7 per cent of the constituency vote in 1999, and 23.8 per cent in 2003). The breakthrough came in 2007 when it won power by one seat, and 32.9 per cent of the votes, and governed as a minority until 2011 when it won 45.4 per cent and a majority of seats (sixty-nine), rising to 46.5 per cent in 2016 (and sixty-three seats), and 47.7 per cent in 2021 (sixty-four seats); in both cases just falling short of a majority.

The rise of the SNP meant that the main battleground of Scottish politics was between the nationalists and Labour. Both tapped into left-of-centre policy preferences, and competed for similar voters who were broadly leftist in ideology and liberal in social values. The 2021 Scottish Social Attitudes survey data, for example, showed that in terms of party identification, SNP identifiers were more left-wing, and more liberal in terms of social attitudes, than Labour identifiers, a difference between them which was statistically significant. In terms of voter comparisons, at the 2019 British general election, and the 2021 Scottish parliamentary election, the differences were broadly significant though less clear-cut.[12] All this suggests that what marks out Labour and SNP voters are differences on the constitutional question, and not on ideological issues. Broadly speaking, left-nationalism is the core set of political beliefs north of the border, which both parties sought to make their own.

THE REFERENDUM DECADE

Consider Table 7.1 showing constitutional preferences in Scotland in the second decade of the new century.

When the Prime Minister David Cameron agreed to allow a referendum on Scottish independence, it possibly seemed a safe bet that it would be defeated, given that in early 2014 only one-third of people in Scotland supported it. Cameron was not to know that this would rise to 45 per cent in the actual referendum, which, though a defeat for the Yes campaign, gave added momentum to the campaign for independence. The lesson that referendums are binary devices which shoehorn opinions into for and against, squeezing out the nuances, was lost, but not until Cameron had blundered into holding a second referendum on the UK leaving the EU, held two years later. Both referendums were to have dramatic effects on public opinion, especially in Scotland, as they changed the relationship between national identity and constitutional preferences (see Chapter 6). Scholes and Curtice drew these conclusions:

> Scotland's political parties are addressing an electorate whose sense of Scottish identity has become more entwined with support for Scottish independence, a link that has seemingly been galvanised by both the 2014 independence referendum and the outcome of the 2016 EU referendum. Meanwhile, Brexit has ensured that support for independence is now more common among those with a liberal outlook. Between them these two developments have resulted in a sharper division between those who support independence and those who do not in terms of both identity and ideology. At the same time, bigger differences have opened up in the character of party support. The link between support for independence and voting SNP became much stronger in the wake of the 2014 independence referendum,

Table 7.1 Constitutional preferences, 2010–19

% by column	2010	2011	2012	2013	2014	2015	2016	2017	2019
Independence	23	32	23	29	33	40	46	46	51
In UK with devolution	61	58	61	55	50	49	42	41	36
In UK no devolution	10	6	11	9	7	6	8	8	7

Source: Scholes and Curtice, 2020.

while the EU referendum saw the parties' supporters become more distinctive in their stance on the liberal-authoritarian dimension. At the same time, the left-right divide does not appear to have become any less important. (Scholes and Curtice, 2020: 12)

As we saw in the previous chapter, there has been a tightening up of the relationship between constitutional preference and national identity. At the beginning of the decade, a minority, 44 per cent, of those describing themselves as 'Scottish not British' were in favour of independence. By 2019, this had risen to 77 per cent, and while over that decade there was a rise in support for independence among those who thought of themselves as 'mainly British' (from 7 per cent to 23 per cent), it is the differential between the two identity groups which shows the biggest increase after 2014. Similarly, those 'liberal' in their social values moved disproportionately to support independence compared with 'authoritarians', even though at the start of the decade there had been no relationship to speak of between social values and voting.

There is also strong evidence that increased support among liberals for independence was driven by attitudes to the EU, and more strongly associated with Remain voting in 2016. Similarly, those who express left-wing attitudes moved significantly to support independence, from 34 per cent in 2010, to 62 per cent in 2019, while the shift among the 'right' is less clear-cut (from 18 per cent in 2010, to 40 per cent in 2019), a greater differential between right and left than at the beginning of the decade (+16, compared with +22). The proportion of support for the SNP that comes from supporters of independence also increased markedly, from 55 per cent in 2010, to over 80 per cent in 2017.

The Conservatives, on the other hand, spotted quite early in the decade that political space had opened up for them to appeal to opponents of independence, to those with more authoritarian views,[13] and to people on the Right. This it did successfully, doubling support among 'authoritarians' (from 17 per cent in 2011, to 34 per cent in 2017), and with greater appeal on the Right (from 27 per cent in 2010, to 47 per cent in 2017).

We can now appreciate why there was a rise in support for the Tories, which we saw in Figure 7.4, the result of a strategy to align social and political values, constitutional views, as well as national identity, particularly among those who thought of themselves as 'equally British and Scottish'. Even at elections which had nothing ostensibly to do with constitutional matters, such as the local council elections in 2022, this was designed to maximise the unionist vote. It was a measure of expected success of the strategy that the Tories were disappointed at getting 19.7 per cent of first preference votes at those elections (only 2 percentage points behind Labour) and that they described it as a 'disappointing result'; they had expected to do better.

Labour? Much like the Tory devolutionists in 1997 who deserted the party to find a more congenial home for their beliefs, so Labour lost the support, to the SNP, of those who had voted Yes in the 2014 referendum on independence. In 2010, Labour voters comprised 28 per cent of supporters of independence, and SNP voters 55 per cent. By 2017, they represented 18 per cent (down 10 percentage points) – and the SNP could count on 72 per cent of pro-independence supporters. The Conservatives, meanwhile, had become the largest anti-independence group (37 per cent, to Labour's 36 per cent, contrasted with 2010 when Labour supporters were the largest bloc (44 per cent, to Tories' 20 per cent) (Scholes and Curtice, 2020: table 5). Labour's problem was that, in contrast to the SNP and the Conservatives, they were not in a position to take a strong stance on constitutional options shaped around pro-and anti-independence. For example, of those who said they had voted Labour in 2005, 37 per cent voted Yes in the 2014 independence referendum. Of those voting Labour in 2019, only 26 per cent reported voting Yes, a substantial drop of 11 percentage points. In contrast, both Tories and nationalists were solid No and Yes voters respectively, so the politics for these parties were more straightforward.[14] Labour voters' views on Scottish sovereignty were more nuanced, less clear-cut than their main rivals, and it is to matters of sovereignty that we now turn.

SOVEREIGNTY MATTERS

The claim that Scotland is a nation, not a region of the UK, rests upon claims to sovereignty, that Scotland was a founding partner of Great Britain through the Treaty of Union in 1707. Claims to sovereignty usually rest in legal theory, the most famous in the Scottish case, the *obiter dicta* of Lord Cooper in his judgment of 1953 in the Court of Session, that because the pre-Union

Scottish parliament had never exercised untrammelled sovereignty, it could not have passed it on to the parliament of Great Britain created by the Union of 1707. The Scotland Act of 1998 which set up the devolved Scottish assembly/parliament affirmed the Westminster doctrine of absolute sovereignty in clear terms, despite most Scottish MPs, excepting Conservatives and a single Labour member, Tam Dalyell, having signed the Claim of Right in 1989. In effect, the question of sovereignty has never been resolved in Scotland, except in strict legal(istic) terms.[15]

The Westminster doctrine that the Crown-in-Parliament is sovereign was challenged, by default, by the 1989 Claim of Right, and explicitly by the SNP, notably over who has the right to decide Scottish matters. What of the people? Where do they think 'sovereignty' rests? In the British Election Study of 2019, and again in Scottish Social Attitudes survey of 2021, we measured that using two questions: 'People in Scotland should have the ultimate right to decide for themselves how they should be governed.' The second placed the constitutional onus on Scotland to accept the UK Brexit vote as a whole, as opposed to Scotland having the right to go its own way: 'Because a majority of people in the UK voted to leave the EU in the 2016 Referendum, people in Scotland should accept that decision.' The first question forefronted the sovereigntist position, and the second, the unionist one. In the 2019 survey, there was strong support for the former, with 60 per cent agreeing/strongly agreeing, and 17 per cent disagreeing/strongly disagreeing, a ratio of more than three to one.[16] On the second question, also in 2019, opinion was evenly split, 43 per cent (the sovereigntist stance) disagreeing with the proposition that Scotland should accept the UK decision to Leave, and 41 per cent arguing for acceptance. Of the sample in 2019, 41 per cent were 'sovereigntists' and 15 per cent 'unionists', with 16 per cent 'semi-sovereigntists', that is, sovereigntist on the first question, and unionist on the second.

Repeating the questions two years later, in the 2021 Scottish Social Attitudes survey, confirmed similar results: over 40 per cent were sovereigntists (on both questions), 18 per cent were unionists and 26 per cent were semi-sovereigntists. The outcomes were clear: around four out of ten people in Scotland are sovereigntists, around one in six unionists, leaving around 40 per cent somewhere in between. Using slightly different formats (agree/disagree rather than a five-point scale from strongly agree to strongly disagree) and excluding 'don't-knows', the 2021 data suggest Scottish sovereignty is supported by well over 40 per cent, and British unionism by 20 per cent of the sample, with about 25 per cent semi-sovereigntists.

Scottish sovereigntists were defined by strong identification with the SNP (74 per cent), voting Yes in the 2014 independence referendum (71 per cent), voting Remain in the 2016 EU referendum (86 per cent) and being on the Left of the political spectrum (96 per cent).[17] British unionists, on the other hand, were mainly Conservatives (70 per cent), No voters in 2014 (89 per cent), on the political Right (85 per cent), and Leave voters in 2016 (60 per cent, but note that 40 per cent of Tory voters in Scotland voted Remain).

So it was that the two hitherto marginalised political parties, Tories and nationalists, who were also-rans as recently as 1999 came to dominate Scottish politics in the decade of referendums, in 2014 and 2016. Issues of sovereignty and legitimacy were crystallised by those two referendums, which realigned politics as a struggle between nationalists (SNP) and unionists (Conservatives), the latter seeing their opportunity to come in from the margins and try to harness the twin horses of unionism and Brexit, even though most of their Scottish supporters had voted Remain (55 per cent).

And Labour, which had dominated Scottish politics up until the late 2010s? About a third of Labour supporters were Scottish sovereigntists, and just over one in ten were 'British unionists', which meant that most were somewhere in between, and there was no clear-cut constitutional position for Labour to take. Between 2015 and 2019, Labour retained only half its sovereigntist vote, the rest going to the SNP. The damage had in fact been done between 2015 and 2017. While it retained most of its vote thereafter, between 2017 and 2019, it lost those which had switched to the SNP. As far as Labour supporters of the Union were concerned, there was also attrition, this time towards the Tories. Of those who voted Labour and expressed 'unionist' views as we have measured them, as many as 60 per cent of those who had voted Labour in 2015 had switched to the Conservatives in 2019. Furthermore, between 2015 and 2017, a greater proportion of Labour's unionist vote in 2015 went Tory (49 per cent) than it was able to retain (45 per cent). By 2021, the two largest categories of Labour supporters were Scottish sovereigntists (33 per cent), and British unionists (22 per cent), which underpins Labour's ambivalence – or nuance – on constitutional matters. Furthermore, in terms of ways of measuring support for sovereignty, the 'ultimate right' question, and the 'reject UK Brexit vote' question, almost two-thirds of Labour supporters supported the former, and just under half (45 per cent) supported the latter, which placed them almost equidistant between SNP and Conservative supporters.[18]

Political Ambivalence

In spite of two seemingly strong constitutional positions, sovereigntism and unionism, there is in fact considerable ambivalence about who, ultimately, should make important decisions, even among sovereigntists and unionists; bearing in mind too that a sizeable minority, around 40 per cent are in neither camp. We might ask: sovereigntist and unionist with regard to *what*, exactly? So we included a set of hypotheticals to see how well they correlated – and found that by and large they do not, except in general directions of travel:[19] 'Scottish sovereigntists' are defined by a belief that an independent Scotland should be in the EU; that it should have its own currency; that farming decisions should be made by Scottish government; a strong SNP vote in the British general election of 2019; and Scottish control over immigration policy, especially to make it easier. 'British unionists' are defined by their hostility to the idea of an independent Scotland being in the EU; their belief that the UK government should make decisions for Scotland; and that it should make decisions about farming. Unionists have a strong 'British' identity; voted overwhelming No in the 2014 independence referendum; and think that only the UK government should decide whether and when to have another Scottish independence referendum.

Nevertheless, while the associations are much as expected, there is considerable cross-over in views on these polar positions:

For sovereigntists:

- More than half (53 per cent) would accept a shared currency with the rest of the UK (rUK) in the event of independence.

- A substantial minority, 37 per cent, would support sharing armed forces with rUK.
- 42 per cent would accept the UK government being able to spend public money in Scotland.
- On immigration, 29 per cent would accept having same rules as rUK.

For unionists:

- More than half (58 per cent) accept that government decisions for Scotland should be shared (with the Scottish government making some, and the UK government others).
- Marginally more (38 per cent) accept sharing decisions on taxes than seeing it as sole UK government responsibility (32 per cent).
- Most – 59 per cent – accept a joint or a shared responsibility for welfare benefits in Scotland.
- 40 per cent think that the right to decide on a second independence referendum should be shared between the Scottish parliament and the UK parliament.

In terms of political party support, we can compare these features in Figure 7.8.

What is clear in the graph in Figure 7.8 is how both SNP and Conservative supporters frame the extremes (the top and bottom graph lines). Note, however, that Labour is much closer to the national average than either of them (the middle two graph lines). We can read this in two ways: that Labour voters are unsure as to where they stand, or that they are more nuanced about sovereignty. The graph in Figure 7.9 shows the same data in Pareto form for Labour.

We can see from Figure 7.9 that Labour supporters are mainly defined (that is, to the left of the curve) by support for independence in the EU, the belief that decisions on farming and welfare benefits should all be made by the Scottish government, and that they think of themselves as 'very Scottish'. On the other hand, those factors to the right, and below, the Pareto curve show them to be *less* defined by voting Yes in the 2014 Scottish independence referendum (only 21 per cent of Labour supporters did so), and being less supportive of a separate Scottish currency or of immigration rules being easier than in the rest of the UK.

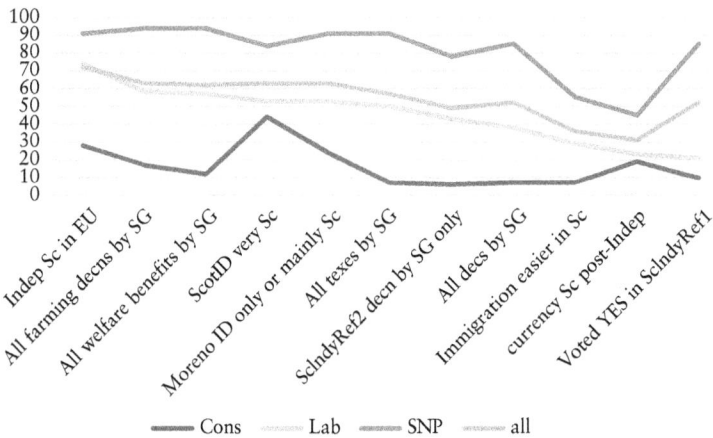

Figure 7.8 Measuring sovereignty by party supported
Source: McCrone and Keating, 2023.

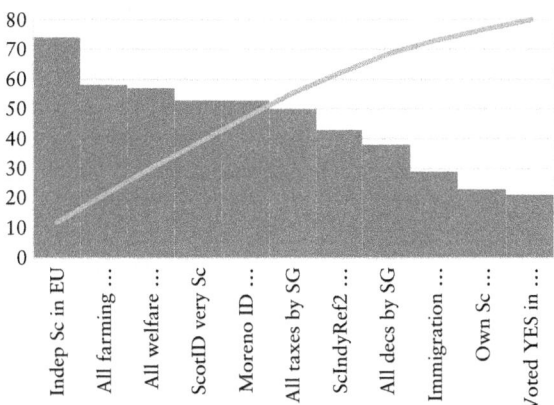

Figure 7.9 Where Labour supporters stand (Pareto chart)
Source: McCrone and Keating, 2023.

We might interpret low levels of support for Yes in the 2014 Scottish independence referendum among Labour supporters as both cause and effect of *not* shifting to supporting the SNP. Labour can be described from those data as closer to the SNP on being in the EU, on welfare being run from Holyrood, but closer to the Tories on Scottish identity (being British in some degree), on currency post-independence, and voting No in 2014; and equidistant on farming, taxes, immigration and that the Scottish government should be mainly in charge of decision-making.

It remains to be seen what effect Labour's resurgence in the opinion polls from 2023 has had (claims, for example, that 'soft nationalists' have gone to Labour), when support for independence in particular (and even for the SNP) has not dramatically fallen (see John Curtice's analysis for correcting such claims in https://www.whatscotlandthinks.org).

In any case, public attitudes in Scotland to issues of sovereignty and independence remain complex and nuanced. Using data from the Scottish Social Attitudes surveys in 2016 and 2019, Lindsay Paterson identified two groups who are ambivalent about independence: 'doubtful nationalists', who support independence but nevertheless believe that the UK government should still have some responsibility for policy decisions affecting Scotland; and 'uncertain unionists', who are people who do not support independence but nevertheless believe that the Scottish parliament should be responsible for all policy decisions affecting Scotland. He observed: 'doubtful nationalists are independence supporters who might be most open to being persuaded not to support independence. Uncertain unionists are opponents of independence who might be most open to being persuaded to support independence.' Doubtful nationalists tend to be older than independence supporters on average, while uncertain unionists tend to be younger than people who oppose independence. Furthermore, graduates of higher education tend to be less likely to have doubts, whether about nationalism or about unionism. But among young graduates who are nationalists, a relatively high proportion have doubts about independence. Doubtful nationalists are more common among people who identify as British rather than Scottish, whereas uncertain unionists are more common among people who identify as Scottish rather than British. Doubtful nationalists are more common among people who are economically right-wing, whereas uncertain unionists are more common among people who are economically left-wing. Social liberals are the least likely to have doubts about their views on independence.

This analysis of the Scottish Social Attitudes survey data complements what we found in our work on Scottish sovereignty, namely, that lying behind expressions of sovereignty and unionism is a complex set of attitudes which find themselves squeezed into binary divides for the purposes of public referendums. We know that on matters of Scottish self-government, there is a spread of opinion:[20] from independence outwith the EU (10 per cent); independence within the EU (38 per cent); a Scottish parliament with some taxation powers (37 per cent); a Scottish parliament with no taxation powers (6 per cent); through to no devolution at all (8 per cent). Voting Yes or No to something called 'independence' is itself a matter of degree rather than kind, and subject to the kind of nuances we have discussed here. We might ask whether being independent in the EU constitutes 'independence', and this raises questions about 'post-sovereignty' (see, for example, MacCormick, 1999).

Behind narrow debates about constitutional futures lies something more fundamental: what Scotland is, and where it might be going. Social change – reflected in age cohorts armed with higher levels of education, and reflected in more leftist and liberal values – has been the driver of politics in Scotland. The key point is that '... if the movement for Scottish independence is a rebellion against elites, it is not based on the low-educated and the old' (Paterson, 2023b: 537). True, 'as late as 2004, more than 40 per cent of independence supporters had low or no formal [educational] attainment and only a quarter had higher education. By 2014, and later, the position had reversed (respectively a quarter and 40 per cent).' (ibid. 535) By the 2014 referendum, a process of generational replacement had taken place[21] such that the electorate was composed of more young people with more education who were more likely than older cohorts to support independence.

CONCLUSION

This chapter has focused on the changing social base of politics in Scotland, on the grounds that parties are vehicles for expressing the values and attitudes of voters. This approach is better able to identify how social structural changes which we spelled out earlier in the book impact upon, and work their way through, the political system.[22] In this regard, 'politics' is neither the cause nor effect of social change; rather, it is the medium through which social change is read and expressed. Parties succeed, by and large, when they articulate voters' values and attitudes, and make them appear 'natural'. Thus, the argument in this chapter is that the Scottish National Party was able, from the 1970s, to appeal especially to those voters who were swept along by change: the young, and the socially and geographically mobile. That is why we can think of the SNP as being in the right place at the right time. That may sound as if success was a matter of chance and not volition, that somehow the party was not aware of what it was doing, but that would be the wrong conclusion to draw. The skill was positioning itself to take advantage of political opportunities.

Much depended on what its political competitors, Conservative and Labour, got up to. The problem for these parties was that their trajectories were set in a different direction. The Tories' success, even in the post-war period, derived from hitching their star to the nexus of religion–empire–war, thus appealing to a generation to whom this nexus was especially relevant. And as Bill Miller observed, Tory success went beyond their expected class base. Labour too had inherited a mantra: state-driven 'modernisation' using the instruments of the British state but in Scottish clothing. Into a two-party system based on first-past-the-post elections, smaller parties such as the Liberals and the SNP were squeezed out. The former made the breakthrough in the 1970s south of the border, appealing to the young and mobile, and while in Scotland they managed to pull back support in places like the Highlands and the Borders, small-town and rural Scotland, they lost out to the SNP who emerged more dramatically to prominence in the 1970s. Ironically, long-term Liberal support for Home Rule was overtaken by something more robust such as constitutional independence, even though devolution in Scotland owed far more to the Liberals' long march to a Scottish parliament. Liberalism, however, did not have the appeal to the young which the SNP had as it mobilised a new iconography of politics. Liberalism's rural and small-town social base was amplified by eventual success in suburbia, as well as patient attention to 'pavement politics'.

It would be misleading to suggest that 'old politics', especially the two-party variety held in place by an electoral system designed for two-party competition, is dead, for old parties do not disappear but reinvent themselves in order to survive. Home Rule politics has never gone away, and it became a beacon for Liberals, who long believed in it; Labour, who gave it up in 1945 only to rediscover its virtues in the 1970s; while the Tories struggled to make it relevant in the context of Mrs Thatcher's liking for centralised neo-liberalism. The Scottish parliament, and Home Rule, which they opposed, has allowed them to reinvent themselves.

The battle for Home Rule throughout the 1980s and 1990s was as much about street-politics as the institutionalised variety. Labour was responsible for the ill-fated proposal for a Scottish Assembly in the 1970s, and its minority status for the second half of the 1970s made it vulnerable to ambush by opponents both inside and outside the party. Finding its feet again in opposition in the 1980s as a party of Home Rule – Pat Kelly's description of 'the overwhelming feeling with the Labour Party drifted towards home rule' gets it right – its alliance with Liberals, and under Donald Dewar's sure-footed leadership, it became the obvious party to shape the new parliament in 1999. The fact that from that date onwards the parliament and government were deemed by the Scottish public as responsible for the successes and virtually none of the failures – the devolution conundrum – attests to that (see McCrone, 2019a). The Conservatives, on the other hand, struggled for relevance, and is the only major party not to have been in government at Holyrood – Labour, Liberals, Nationalist and even Greens have all been there. The Tories were saved by an electoral system they did not vote for, for an institution they did not believe in, and at a time in political history where policy was dictated elsewhere; by a right-wing government at Westminster. Small wonder that they struggled to speak with an authentic voice, except when the party hitched its star to 'unionist' politics of the more 'muscular' kind: anti-independence, anti-EU, too similar to its southern big brother for that to be anything other than a political cul-de-sac in Scotland.

The Nationalists virtually became the 'natural' party of the Scottish government, but that did not happen until 2007 – and, in fact, not until the second decade of the new century, and even then, masked by the steamroller effects of the first-past-the-post electoral system. They benefited from the 'referendum decade', even though both causes on which they fought, Scottish independence in 2014, and Brexit in 2016, were lost. By the start of the second decade, their star began to wane, trammelled by policy troubles and constitutional contradictions; how to obtain and win a second referendum on Scottish independence, in which, ironically, they would have a much better chance of success than at the first. So why, the unionist parties thought, should Westminster grant their wish for a second referendum when the chances of a Yes vote second time round are greater?

Understanding nationalism in Scotland is bedevilled by easy and misleading accounts elsewhere. Consider this comment[23] from the political commentator David Goodhart: 'Brexit was a movement to regain control/sovereignty from a supranational EU and the SNP is a movement to reclaim control/sovereignty from a multinational United Kingdom' (2017: 53); pleasing in its symmetry, but wrong in its analysis. Something similar seems to be implied in Sutcliffe-Braithwaite's comment on the propensity of 'SNP and UKIP voting among the working classes' (2018: 5). It is a false parallel to equate nationalism in Scotland with populism elsewhere, for the SNP is a centre-left party, espouses civic not ethnic values, and has a much more 'progressive' social base than Goodhart implies. It is also a false dichotomy to claim that it is an expression of 'identity politics' rather than the material kind, for one is the expression of the other.

At the heart of Scottish politics, arguably any politics, is a tension between the utopian and the practical. Scotland has practised 'zig-zag' politics whereby progress is made incrementally as a way of resolving bigger demands: devolution over independence, for example – especially as these are, in essence, *degrees* of Scottish autonomy. Where we are at any moment depends on a series of compromises. Lindsay Paterson has observed that 'radical challenge is followed by pragmatic adjustment as the state cedes just enough power to keep the Union intact for the time being, a compromise which sows the seeds of the next phase of radical rebellion'. (Paterson, 2015: 1).

We can understand successive events in post-war Scottish politics as key points of 'crisis', in the original meaning, a Greek word for a turning-point. The Scottish Covenant in 1949, with its 2 million signatures was one: ignored by the UK Labour government, but remembered in the long haul to greater self-government. The second 'crisis' or turning-point culminated in the first devolution referendum in 1979, defeated by an invented 'rule' of 40 per cent, but entering the radical narrative of the long haul, a moment of perceived betrayal by the British state. This then was knitted into the long campaign for Home Rule, hopes raised and then dashed by the failure of Labour in the early 1990s to get elected, and civic Scotland taking on the task unto itself. By the end of the decade, a Scottish parliament had been created, and a mere fifteen years later, another referendum, this time on independence, lost, but a marker further along the road. Lindsay Paterson expresses it thus:

> Throughout the last three centuries, the story has recurred: dissatisfaction grows, often to an intensity that threatens to destroy the Union, at least among the politically active and vociferous. The ground of that protest is always that Scots are not being treated equally, with respect, with regard to their rights. But then the UK state remembers its inherent flexibility and pragmatism, and concedes just enough not just to placate the discontent for the time being – which would be merely cynical – but actually, wisely enough, appreciating what the real discontent is, which is not about constitutional structures but about social, economic and political issues.
> ...this whole period from the 1960s to the end of the century showed the characteristic features of Scottish development quite graphically: utopian articulation leading to radical protest, met eventually by a Britain grudgingly remembering that its very essence has been a kind of muddled pragmatism, but the compromises of which then store up the pressures that lead to the next phase of protest, which is now. (Paterson, 2015: 5)

Two key points are worth making: first, that change derives from the tension between the utopian and the pragmatic, that these are not separate elements. Second, that 'sovereignty' and 'independence' are not the same thing: there is little doubt about the extent of the belief that Scots have the right to determine how they are to be governed (sovereignty), but that this does not imply having an independent state, which, in any case, is a matter of degrees of self-government; object rather than subject. Hence the two stories, utopian and pragmatic.

This combination of disappointment and expectation is baked into Scottish politics, but not simply 'politics' narrowly defined but the nature of the nation itself, a debate which it has had with itself long before even the Union with England in 1707. It is not a matter of narrow constitutionalism, but of the nation's narrative, a struggle between contradictions. It is not a coincidence that Gregory Smith's notion (1919) of the Scottish antisyzygy, a zig-zag, a union of opposites, of contradictory forces, continues to have currency in debates about the nature of Scotland and its futures; we will examine this in Chapter 8. While Smith's concept was invented in the context of a debate on Scottish literature and culture,[24] it has much wider traction, given that culture, society and politics have leaked into each other over the past century.

Furthermore, if, at the time of writing (2024), the SNP's political star is on the wane, then support for greater Home Rule, and even independence, whatever that may come to mean, is not (see Scholes and Curtice, 2020). The movement and the party are, at least for the moment, not in alignment. This, to be sure, is not new. Back in the 1990s, when Labour, against expectations, failed to win the 1992 Westminster election, it was civic society in Scotland with its array of organisations and institutions who worked out what Home Rule would mean, and how it might be achieved. Political parties were merely the means to ratified achievement. Nothing could, arguably, express more clearly the argument of this book. Social change, in its widest senses, is what drives politics, that the political process is the expression of social change. Politics matters, but only in that sense, that we read through it the impact of social change. And the key mechanism which connects the social and the political is culture, and it is to that issue we turn in the next chapter.

NOTES

1. Because Scottish parliamentary elections use the Additional Member System (AMS), with two votes, one for the constituency and one for the regional vote, the simpler measure for our purposes is the former.
2. The use of 'Britain', rather than the UK, is deliberate, focusing on the 'mainland', in that the politics of Northern Ireland were *sui generis* and defined by Partition; the Ulster Unionist Party taking 50 per cent of the vote in 1945, and its closest rival, the Northern Ireland Labour Party, 18.5 per cent.
3. For example, in 1945 Labour's advantage in Scotland was -0.9 (that is, they were doing less well in Scotland than in the rest of Britain). The Conservative shortfall in 1945 was also -0.9, a combined gap of 1.8.
4. On strict proportionality, Labour would have won twenty seats, and the SNP seventeen.
5. By a quirk of political irony, the UK vote for Brexit in 2016 was exactly 52/48 in favour of Leave, but there was no suggestion on that occasion that the Brexit vote had failed to meet any kind of voting threshold. If a 40 per cent rule had obtained, the Brexit referendum would have failed, as only 37.4 per cent of the electorate had voted Leave.

6. Callaghan observed: 'You know there are times, perhaps once every 30 years, when there is a sea-change in politics. It then does not matter what you say or do. There is a shift in what the public wants and what it approves of. I suspect there is now such a sea-change – and it is for Mrs Thatcher.' (quoted in Kenneth Morgan's book, *Callaghan: a life* (1997: 697).
7. Grimond, educated at Eton and Oxford, came from a jute-owning family in Dundee – known as Juteopolis.
8. Calling her address 'The Sermon on the Mound' was a journalistic invention, neither hers nor the Kirk's, and described as 'tasteless' by the Thatcher Foundation.
9. In the thirty years after 1945, Labour support in England fell below 40 per cent only once, in February 1974.
10. <https://www.scottishleftreview.scot/the-campaign-for-a-scottish-parliament/>.
11. Of those who voted Tory in 1997, 30 per cent were in favour of a 'Scottish Assembly' with or without tax-varying powers, within the UK, and hence were at odds with the party's position (Scottish Election Study, 1997).
12. At the time of writing, data with which to analyse the 2024 election in detail were not to hand.
13. British, and Scottish, Social Attitudes surveys have long carried composite scales, from Right to Left, and from Liberal to Authoritarian, constructed from suites of attitudinal questions.
14. Only about one in seven Tory voters were Yes voters; and one in five SNP voters voted No.
15. See Supreme Court rulings July 2018 (Case No. UKSC 2018/0080); and Nov 2022 (UKSC31).
16. Eighteen per cent neither agreed nor disagreed.
17. These were the variables which most explained, in terms of the binary logistic regression models, what made people Scottish sovereigntists; British unionists were defined by voting Leave, voting Tory, and being British as well voting No in the 2014 referendum.
18. On the 'ultimate right' question, 95 per cent of SNP voters and 37 per cent of Tories accept that 'people in Scotland have the ultimate right to decide how they are governed'. On the 'reject UK Brexit vote' question, 82 per cent of SNP and 9 per cent of Tories agree with the 'sovereigntist' position, putting Labour voters midway between their main political opponents.
19. These features are the statistically significant ones when modelled using binary logistic regression.
20. These data are based on Scottish Social Attitudes surveys for 2016 and 2019, and are broadly indicative of public attitudes on how Scotland should be governed.

21. Reinforced by allowing 16-year-olds to vote.
22. An alternative approach is to chart the organisational history of political parties, the 'supply' side of politics, rather than, as here, the 'demand' side of politics, how voters use politics to express values and beliefs.
23. Cited in Paterson, 2023b: 526.
24. Smith invented the term in his book *Scottish Literature: Character and Influence* (1919). He wrote: 'We need not be surprised to find that in his literature the Scot presents two aspects which appear contradictory. Oxymoron was ever the bravest figure, and we must not forget that disorderly order is order after all.'

8

The Cultural Turn

> Scotland is the land where ideal has never, even for an instant, coincided with fact.
>
> (Tom Nairn, 1968)

In this chapter, I explore the relationship between politics, culture and society, and in particular the view that the Scottish Question has never really been about the constitution as such, but the very existential reality of Scotland itself. The point is a simple, but important, one: social change does not impact directly on to social behaviour and attitudes, but is refracted through the cultural prisms available. How we see ourselves, and who we aspire to be, are key mechanisms of the changing world around us; and 'culture' in Scotland has, we might conclude, a lot to answer for.

There is a powerful pedigree of cultural pessimism in Scotland, tantamount to a claim that its culture is so tainted and deformed that it is beyond redemption (note the quasi-religious redemptive concept, a running theme in this critique). The dominant figure in this argument is the late Tom Nairn who died in early 2023, described by Pat Kane as the 'theoretical godfather' of the independence movement (Kane, in *The National*, 18 November 2023). Few would cavil at that. When he died in January 2023, *The Herald* also referred to him as the 'godfather' of Scottish nationalism.

And yet that is insufficient, because Nairn's focus was much more on the perceived deformities of Scottish culture, rather than what he dismissively called 'mere constitutionalism', and the 'tired legalistic arguments for independence' (see Paterson, 2015).

In other words, if Nairn was indeed the godfather of Scottish nationalism and a putative nation-state, then it is fair to say that he was far more interested in the 'nation', the cultural dimension, than the 'state', the political one.

This chapter, then, places the analysis of Nairn's views, and his belief that Scotland suffered from a 'pathological discourse', at the centre of the argument about Scottish culture. How does this connect up with the argument of this book, namely, that from the 1970s fundamental social, political, and indeed cultural shifts took place so as to transform Scotland in a way hitherto unseen? I will argue that Tom Nairn's Scottish 'pathology' was to a large degree overturned, at least in making sense of transformations in the political-constitutional sphere, notably the long haul to Home Rule in 1999, and the Scottish referendum debacle in 2014, to say nothing of the political hegemony of the Scottish National Party from 2007 until 2023. Put simply, it seems that the old wisdom that Scottish culture was ineradicably deformed, thus preventing 'proper' political change, shifted to the assertion that it was cultural change which was responsible for bringing about these political-constitutional changes. That old argument, in other words, was turned on its head. If 'culture' had prevented political change, then in post-1970s Scotland, it was deemed responsible for making political change happen. That, at least, was the claim. It fitted in with the shift in intellectual perspectives generally that 'culture' rather than 'structure' explained social change; what became known as the 'cultural turn'.

To prefigure my argument: both assertions, the old and the new, seem to me too stark, for they attribute the key relationship as that directly between culture and politics without much in between. Above all, they are a-sociological, and pay very little attention to the kinds of social structural changes I have described in this book. What is missing in particular is the concept of 'civil society', that relatively dense network of social institutions which permeate any society, and which act as a transmission belt for cultural and political change. Readers will recall that Chapter 2 of this book made the case for Scotland as a society in those terms. To reinforce the nub of the argument: without a sociology of Scotland we cannot make proper sense of the relationship between its culture and its politics. Nevertheless, this relationship between culture and politics is a key part of Scotland's transformation, and we can read cultural change from the 1970s as on all-fours with that transformation, even though we might disagree as to its nature and influence.

UNDERSTANDING CULTURE

But what do I mean by 'culture' anyway? This is not a chapter specifically about capital-letter 'Literature and The Arts'. It is about culture as used in the social scientific sense, and particularly derived from the discipline of social anthropology; in the words of Clifford Geertz, '... man (sic) is an animal suspended in webs of significance he himself has spun ... these webs constitute "culture", whose analysis is not an experimental science in search of a law but an interpretative one in search of meaning' (A. Cohen, 1986: 17). Anthony Cohen was pointing out that Geertz's definition contains three interrelated and powerful principles: first, that culture as a 'web of significance' is created and continually recreated by people through their social interaction, rather than imposed upon them; second, that, being continuously in process, culture has neither deterministic power nor objectively identifiable referents (such as law); and third, that culture is manifest in the capacity with which it endows people to perceive meaning in, or attach meaning to, social behaviour. In other words, behaviour does not contain meaning intrinsically, but is found to be meaningful by an act of interpretation: *we* make sense of what *we* observe. Thus, says Cohen, 'we should not confuse an increasing similarity in the machinery of people's lives with their response to it' (ibid. 2). The interpretation is symbolic, rather than structural, in such a way that 'we look for the boundaries of people's worlds of identity and diversity so that people hold the form of a symbol in common, while investing it with different meanings.' (ibid.)

There is also the double-edged character of 'culture'; that it is both descriptive *of* a society, but also prescriptive *for*, in terms of what its desired values are deemed to be.[1] To take a Scottish example to be developed later in this chapter: the 'lad o'pairts' is an icon in terms of what lies at the heart of Scottish education and culture, if somewhat eroded by age and experience. It is also prescriptive in the sense that it operates as a goal still to be achieved; thus iconic in both senses. We might also ponder the singularity of 'culture' in this context, even though we may wish to argue that 'Scottish culture' should be pluralised, given the multiplicity of symbolic systems. Nevertheless, insofar as 'culture' is the essence of 'nation-ness', and, by and large, arguments about Scotland relate to the singularity of its culture in the round, then that is how I address it here. Nor is 'culture' a unity, still less an 'organism'. As Cairns Craig (1999) pointed out, it is the site of a dialogue. We shall return to that argument shortly.

For our purposes, Scottish culture has a set of broad symbols in common (such as language, landscape, flags and emblems), but we cannot be certain that their meanings are shared analogously with others. Nevertheless, because people construct their community symbolically ('Scotland', in this case), they make it a resource and a repository of meaning. That is threaded through national identity, how people see themselves and others in relation to key markers such as birth, accent, ancestry and so on. National identity is both a personal matter, and an institutional one, for institutions and organisations carry identities, none more so than the Scottish parliament, which is both a political institution, but also *par excellence*, the prime institution in Scottish civil society.

The concept of 'nation' carries much of the weight of cultural difference. That Scotland as a nation relies on the notion of it being an 'imagined community', in Benedict Anderson's phrase, even though Anderson expressed the view that 'already in the 17th century large parts of what would one day be imagined as Scotland were English-speaking and had immediate access to print-English provided a minimal degree of literacy existed' (Anderson, 1996: 90). Anderson's imputed claim that Scotland was insufficiently different in cultural terms, can be contested in a number of ways: in the first place, Scotland had a long pedigree of nation-state-ness pre-1707 ('one day be imagined as Scotland' can be read as not having been so in the past); its language, Scots, is a cognate of 'English', and in any case, sharing the same language has never been a barrier to political and cultural difference (witness, for example, the USA, Canada and Australia). The reader might bear in mind the extent and nature of national identity in Scotland (see Chapter 6); and suffice it to say that its 'nation-ness', its sense of cultural difference, is not in dispute. What is disputed, however, is the substance of 'nation', which equates directly with 'culture', and which is the central aspect of this chapter. The dominant wisdom about Scottish culture is that of Tom Nairn, and we begin with an exegesis of his relevant writing.

Scotland as Dream Country

The first manifestation of Nairn's significant writing on Scottish culture appeared in *New Left Review* in May/June 1968, a key moment in history, if somewhat coincidental to *les événements de Mai 68*, while part of a more general political-cultural shift in western Europe. Nairn's essay was called 'The Three Dreams of Scottish Nationalism', and the dream motif was a constant throughout his writing on Scotland in the subsequent decades. Nairn nailed his colours to the mast: 'Scotland is the land where ideal has never, even for an instant, coincided with fact. Most nations have had moments of truth, alas, Scotland never' (1968: 3). The 'dream pathology' (his term) was a constant in his writing about Scotland.

There were, in Nairn's view, three dreams. The first related to the Reformation, and its role in 'Scotland's long and stagnant twilight', where the Kirk was a substitute of sorts for national identity. Nairn thought the Kirk's influence on Scottish culture iniquitous as well as ubiquitous. Famously, he observed that 'As far as I am concerned, Scotland will be reborn when the last minister is strangled with the last copy of the *Sunday Post*' (in Karl Miller's *Memoirs of a Modern Scotland* (1970)). The second dream related to cultural movements, notably Romanticism, 'still implanted in the subsoil of Scottish consciousness'. The third dream was about nationalism, 'basically a dream of redemption', and based on 'sporranry, alcoholism, and the ludicrous appropriation of the remains of Scotland's Celtic fringe', plus 'sickening militarism'. Nairn excoriates Scottish nationalism in this 1968 article: 'SNP Nationalists are merely lumpenprovincials whose parochialism finds its adequate expression in the asinine idea that a bourgeois parliament and an army will rescue the country from provincialism' (ibid. 17). If Nairn was the 'godfather of Scottish nationalism', this amounts to disowning one's offspring. Nationalists, at least in the late sixties, are described by Nairn as 'a junta of corporal-punishers and Kirk-going cheese-parers'. He cites in co-disapproval the work of literary scholar David Craig 'who has outlined the problem [of deformed cultural expression] with admirable precision'. Craig, however, was no (Scottish) nationalist. Consistent in his beliefs, he wrote in *London Review of Books* in 2014 at the time of the Scottish referendum that he 'mistrusted any party which is founded on nationhood as such ... and for that reason, if I still lived in Scotland, I would vote No' (*London Review of Books*, Sept 2014: 13–15).

Tom Nairn's views on Scotland are well-known, at least in his homeland. He was the inventor of 'the tartan monster', if not literally, then of its powerful avatar. Nairn never gave up on the idea that Scottish culture was deformed, that it manifested itself in tartanry and kitsch. His essay 'Old and New Scottish Nationalism', reprinted in *The Break-Up of Britain* (1977), first appeared in Gordon Brown's edited book *The Red Paper on Scotland*, in 1975. Nairn averred: 'Tartanry will not wither away, if only because it possesses the force of its own vulgarity – immunity from doubt and higher culture. Whatever form of self-rule Scotland acquires, this is a substantial part of the real inheritance bequeathed to it' (1977: 155). In his essay 'Empire and Union' (Nairn, *Faces of Nationalism*, 1997), he speaks of 'Kitschland which now stands in for Scotland in the world's consciousness' (ibid. 207).

How did Nairn think this had come about? He put it down to Scotland's peculiar history. Thus, 'a previous history of independence [pre-1707] made assimilation [to the UK] impossible; and yet the imperial alignment with England and a habitual posture of universalism made ethno-national liberation difficult too.' (ibid. 180) The bourgeois cadre which would have led an independence movement in 'normal' places had no need to do so because they were in charge of domestic governing institutions, and, in his view, 'a famously educated culture produced no intelligentsia' (1997: 204). Those are strong statements, and many dissented from them. One of the dissenters, Lindsay Paterson, is taken to task by Nairn for his argument in his book *The Autonomy of Modern Scotland* (1994), that Scotland had considerable institutional autonomy within the British state, and in any case, the time-sequence whereby political nationalism as an ideological movement came after this was in place meant that 'independence', in conventional terms was deemed not necessary. Nairn did not think much of this 'institutional identity', and poured scorn upon the notion, and upon ideas of 'civil society', which he called the poor relation of 'political society' (see, for example, his short essay, 'La société civile: un mythe écossais', *Liber*, 24 October 1995). Crucially, in his view, 'real [national] identity' could not surface, and thus a 'display identity is needed to fill the gap' (ibid. 207). Thus was *Kitschland* created.

Throughout his writing career Nairn never gave up on this notion. He took the view that Walter Scott showed us, sentimentally and politically, in the early nineteenth century how *not* to be nationalists in an age of ascendent political nationalism. Scott, in his view, enabled its history to be 'politically null', firmly separating historical consciousness from political action, or put famously, separating 'its heart from its head' (Nairn, 1977: 150). Here is a familiar trope in Nairn's work, and 'split personality', notably Robert Louis Stevenson's Dr Jekyll and Mr Hyde, figures prominently, as does the poet C. M. Grieve (judged by Nairn to be 'lucid') becoming separated from his nom-de-plume 'Hugh MacDiarmid' (judged 'demented') (Nairn, 1997: 169). Nairn's liking for psychiatric metaphors (more trope than metaphor) runs throughout his writing.

We can see in his account of 'deformed' Scottish culture his attraction to deep psychology, which surfaced in his later book *Faces of Nationalism* (1997). There is, however, historically deeper form here. In 1919, Gregory Smith's term, the *Caledonian Antisyzygy* – the juxtaposition of opposites – was described by Nairn, revealingly, as a 'curious bacillus' (1977: 112). The antisyzygy was kept alive by the poet Hugh MacDiarmid 'to provide the disruptive creative licence and Scottish national difference that his brand of modernism and nationalism required' (Carruthers, 2009: 13) and in implicit form by Robert Louis Stevenson in his celebrated novella *Dr Jekyll and Mr Hyde*. Nairn described 'the Jekyll-and-Hyde physiognomy of modern Scottishness' (Nairn, 1977: 136), and the 'Jekyll-and-Hyde fragmentation of modern Scottish culture' (1977: 157). He also employed Christopher Harvie's distinction between 'red' and 'black' Scots (acknowledged on p. 168) taken to exemplify emigrant, progressive Scots ('red') as distinct from the 'black' parochial variety who stayed at home to nurse the tartan monster.[2]

Characterisation is almost all, for there is nothing that can be done meaningfully, given the depth of this psychology, to 'prove' the existence and effects of this cultural deformation. Whatever their dubious truth-status, 'deformation' and 'cultural cringe' have been constant bedfellows in the analysis of Scottish culture and nationalism. Similarly, Nairn employed the concept of 'neurosis', whereby in the nineteenth century the Scottish bourgeoisie had to 'sublimate' (another psychiatric trope) because 'there was no call for the usual services' (Nairn, 1977: 154) of leading the nation to full independence. Thus it was that 'a strange sort of sub-national culture emerged' (ibid. 155), and 'the best title for this is ... cultural sub-nationalism' (ibid. 156). 'It could only be "sub-nationalist" in the sense of venting its national content in various crooked ways – neurotically, so to speak, rather than directly' (ibid. 156). Hence, 'vulgar tartanry' and 'kailyard' (cabbage-patch) became the dominant cultural formations. The latter, kailyardism, 'was the definition of Scotland as consisting wholly of small towns, full of small-town characters, given to bucolic intrigue and wise sayings' (ibid. 158).

In Nairn's view, a figurative schizophrenia (sic) was imposed on the intellectual class, replete with notions of 'ego' (the role of the émigré intellectual in exorcising the kailyard) and 'id' ('the extraordinary blatant [British] super-patriotism'), thus reinforcing the view of Scotland as a psychiatric – Freudian – condition. Scotland's intellectuals were required to be super-British patriots, as well as sentimental nationalist Scots, albeit of a firmly non-political nature. And lest we think that this is an imposed reading of Nairn, he himself spoke of the 'lacerating contradictions' forced upon Scotland by its anomalous mode of development, having crossed over into modernity before the ideological onslaught of nationalism and nation-making. Furthermore, 'it is hard to avoid the metaphor in describing the situation – "decapitation", "neurosis", and even "schizophrenia", and so on' (ibid. 172).

So what took Scotland so long for the belated modern version of nationalism to emerge? 'The puzzle is less why the SNP took half a century to break through than why it broke through at all' (ibid. 175). Indeed, the 'split personality' is reproduced in the nationalist movement itself, notably in the chronic division between 'politics' and 'culture', and above all, to explain why the SNP owed more to the former than the latter, and is famously a-cultural. As Cairns Craig observed: '... there is probably no nationalist party in the world that has been less focused on mobilising culture as part of its political strategy than the SNP' (C. Craig, 2018: 20).

The causes of the rise of nationalism in Scotland, Nairn argued, were external, political and contextual: the decline of the British state and its empire, the windfall of North Sea Oil, and the degeneration of British politics, reflected in the 'enchanted glass' of the British monarchy (Nairn, 1988). Twenty-five years on, in 2004, Nairn's views about Scotland had not changed fundamentally, even with a devolved parliament in Edinburgh. 'If there is one thing that the Scots in particular know all about, it is self-colonisation. They lived it for three hundred years after the Treaty of Union in 1707' (Nairn, 2004: 25). Little, in his view, had altered:

> The sententious moralism of the marginalised; disregard of democratic deficit for economic opportunity; cultural over-compensation and romantic chest-beating, to efface or embellish powerlessness; over-effusive loyalty to a distant cause and metropolis, welcomed yet never welcome enough – all these tropes of a supposedly postnational world are, alas, tired old family skeletons in Edinburgh and Glasgow. (Nairn 2004: 26)

Given the depth of self-colonisation attributed by Nairn to Scotland and the Scots, we might wonder why they voted for a (devolved) parliament in 1997, except that it *was* devolved and not independent; and when it came to a direct plebiscite in 2014, the Scots backed off full independence. Perhaps, however, it depended on who Nairn's audience was. In 1977, when the *Break-Up of Britain* was published, the political writer Bernard Crick observed perceptively in his review that 'much of his book is a protest against those of his fellow socialists who would lump together in *a priori* abstractions all forms of capitalist state and all forms of nationalism rather than examining particular variants historically and sociologically' (Crick, *Times Higher Education Supplement*, 4 Nov 1977). Crick noted, presciently, that 'the breakdown' of the British state might lead more convincingly to an English 'conservative-nationalist' reaction. Crick credited Nairn with seeing, correctly, that 'England herself is the weak link in any chain of hope for peaceful transition [to federalisation of the UK]' (ibid.). The Brexit referendum in 2016 and its messy aftermath would seem to support Crick's view.

The Transition to Modernity

What, according to Nairn, was it that lay behind this deformation of Scottish culture? In large part, it was because Scotland had made the transition to modernity before nationalism emerged as the key ideology: 'Only one land [Scotland] crossed the great divide before the whole condition of European politics and culture was decisively and permanently altered by the great awakening of nationalist consciousness ... it was Scotland which enjoyed (or suffered) this solitary fate' (Nairn, 1977: 108). There is consensus among writers that the transition to modernity was effected by the Union of 1707, and that the empire state of Great Britain thereafter provided untold opportunities for Scotland's elites, and above all, its intelligentsia. We will explore the argument later in this chapter, but what concerns us here is Nairn's contention that this led ineluctably to a residual, deformed culture in Scotland. He was arguing that, as a result of modernity through Union, 'no new intellectual class, at once national in scope and basically disgruntled at its life-prospects arose' (ibid. 119), and furthermore, '*if only* [his emphasis] the intellectuals had behaved differently, then our national history might have left its banks and changed its course' (ibid. 120).

Nairn relies for evidence on David Craig's book *Scottish Literature and the Scottish People* (1961) where he asserted that 'during the 19th century the country was emptied of the *majority* [Nairn's emphasis] of its notable literary talents – men who, if they had stayed, might have thought to mediate their wisdom through the rendering of specifically Scottish experience' (124). Craig had in mind the Mills (James, and son John Stuart), Macauley, Carlyle, Ruskin and Gladstone, although of these, only James Mill and Thomas Carlyle were born in Scotland, and Craig is surely stretching the notion of 'Scots' here rather too far, and for his own purposes.[3]

What Nairn was doing was setting up a thesis about the role of the intelligentsia in constructing the nation. If their services are not called upon – as in Scotland – then there is a lack of wholeness, of bringing together culture and politics in a society in which there was no shortage of appropriate 'history'. He commented that 'the one thing the Scots can never be said to have lacked is identity' (ibid. 131), and that identity is built on substantive amounts of 'history', but of the wrong sort: 'only in retrospect from the point of view of the age of nationalism, did the loss of statehood seem to overshadow the country's history so completely, condemning it to eccentricity and oblivion' (ibid. 135). Paradoxically enough, we might say that Nairn thought that there was too much history, at least as managed by Walter Scott who was a supporter of the Union (being a Tory) and not its opponent. Scott, we have noted, rendered Scotland's history in Nairn's view as 'politically null'. Left to its own devices, Scotland (at least in the form of Stevenson's Mr Hyde) produced a deviant and distorted form of history, reflected in two cultural formations: Highlandism ('the cultural sub-nationalism of tartanry') and Kailyardism ('Scotland as consisting wholly of small towns full of small-town "characters" given to bucolic intrigue and wise sayings') (ibid. 158).

It turns out, however, that the 'kailyard' is misplaced here, for it was peculiar in time and place, an *émigré* literature aimed at a wider British and American market in the late nineteenth century. Willie Donaldson's definitive study of this cultural formation contradicted Nairn, and concluded:

> On the whole, popular fiction in Victorian Scotland is not overwhelmingly backward-looking; it is not obsessed with rural themes; it does not shrink from urbanisation and its problems; it is not idyllic in its approach; it does not treat the common people as comic or quaint. The second half of the 19th century [the heyday of 'Kailyard'] is not a period of creative trauma or linguistic decline; it is one of the richest and most vital episodes in the history of Scottish popular culture. (Donaldson, 1986: 149)

What of the other deformed cultural formation – tartanry and Nairn's tartan monster? Tartanry was never treated as seriously as the kailyard by Scottish intellectuals; perhaps it was considered too unspeakable to be worthy of their analysis, although they are often linked conceptually together, as in this comment by Christopher Harvie: 'Tartanry attained its fullest extent in the shrewd marketing of the Kailyard authors in the 1890s' (Harvie 1988: 27). The most notorious account is by English historian, Hugh Trevor-Roper (Lord Dacre) in his chapter in the Hobsbawm and Ranger's collection *The Invention of Tradition* (1984), in which he attempts a demolition job on tartan itself. The kilt, he claimed, is a purely modern costume, first designed and first worn by an English Quaker industrialist, and it was bestowed by him on the Highlanders in order not to preserve their traditional way of life but to ease their transformation: to bring them out of the heather and into the factory, presumably because they did not have the wit to do that for themselves. (1984: 22).

It is not difficult to demolish Dacre's account of the origins of tartan (Bill Ferguson's *Identity and the Scottish Nation* (1998) does so comprehensively), and he certainly had political and cultural axes to grind. Neal Ascherson commented:

> Trevor-Roper's Scotophobia, evident even in the letters he wrote as a boy from a Scottish prep school, was not entirely rational. *The Invention of Scotland*, a posthumous selection of some of his essays on the country, is fun to read but spoiled by ignorance of the background, unfamiliarity with recent Scottish research and malicious interpretation. The fact is that he was out of his depth, as he often was when he stepped beyond about 1760.[4]

Nevertheless, Tom Nairn resisted the view that neither kailyard nor tartanry were as powerful and significant tropes as he made out. His thesis came under attack from a more conventional nationalist quarter. Beveridge and Turnbull, writing in 1989 and again in 1997, promoted as the central task of cultural nationalism, 'the recovery of Scottish cultural practices', which have to be rescued from the metropolitan-influenced analysis of Scotland. Intellectuals like Tom Nairn were accused of a 'deep aversion to everything native and local' (1989: 58), which in turn derived from longstanding processes of 'cultural colonisation'. Such processes inflict a manichean view on Scottish culture. 'In Nairn's description, there are no shades or contours; everything stands condemned' (ibid.). Beveridge and Turnbull turn the tables in this argument about 'the eclipse of Scottish culture', the title of their 1989 book. They criticize 'the Scottish intelligentsia on "tartanry" namely as another instance of the Scottish intelligentsia's readiness to embrace demeaning conceptions of national culture – in other words, as an expression of inferiorism' (Beveridge and Turnbull, 1989: 14). Beveridge and Turnbull set themselves the task of identifying and promoting Scottish cultural traditions, untainted by the 'anglicised traditions' of the universities in Scotland (not, in their view, properly *Scottish* universities anymore). For this they relied on the work of George Davie in *The Democratic Intellect* (1961) in which he argued that Scottish higher education underwent an unprecedented and fatal anglicisation in the late nineteenth century, a thesis described by Lindsay Paterson as persuasive and usually undisputed, but quite wrong in its interpretation of events and processes (1994: 66).

Furthermore, Lindsay Paterson developed a powerful counter-thesis that the lack of self-government in formal terms was a reflection of *de facto* autonomy for Scottish civil institutions. He observed:

> these institutions are much more subtle and complex than merely a parliament, and this is as true of Scotland as of nations that are formally independent: they are the schools, universities, media, churches and the myriad daily practices that develop informally and slowly. In that sense, nationalists have been successful: they, whether official or oppositionist, have created a world of dense Scottishness which creates a feeling of natural allegiance in nearly everyone who is brought up here, or who has lived here for an appreciable length of time. (Paterson, 1994: 181)

Both Nairn's and Davie's theses have been powerful in their impact, and plausible in their effects. The problem is that each rest upon dubious evidence, if evidence there be. Whatever their truth status, they have dominated discussions about Scottish culture, in Nairn's case that it is pathological in its effects, and in Davie's, that the distinctiveness of Scottish educational traditions, and more generally of culture, have anglicised Scotland. We now turn to other accounts of Scottish culture to examine their effects, especially on Nairn's.

UNIFYING CULTURE

From the 1980s, there were attempts to replace tartanry and kailyard with a more progressive cultural formation – labelled Clydesidism, which had in its favour its construction 'from 'real' images of working-class life, from the discourse of class, and from naturalism. As we saw in Chapter 5, this has been a powerful trope for understanding Scotland. Its language was redolent of early twentieth century Clydeside, with its appeal to the 'industrial masses' and to skilled masculine culture. This resonates with the discussion of 'coal culture' and de-industrialisation discussed previously, which is a good example of the genre. It was fine, said Cairns Craig, to break out of the mental traps of the historic myths of tartanry and kailyard, to imagine a future, even a revolutionary future, through which to overcome the static quality of the dominant myths, but we risked embracing a myth based on a fast-disappearing working class culture.

One might argue that the point was not to find a new, pure, Scottish national culture fit for the twenty-first century, but to recognise that the relationship between cultural forms and political movements is never going to be straightforward. It is tempting to reach back for the classical nationalist formulation of the late eighteenth and nineteenth centuries whereby 'a people', unique in their culture, reach for political self-determination as an expression of that culture. However, rather than there being a single people with a single culture in Scotland, there seemed to be advantages in diversity and fragmentation, as Cairns Craig observed:

> The fragmentation and division which made Scotland seem abnormal to an earlier part of the 20th century came to be the norm for much of the world's population. Bilingualism, biculturalism and the inheritance of a diversity of fragmented traditions were to be the source of creativity rather than its inhibition in the second half of the 20th, and Scotland ceased to have to measure itself against the false 'norm', psychological as well as cultural, of the unified national tradition. (C. Craig: 1987:7)

In his later book *The Wealth of the Nation* Craig notes that 'culture is not only fundamental to the wealth of the nation but fundamental to its self-perception as a nation' (2018: 20) but he argued that few historians of Scotland deal much, if at all, with Scottish culture. Thus, since the 1960s and the rise of modern Scottish nationalism, Scotland's 'absent nationalism' in the nineteenth century has been an issue which has both inspired and perplexed many historians and theorists such as Tom Nairn. Craig cites politician Gordon Brown's view that a Scottish nationalism would have made sense in the nineteenth century, but not in the twentieth (considered by Brown 'a political mistake'). Craig argues that twenty-first century historiography is mindful of the role of the Scottish diaspora in the British Empire, 'a territory full of intellectuals and intellectual energy busy promoting Scotland's cultural inheritance and engaged in making Scottish culture foundational to the new nations which it was helping to build' (ibid. 60), and that '... Scottish nationalism did not need to assert itself in the British state because "the world was its field", and its aim was to make Scotland the spiritual core of the imperial project' (ibid.73). Thus it was that Scotland did not need a 'resistant nationalism' because its 'imperial nationalism' 'was projected outwards to allow it to demand recognition as a cultural force quite separate from that of "Anglo-British imperialism"' (ibid. 73). As an imperial nationalism rather than a unionist nationalism (Morton, 1999) it was based on consolidating Scottish values across the globe, notably in what is called nowadays the 'anglosphere' (thus including the United States).

Cairns Craig pointed up the significance of cultural pessimism about Scotland, what he calls 'nostophobia' (phobia of home). He has this to say about his namesake, David Craig:

> Craig's study [*Scottish Literature and the Scottish People*, 1961] is a study of the decline of Scottish culture as it moves from the integrated popular culture that the Reformation destroyed through the narrowing achievements of the 18th century literati to the work of Burns and Scott, each figure representing, despite individual successes, a further symptom of the disintegrative environment in which they worked. (2018: 185)

He acknowledged the nostophobia of modern commentators such as writers John Lloyd and John Herdman, Tom Nairn, 'the true nationalist's irrepressible gloom in our land', as well as George Davie:

> If, as is often claimed, 19th century Scotland was the country of nostalgia, then for most of the 20th century Scotland has been the country of nostophobia. Far from being the minority opposition in modern Scottish culture, nostophobia was, in fact, the ideology of much of the cultural 'establishment'. (2018: 188)

Pointing out that nostophobia covered the political spectrum – Allan Massie, who had written the introduction to the 1982 reprint of Edwin Muir's *Scott and Scotland*, asked rhetorically 'how do you write about a second-hand society?' – Cairns Craig argued that the years after 1979, and the 'failure' of the referendum that year, saw a change; 'as though in defiance of the stalled political reality in which it is trapped, Scottish literature of the 1980s and 1990s drew its energy from discovery of a variety of routes into alternative ontologies where the imaginary can become real' (2018: 226). The implication was that precisely because of the failure of 'politics' to solve the Scottish conundrum of greater self-government, it stimulated writers such as Alistair Gray (*Lanark*, 1981) and the poet Edwin Morgan, to 'write a lot'. Commented Morgan: 'by 1996 Scotland had neither a Parliament nor a National Theatre, but it had a voice; in fact it had a wealth of voices' (2018: 259).

What brought about this apparent cultural transformation? Cairns Craig put it down to three factors: the secularisation process in the 1960s whereby the Church of Scotland was no longer the 'pulpit' for Scottish talk (if it ever had been); the end of empire, and with it, union in its older form; and related to that, the failure to create a 'British culture'. With hindsight, John Maynard Keynes' resistance to a distinct Scottish version of the Arts Council (originally called CEMA, the coyly named Committee for the Encouragement of Music and the Arts) reflected that (McArthur, 2013). So did the BBC's uncertainty whether to call Scotland a 'region' or a 'nation' (even an oxymoronic 'national region') and its resistance to anything called a Scottish national TV early evening news programme (the so-called Scottish Six). Cairns Craig concluded his 2018 book, *The Wealth of the Nation*, as follows: 'without cultural independence a country ceases to exist: the achievement of Scotland since 1707 or, more recently, after 1979, is that it has established the value of the culture on which its independence, whatever its political environment, can be maintained' (2018: 291).

Inventing Literature

There is a further argument which is relevant here: Robert Crawford's claim that the subject of 'English Literature' was a Scottish invention. In his book *Devolving English Literature*, Crawford argued that university teaching of 'Rhetoric and Belles Lettres', the forerunner of English Literature, was actually Scottish. Thus: 'Scotland can claim much of the credit for inventing "English literature"; it can also claim, in common with all other societies which are sometimes labelled "provincial", to have felt the need to try to escape from that invention' (Crawford, 1992: 44). Better, thinks Crawford, to consider Scottish literature entering a British phase in the eighteenth century, post-Union. The point is that Scottish writers saw huge opportunities in writing furth of Scotland, and in the context of what might more accurately have been called British Literature.

The term English Literature, in any case, has a useful ambiguity about it. It can mean the literature of the English (people), as well as literature written in English (language). Crawford observes that Scottish writers in the eighteenth and nineteenth centuries were able to take advantage of burgeoning Britain while avoiding anglocentricity. It was not simply the imperial context, but, in the proper sense of the term, the anglosphere of shared written culture. Consider, for example, the perceived influence of Robert Burns on the American poet Walt Whitman: 'for Whitman, who replied with gleeful affirmation to the question "Do I contradict myself?", that mention of Burns's contradictory nature is a final gesture of identification with the Scottish poet' (Crawford, 1992: 213). Crawford also makes the point that there was a general role of 'outsider-insiders' in English Literature (such as Joseph Conrad, T. S. Eliot and many more), as well as a strong 'provincial' emphasis in England itself (consider Jane Austen, the Bronte sisters and Thomas Hardy). The case of Irish writers making a significant contribution to 'English' literature reinforces the point that such literature was, and is, global in its context. David Hume's *History of England*, published in six volumes between 1754 and 1762, is an example of 'England' being employed to mean 'Britain', a far more acceptable equation at the time than it is today. Furthermore, Robert Crawford counsels that 'to many it appeared that the way to advance as a Scot was to appear as English as possible, while at the same time upholding an ideal of Britishness in which Scotland would be able to play her full part' (ibid. 24). This, manifestly, is contextualised historically, for, as Crawford points out 'Scotland and Scottish culture, like all nations and cultures, require continual acts of re-imagining which alter and develop their natures' (ibid. 15).

From the perspective of the late twentieth century, the literary imaginaries had moved on, making such dovetailing of Scottish and English literatures seemingly redundant. In his essay on twentieth-century Scottish literature, Cairns Craig observed: 'When TS Eliot, in a review in 1919, asked, "Was There a Scottish Literature?", the past tense perspective seemed all too appropriate to the possibilities of Scottish literature surviving into the twentieth century as an independent cultural force.'

(C. Craig, 1987: 1). What Scotland was *not* considered to be was an 'organic whole', a vibrant literature and culture which sustained a sense of cultural identity, and which stimulated a greater political one. In short, much of the writing about Scottish culture and politics in the twentieth century assumed that 'Scotland' had effectively ceased to be; it had come to an end. It was common to see Scotland's literature as 'fundamentally a dead literature, the literature of a nation which once existed but now has no independent identity' (C. Craig, 1999: 16). Much of the commentary was elegiac, which saw Scottish culture as doomed to failure, conspiring to produce a cultural wasteland.

The quest for Scottish cultural independence from a culturally suffocating and homogeneous Anglo-British one ignored the fact that the latter had itself fragmented. Craig argued that the post-1918 period saw the collapse of the English cultural imperium, meaning that 'English culture' could no longer be equated with 'the culture of England'. In most English-speaking countries, there was a burgeoning of indigenous literature – in Canada, Australia, South Africa, New Zealand, the United States and Ireland. Craig commented: 'At no time in its history could Scotland have been described as "organic" or a "unified" culture: it could never have been envisaged as one "comprehensive" mind transcending the "prejudices of politics and fashions of taste" of particular periods' (C. Craig, 1996: 15). He borrowed the phrase 'being between' from the poet Sorley MacLean with reference to the mediums of Gaelic and English, This is the context for Craig's comment, mentioned earlier, that: 'Culture is not an organism, nor a totality, nor a unity: it is the site of a dialogue, it is a dialectic, a dialect. It is *being between*' (C. Craig, 1999: 206). What this condition signifies is not a divided, but a diverse culture, which Scotland had to be from its earliest forms of statehood. It was neither feasible nor desirable to impose a single, uniform sense of culture. If we take that as our perspective, we can read Scottish culture differently.

The Question of Language

Recall Benedict Anderson's observation earlier in this chapter that Scotland laboured under sharing a common language with England, and thus was inadequately distinct from its southern neighbour to be considered a separate nation in its own right.

Recall too Robert Crawford's argument that the teaching of 'Rhetoric and Belles Lettres' – what became known as the study of English Literature – was a Scottish invention. What was perceived as a weakness – Scots, by and large, spoke and wrote in English – can be considered a strength in that there were fewer barriers to be considered 'Scottish'; the tariff to belonging was, so to speak, sufficiently low. Hence, externally, there were few barriers in imperial influence to Scots on the make. Internally, it mattered too, because territorial inclusion rather than ethnic belonging, as expressed through language, was easier to effect.

On the other hand, language was a double-edged sword. Too little difference from 'the English' in that regard allowed the argument to be made by Benedict Anderson that to all intents and purposes Scots differed little from their southern neighbours, and the basis of its nation-ness was thereby weak. Language in any case is not simply a carrier of thoughts and ideas, the means for expressing them, but also the substance of 'national culture'. Consider the significance of literature in the round, as well as spoken and written speech. Few can doubt that Catalans and Quebecois are 'different' culturally, living as they do in states where 'national' languages, Spanish/Castilian, and English respectively, are the norm. Similarly, on the British island, Welsh is spoken by around 30 per cent of the population of Wales, while the 2021 census reported that three-quarters said they had no Welsh language skills to speak of. In these cases, a substantial proportion of the populations of Wales, Catalonia and Quebec are somewhat at a disadvantage in terms of being considered 'non-nationals' if they do not speak the language.

In Scotland, despite periodic attempts to turn Gaelic and Doric/Lallans into national languages, they are most obviously 'regional' in their usage, associated with the country's north-west and the north-east respectively. By and large, there is no linguistic tariff for incomers to pay in Scotland in terms of language, leading to claims that Scottish national identity is 'civic' rather than 'ethnic', and hence inclusive. On the other hand, claiming to be a nation is made more difficult, ostensibly, without a significant linguistic difference, or at best, differences of degree (accent or vocabulary, for example) rather than kind. To be sure, people on the other island of Ireland were also faced with similar challenges, and after Independence in 1921 'Irish' was a badge of difference culturally in the Gaeltacht but failed to become *lingua franca* throughout the state.[5] On the other hand, the point has been made that 'English' as a vernacular and a global language has many variants: most notably in North America, Australia, New Zealand, Ireland but throughout the world and known as 'global Englishes'; see, for example, the 1986 BBC series and accompanying book *The Story of English* by Robert McNeil, Robert McCrum and William Cran.

More to the point: what are we to make of the undoubted fact that, for much of its history, the Scottish school curriculum was centred on the study of 'English'? Lindsay Paterson has observed that 'the inter-war period settled the definition of secondary education in Scotland: for the rest of the century, it was to be liberal, academic and centred on English (Paterson, 2004: 72). Examining the 'English' curriculum in Scottish schools in the 1920s, he found that, in terms of examinations:

> Apart from Chaucer (on whom there was a question every year), there were few medieval authors. There was a question on Shakespeare every year too, and other sixteenth- and seventeenth-century English authors included Spenser, Bunyan, Milton, Malory, and Marlowe, There were always questions on eighteenth century English poetry: the authors included Dryden, Gray, Pope and Goldsmith, The greatest number of poets was from the nineteenth or late-eighteenth century: for example, Shelley, Keats, Tennyson, Wordsworth and Coleridge, Eighteenth- and nineteenth-century English novelists featured regularly, for example Austen, Dickens, Charlotte Bronte, Hardy, George Elliot, and Thackeray, There was also always a question on the English essayists, such as Samuel Johnson, Addison, Charles Lamb, Swift, Hazlitt, Macaulay, Matthew Arnold, Ruskin and Charles Darwin, It would also usually have been possible to answer on modern novelists, poets and playwrights, such as Conrad, Galsworthy, Shaw, Bridges and Sassoon, Scottish authors were not absent: Burns, Scott (as both poet and novelist), Stevenson, Neil Munro, Thomas Carlyle and Hugh Miller. There was also always at least one open-ended question on such topics as travel, natural history, biography or science, and often a question on particular genres such as the lyric, ballads and 'the romantic revival'. (ibid. 66)

This was not teaching Scottish pupils to 'become English', however, for there was a specifically Scottish approach to the study of English in schools: 'the structure of the Scottish Leaving Certificate perhaps managed to combine a modern breadth and – through English literature – a liberal humanism that was not enforced on all secondary tracks elsewhere.' (2004: 70). Thus, the Scottish curriculum had similar aims to the French inculcation of *culture générale*, or the concept of *Bildung* (roughly translated as personal education) in German secondary education: 'The moral philosophical legacy of Adam Smith and of the rest of the Common Sense school left an inclination to interpret education as having a social purpose, and the social uses of English that were emerging in the late-nineteenth century seemed to suit that well' (ibid. 72).

The point Lindsay Paterson is making is a crucial one; putting 'English' at the centre of the Scottish school curriculum is not about making Scottish pupils 'English', but in using the study of English literature, which, according to Robert Crawford, Scots had invented, to teach the values of liberal humanism.

NEW IMAGINARIES

In many ways, the strong tradition of cultural pessimism, which had been so dominant for much of the twentieth century, was eroding in the final quarter, and as we shall see later in this chapter, there were even attempts to explain political change in terms of cultural shifts; a radical leap from pessimism to optimism. A more sociologically informed account of Scottish culture can be found in Andrew Blaikie's *The Scots Imagination and Modern Memory*. He commented: 'Our social imagination – fragmented and multifarious, certainly plural – means not only that each of us, Scots-born or otherwise, perceives this place in a particular way, but also that in establishing our belonging to the country we identify connections to the past through specific kinds of narratives' (Blaikie, 2010: 2).

Blaikie is critical of Tom Nairn's sub-cultural nationalism, labelling it an analysis 'from above', and he observed:

> My contention here is that in finding a legacy of escapism in the debased offerings of mediated mass culture, those latter-day critics who point to the Kailyard school and its offspring as the basis of a culturally deformed 'sub-nationalism', reify a misplaced historiography while underestimating the self-awareness of the consuming public. (2010: 99)

Hence, the products of the kailyard should not be thought of in terms of passive consumption, but as part of a process of active and critical renegotiation. Blaikie used the work of the social anthropologist Michael Herzfeld on 'cultural intimacy' to make the point that there are aspects of cultural identity which are considered a source of external embarrassment but which provide insiders with assurance of common sociality. In any case, the cultural pessimism of the likes of Edwin Muir was suffused with anti-urban and anti-industrial animus, and the projection of personal discontents onto the national scale (see, for example, his book *Scottish Journey*, 1935). Perhaps better to treat what passes for Scottish culture ironically, as the cultural historian Angus Calder did:

> It is easy and indeed necessary to jeer at the nineteenth century exploitation or invention of such symbols as the tartan, the kilt, the Burns cult, the lad o'pairts: yet perhaps one should be furtively grateful that the Victorian Scottish bourgeoisie felt that needed a distinctive methodology and provided us with a national 'image' which we can debunk for intelligent foreigners. (Calder, 1994: 62)

What D. C. Thomson products (such as *The Beano*, *The Dandy*,[6] *The Sunday Post* and *The People's Friend*) have in common is that they purvey 'so much folksy pabulum, but their popularity cannot be wished away as culturally irrelevant or ushered into place as de-politicised "sub-nationalism". To do this is to misunderstand cultural intimacy' (Blaikie, 2010: 121). Accusations of 'involuntary parochialism' fail to read the ironic sense of people's own narrative, as well as the 'structural nostalgia' of the moral community which always entailed some measure of mutuality. Recall the elegiac accounts of the demise of the 'coal community', of heavy industry, as well as 'highlandism' which, says Blaikie, 'persists today because it is a reflection of a popular *mentalité* in which Scottishness is imagined not just by seeing landscape in particular established ways, but through using it symbolically to connect personal, social and national identities' (ibid. 137). Landscapes in particular became symbolic of Scotland and its identity; and that is as true of pit bings (coal tips) as it is of Highland estates. However, Blaikie reminds us: 'the sublime irony is that in "looking upon a land devoid of cultural reference" we are doing something that is, of course, supremely cultural' (ibid. 166).

Nevertheless, landscape has deep cultural meaning. For example, in our work on national identity, we found that two-thirds of people in Scotland said they felt more Scottish when they saw or visited the countryside – in England it was little over half (see McCrone and Bechhofer, 2015: 64). Blaikie ends with Norman MacCaig's comment in his poem *Voice Over* (1988): 'The little plot – do I belong to it or it to me? No matter. We share each other as I walk amongst the flags and tombstones'. Scotland, then, is a landscape of the mind.

Forging a New Way

The road to Home Rule in the final quarter of the twentieth century led in new directions for writers on Scotland. Scott Hames's book *The Literary Politics of Scottish Devolution* juxtaposed 'the dream' and 'the grind' as follows:

> 'The Dream' is a story of cultural vanguardism in which writers and artists play the starring role in the recuperation of national identity, cultural confidence and democratic agency. It contrasts sharply with the less inspiring story I will call 'The Grind': the longer, thinner political history of devolution as a shrewd and sometimes grubby saga of electoral expediency, characterised less by stirring visions of democratic rebirth than ploys of cynical circumspection appointed to do or rather recommend, as little as politically possible. (Hames, 2020: xii)

Hames captures an interesting moment in the relationship between culture and politics in Scotland. There was an almost imperceptible shift away from cultural pessimism, with Tom Nairn as its leading tribune, to one where writers took on a role of cultural leaders on the road to Home Rule. Consider, for example, the writer Andrew O'Hagan, who in 2002, shortly after the Scottish parliament was set up, observed: 'the half-hearted nation [Scotland] will want to hold fast to its grievances ... the problem is not the parliament, it's the people, and the people's drowsy addiction to imagined injury' (quoted in Hames, 2020: 20). There are echoes here of Bertolt Brecht's comment in his poem *The Solution*: 'Would it not be easier in that case for the government to dissolve the people and elect another?', and the highly literate O'Hagan would have been aware of that. By 2017, O'Hagan (and Scotland, presumably) had moved on. In a lecture at the Edinburgh Book Festival that year, he recanted (a good word with appropriate religious overtones), saying that

'Scotland itself, these last 15 years, has moved on from the old stasis I used to criticise' (Hames, 2020: 21). More to the point, 'Britain has mismanaged itself out of existence, and Scotland may not be the beneficiary, but it can certainly be the escapee, free to succeed or to fail in its own ways' (ibid.).

O'Hagan was not alone. The poet Donnie O'Rourke made the observation in 1994 that: 'Scotland's artists did more than its politicians to dream up a new Scotland' (Hames, 2020: 30): quite a claim, and note the word 'dream'. Academic writers made similar observations. Robert Crawford, in 2000, observed that 'devolution and a reassertion of Scottish nationhood were imagined by poets and writers' (Hames, 2020: 31). And Cairns Craig: 'if politics and votes were the means of bringing the parliament into existence, they were not its direct cause'; he continued, the parliament 'has been built on the foundations of a revolution in the nation's culture' (Hames, 2020: 40).

This is a remarkable turnaround, given that the dominant wisdom had been that Scottish culture as a psychiatric condition was too far gone to be reformed. The tone had been set by Tom Nairn and what Hames calls 'his caustic influence' (2020: 68). The writer John Herdman too had damned the people in the 1970s, referring to 'the impenetrable stupidity and desperate fickleness of the electorate' (Hames, 2020: 69) – another case, evidently, for Brecht. At the time of the 1979 referendum, the novelist Willie McIlvanney had likened Scotland to a lion, albeit a dormant and mangy beast. When Scots voted for a directly elected 'assembly' but in insufficient numbers to meet the gerrymandered threshold, McIlvanney talks of the 'cowardly lion': 'those who loved the lion had nothing to say. For the lion had turned in its cage and slunk away. And lives still among stinking straw today' (Hames, 2020: 121).

Taken together, we can hear echoes of Tom Nairn's Scotland as a psychiatric condition, and as Hames observes, 'the self-laceration of "The Cowardly Lion" moves on the moral-psychological plane' (2020: 121). Tom Nairn himself, Hames observed, was reasonably chipper, seeing the 1979 result as making transparent what had been opaque: cards were now on the table, and dividing lines drawn. Alliance-building began shortly after the 1979 referendum such that campaigning organisations sprung up to campaign for a Scottish Assembly/parliament through the complex of civil society, a notion, recall, that Nairn did not have much time for. Still, we are left wondering how the mangy lion of Scottish culture managed to escape from its cage; and how it was that writers and keepers of this deformed creature/culture did a *volte face* in the final decades of the twentieth century. In short, how *was* that pessimism overtaken by optimism?

The short answer is that neither pessimism nor optimism, nor the supposed connection between culture and politics, were quite as straightforward as they seemed. Above all, arguments were largely bereft of evidence one way or another, and for that we need a more robust and evidenced analysis, and unsurprisingly, a sociological one. Earlier in this chapter, I mentioned Lindsay Paterson's book, *The Autonomy of Modern Scotland*, in which he argued that orthodox nationalism did not arise in Scotland in the nineteenth century because it had little need to do so in a latitudinous British state.

Defending Scottish institutions often had to be done in powerful rhetoric. Paterson gives the example of Walter Scott defending the Scottish currency post-Union in apocalyptic terms: 'I think I see my native country of Scotland ... falling so far as its national, or rather, perhaps, I should say its *provincial*, interests are concerned, daily into more absolute contempt' (Paterson, 1994: 3). Invoking the nation, in other words, even though he emphasises 'provincial', requires strong words. We would not know from Scott's inveigh – he was a supporter of Union with England – that he was talking about the fiscal matter of the issuing of Scottish banknotes. It was necessary, in other words, for supporters of Union to wave the flag with vigour, and in a Scottish way when necessary so as to make it a matter of existence. In like manner, *The Scotsman* newspaper in 1993 carried a weekly feature called 'Fly on the Wall' asking celebrities for their favourite moment in Scottish history. The-then Conservative Secretary of State Ian Lang said that being at the Battle of Bannockburn would have been his favourite moment, which might seem, on the face of it, a curious contradiction for a unionist politician.

The point, however, is a broader one. We do not read social and political change off the page, as it were. What we 'see' is framed by what we expect to see, and how well or badly it fits into our broader expectations, none more so than passing them through 'Scottish culture'. Earlier in this chapter, I alluded to Graeme Morton's concept of unionist-nationalism, by which he meant that 'unionism' and 'nationalism' are mutually interdependent. To be a true unionist it is necessary to consider Scotland a nation; and to be a nationalist, it is necessary to fight Scotland's corner within the Union, acknowledging the limits on sovereignty of small nations in the world. Similarly, the historian Colin Kidd (2008) observed that in the ensuing centuries 'unionists' went to great lengths to assert the theoretical independence of Scotland, while 'nationalists' went to similar lengths to argue for equal treatment under the Union. Much of unionism is tinged with nationalism, and nationalism with unionism. The defence of autonomous civil society with its institutions of law, education, religion and civil life was the achievement of union, and the reason it lasted so long. It follows that these very institutions would also be the means of championing and ushering in a new Scotland.

This independent civil society, however, as Paterson observed, was not a national expression in and of itself. His comment bears repeating: 'The Scots could believe that they had won a great bargain because their culture could flourish and their economy could grow. This was their conception of liberty. It is not ours, nor that of nationalism: there was no mass franchise, nor even the nineteenth century icon, a national parliament' (Paterson, 1994: 45).

In 2018, one of Lang's successors as Secretary of State for Scotland, David Mundell, observed in the House of Commons that 'Scotland is not a partner of the United Kingdom; Scotland is part of the United Kingdom'.[7] This possibly made accurate law, but poor politics in terms of Scotland's place in the Union. The point, however, remains. Union and nation are not polar opposites.

Utopian Pragmatism

Recall Scott Hames's distinction between 'the dream' and 'the grind', whereby there requires to be a grand vision, but also the means to achieve it. In a more sociological vein, Lindsay Paterson (2015) labels similar ideas 'utopian' and 'pragmatic'. They are sides of the same coin, one feeding off the other; the former presenting a vision of where we should go; the latter, how it might be achieved. The effect of this dialectic between utopianism and pragmatism has been a zig-zag journey towards Scottish autonomy. There is a vision, provided by utopians, and pragmatists are concerned with the means for getting there. Consider, for example, the rhetoric employed by Walter Scott in defending Scottish banknotes. This is employing utopian tropes; the end of Scotland as a nation; and how to avoid separation by reform.

Thus it was that in the 2014 independence referendum, dystopias were necessary for each side – Yes and No. In Paterson's words: 'The No campaign's negativity helped Yes along the way' (ibid. 12). This was not unique to the 2014 event:

> Throughout the last three centuries the story has recurred: dissatisfaction grows, often to an intensity that threatens to destroy the Union, at least among the politically active and vociferous. The ground of that protest is that is always that the Scots are not being treated equally, with respect, with regard to their rights. But then the UK state remembers its inherent flexibility and pragmatism, and concedes just enough not just to placate the discontent for the time being – which would be merely cynical – but actually, wisely enough, appreciating what the real discontent is, which is not about constitutional structures but about social, economic and political issues. (ibid. 5)

On that occasion, in 2014, the 'established' position of Scotland in the Union with a devolved government was on the defensive, and hence, at the last juncture produced A Vow (by implication, solemn and binding: a genuflection to quasi-religious language) at the behest of the ineffably Scottish politician Gordon Brown, that further devolved powers might be just around the corner. What we were seeing, then, was an elaborate interaction between 'the vision thing' and pragmatic steps forward, delivered in this case by ostensibly 'unionist' political parties. The fact that as the cliché goes, the losers (Yes) won the rhetorical battle, and the winners (No) lost it, reflects the fact that progress has two sides to the same coin. This utopian/pragmatic dialogue is by no means unique to the Scottish cases for and against independence. It suffuses all forms of politics in the western world: Socialists/Social Democrats; Conservatives/libertarians; and so on. Paterson concludes: '…whatever happens the outcome will continue to be compromise, will continue to generate radical discontent, and thus will never settle the Scottish question to the satisfaction of anyone' (ibid. 18–19).

What makes Paterson's analysis particularly powerful is that he identifies the social base of the Yes movement. The social base of Yes in 2014 was 'strongest among those left-leaning middle-class people who identified with working-class Scots, and among left-leaning working-class people who did not show much solidarity with working-class people across the border [with England]'. The utopian movement among the Yes vote was strong: 'it was their assertion that to be Scottish is to be left-wing that galvanised a campaign which could never have been led by the SNP alone, and it was their radicalism that has kept the SNP marginally on the left, to Labour's discomfort' (ibid. 18). The 2014 referendum was, in any case, a success in terms of turnout: 84.6 per cent, far ahead of the 63 per cent at the Scottish election of 2016, and considerably more than the 1997 referendum on devolution (a mere 60 per cent).

In terms of the debate as to the relationship between culture and politics, there is something of a chicken and egg relationship between them. Writing before the devolution referendum, Lindsay Paterson observed:

> Behind all this overtly political activity has been a great deal of cultural activism. Novels, poetry, theatre, history and music of all sorts have flourished in a way that they had not done at least since the 1930s and in some respects much longer. A lot of this was vaguely political in a loosely socialist and nationalist way: it thus helped to create a new account of Scotland as an essentially democratic place which was opposed to an incorrigibly hierarchical Tory England. (Paterson, 1994: 172)

As grist to that mill, claims were made that Scotland was 'naturally' much more democratic and left-wing than England, which was being read off the 'democratic deficit' whereby Scotland was far more likely to get a government (at Westminster) that it had not elected. Such an assertion had some truth to it. For example, in 2016, the year of the Brexit referendum, in terms of political and social values, Scots were significantly more on the Left than the English. However, as many as *half* of people in England placed themselves on the Left, while in Scotland it was 60 per cent: the former is arguably more interesting than the latter. In terms of social values, Scots were marginally more liberal than the English (on a liberal-authoritarian scale), but the differences were insufficient to explain the distinct voting differences north and south of the border. To put these figures in perspective, in 1997, virtually twenty years earlier, the results were comparable; Scots were more left-wing, and more liberal than the English (Brown, McCrone and Paterson, 1997). Such social and political values were suffused throughout Scotland, for there were few regional variations.

This pointed to a relatively homogeneous and distinctive political culture throughout Scotland, based on the 'myth' of Scottish egalitarianism. Myth here is not used as indicating falsehood, but truths held to be self-evident, that all people are created equal, that we're all Jock Tamson's bairns. Think of myth as a perspective, a guide with which to interpret social reality. Egalitarianism is not to be confused with equality, for it is not difficult to show that Scotland harbours deep and abiding inequalities. However, myths do not require 'facts' to sustain them. Egalitarianism refers to a set of social values which operate notwithstanding social and economic realities. Recall too that a higher proportion of people in Scotland than in England describe themselves as 'working class' despite their ongoing employment status. The 'Scottish myth' also suffuses the education system, which historically has been a key carrier of such beliefs (see McPherson and Raab, 1988). The central figure in the kailyard was the 'lad o'pairts', historically the son (rarely the daughter) of a peasant or crofter with academic ability but not the material means for 'getting on' (McCrone, 2001: ch 4). Robert Anderson described it historically thus:

> The lad of parts (sic) did exist, but they were drawn from the middle rather than the lower ranks; the children of ministers, teachers, farmers, shopkeepers and artisans enjoyed opportunities, especially for entry to the professions, which long had no equivalent in other countries. Scotland was also unusual in providing such opportunities even in remote areas, and it was the rurality as much as the social origins of the lad of parts which attracted attention. (1985: 100)

What is alluded to here is a form of communalism rather than class equality, with a commitment to the 'parish', secular and religious, made up of sturdy and self-sustaining individuals and families. While the social and economic conditions of such communalism have long since been eroded, there remains a sub-structure of beliefs and values in Scotland which break through the surface to make sense of new realities. Above all, such a myth is an ideological device for marking off the Scots from the English, despite social structural similarities, and reflected still in significantly different social and political values, as we saw earlier. It is a conception we have of ourselves; a truth held to be self-evident, and mobilised appropriately. Recall too Anthony Cohen's observation that 'people construct community symbolically, making it a resource and repository of meaning, and a referent of their identity' (A. Cohen, 1985: 118). In this regard community equates to nation and national culture.

Connected to such cultures are traditions, or more precisely, selected traditions, in Raymond Williams' words: 'an intentionally selected version of a shaping past or a pre-shaped present, which is then powerfully operative in the process of social and cultural definition and identification' (Williams, 1977: 115). Jonathan Hearn has made the point that the metaphor of the 'covenant' is a thread running through Scottish politics which has a rich and concrete history with particular reference to three relationships: labour to capital, citizen to state, and Scotland to England. (Hearn, 2000: 185). Thus, 'the Scottish-English contract is encoded in the long history of covenants, claims of right and declarations, not to mention the Treaty of Union itself, that figure so prominently in the rhetoric of twentieth-century nationalist politics' (Hearn, 2000: 187). The notion of the social contract, then, provides a deep structure to Scottish politics, and bifurcates into 'utopian' (with quasi-religious overtones) and 'pragmatic' versions. Thus, the notion of Scots as a 'covenanted people' stretches back, arguably to the 1320 Declaration of Arbroath (recall its words: 'if he [the king] should give up what he has begun, and make us subject to the King of England, we should drive him out as our enemy and a subverter of his own rights and ours, and make some other man our King'), the Solemn League and Covenant of 1643, the National Covenant of 1689, the Claim of Right of 1842 (a prelude to the Disruption of the Church), the Scottish Covenant of 1949 (in favour of a Scottish parliament), and deliberately echoed in the 1988 Claim of Right set out by the Scottish Constitutional Convention.

Despite the religious origins of these covenants and claims of right, they are threaded into later, secular, ones. Underlying these are two beliefs: the right of Scots to choose their leaders, and the right of Scots to control their own domestic politics. These are, in fact, issues of sovereignty, to which we will return in the next and final chapter. They are premised on two principles:

an appeal to higher authority (God, and latterly, the People), and the assumed, essentialised difference between Scotland and England. Hearn concludes: the cause of the Scottish movement entails imagining a Scotland and its past, but the burden and power of such imaginings is not peculiar to nationalism, but rather falls on any political project, by the very nature of how we collectively think and act in this world' (Hearn, 2000: 197). Note too that such ideas underpin radical social and economic changes such as the decline and demise of the coal and traditional industries as examined in Chapter 5. The notions of 'moral claim' and 'social contract' have a deep Scottish pedigree.

CONCLUSION

The relationship between culture and politics is central to the very notion of Scotland, indeed for that matter, any nation. Hence, much of the debate about that relationship is about whether or not, and in what sense, 'Scotland' exists at all. In that regard, it is about 'the nation' rather than the 'state', and what should be the relationship between them. The thread of cultural pessimism has been the dominant one in such debates, that Scotland seems to be on the verge of extinction, hence Walter Scott's comment that he saw his native country falling 'daily into more absolute contempt'. Being 'stateless', or at least 'under-stated', has meant a degree of vulnerability about its existence and continuation.

Dominating the discourse in recent times has been Tom Nairn with his battery of psychiatric tropes, conveying the powerful sense of a culture deformed beyond repair, and preventing the emergence of something 'healthy'. Even steps towards a devolved parliament, and then a vote on independence in 2014 were considered too little and too late. Pessimism ruled. And then, around the late 1970s and early 1980s, the 'cultural turn' took place. A belief arose that constitutional change was being driven by cultural shifts; that far from grinding pessimism, there were glimmers of light. Partly this had to do with a realisation that the English cultural imperium had fractured, whereby 'English culture' was no longer equated with the culture of England, and out of the wreckage a new sense of Scotland emerged, reflected in the rapid rise of new political formations such as the SNP, though one which was careful not to be overly 'cultural'.

The problem with the thesis connecting culture to politics has to do with what constitutes evidence, at least for the social scientist. Thus, as Andrew Blaikie pointed out:

> national identity is sustained by a complex set of social institutions and organisations, which rear us, educate us, keep us on the legal straight and narrow, and govern us. If anything, being 'national' is the outcome of the process of civil societalisation, and the result mainly of the channels and mechanisms which shape us and make us feel that way. (Blaikie, 2010: 30)

In other words, the institutions and organisations are the carriers of values and tropes, such that civil society represents the sphere of culture in the broadest sense. It is where values and meanings are established, where they are debated, contested and changed. Tom Nairn had little truck with 'civil society', seeing it as a poor substitute for a state, and its practitioners too infected by feelings of inadequacy.

A more sociological reading would argue that the relative density of civil institutions in Scotland are not poor substitutes for state-ness, but the transmission belt between culture and politics. The constitutional impasse of the 1980s and 1990s, when Conservative politicians ran the Scottish Office without a popular mandate – the democratic deficit – helped to bring into being the Scottish Constitutional Convention, made up of civil organisations such as churches, which helped to formulate the demand for a Scottish parliament – historically, Home Rule – which Labour was required to implement when it came to power in 1997. One might argue that this process was as much 'political' as 'social', and so it was. So it was, too, that in 1999 the Scottish parliament became, not only a 'government' in all but name, but the *primus inter pares* of social institutions. And the relationship between culture and the new politics? They are separate spheres which collide with each other periodically, and so inform each other but not in predictable ways. Just how Scotland's 'new politics' emerged and was naturalised is the subject of the final chapter of this book.

NOTES

1. I am grateful to Jonathan Hearn for reminding me of this, as well as drawing attention to its significance in Geertz's writing.

2. In fact, Harvie possibly borrowed, unacknowledged, this distinction from the Australian bush poet, Henry Lawson, in a poem in 1908 called *The Scots*.
3. Craig's descriptor is to those of 'Scottish extraction'.
4. <http://www.lrb.co.uk/v32/n16/neal-ascherson/liquidator>.
5. Thus, Patrick Pearse becomes *Pádraig Anraí Mac Piarais*, and James Connolly, *Séamas Ó Conghaile*, but they are better known, even in Ireland, by their 'English' names. According to the 2022 census, around 40 per cent of the Republic's population claimed some ability to speak 'Irish'.
6. *The Dandy* was published from 1937 until 2010, when it was discontinued.
7. 14 June 2018, vol 642, col 1129 (debate on the European Union (Withdrawal Bill): Sewel Convention).

9

Where To Now?

> The Scottish people do not see their future in a binary way, as an either-or. They simply wish Scotland to run its own affairs, as other nations do. For most people, devolution and independence are little more than different uniforms which can be buttoned over the single reality of self-government.
>
> (Neal Ascherson, *Stone Voices*, 2002)

Where is Scotland going? That may seem an inappropriate question, because Scotland is a place, a territory, rooted in rock; it is not a social actor. It isn't 'going' anywhere, any more than it is 'doing' something. It is a stage on which things, and especially social, political and economic things, happen. It is a small step from there to reifying Scotland, as culture, society and nation. In truth, that is a universal trope, as we deem the world composed of acting nations, even those like Scotland, which are not nation-states. In further truth, however, genuine nation-states hardly exist, in terms of the seamless fusion of nation, as cultural entity, and state, as a political-constitutional one. The nation-state is an imagined entity, a thing of the imagination, for there are few states in the world which map neatly on to 'nation'. It is an aspiration, a claim to justify acting on behalf of a distinct 'people'. Opponents of nation-ness decry the distinctiveness of 'a people', that they are no different from an 'us', and hence they have no right of self-determination. Think, for example, of Russian claims to Ukraine as its territory because it is deemed to be, to all intents and purposes, part of the greater Russian We (Hrytsak, 2023).

In the twenty-first century, few would deny that Scotland is a nation in a world of nations, even though it is not a state; but one with considerably more state-ness in the shape of a parliament and government than it used to have before the turn of the century; let us call Scotland, then, an under-stated nation. There is, however, no inexorable shift to state-ness, and in any case, what constitutes state-ness, conventionally 'independence', is considerably moot. Our research on 'sovereignty' (McCrone and Keating, 2021, 2023) shows clearly that most people in Scotland think its people are sovereign insofar as they have the right to self-determination; it is a theoretical right, not necessarily a desired outcome, in terms of 'independence'. It is not illogical to think that Scotland (to reify this inevitably) has such a right, but not that it needs to be activated. It is, to use Andreas Wimmer's apposite term, a 'nation by will' (*'willensnation'*), a nation by choice. And in any case, what constitutes independence in the twenty-first century is a point for considerable debate. The 2016 vote for the UK leaving the European Union was ostensibly one to 'take back control', but from what, exactly? It is, when all is said and done, a matter of *inter*-dependence.

WHO IS WE ANYWAY?

Nor is it a matter simply of grand constitutional matters. National identity is deeply personal as well as institutional. As Anthony Cohen observed, 'the nation is one of the resources on which individuals will draw to formulate their sense of selfhood' (A. Cohen, 1996: 803). Self and nation are not in opposition to each other. He continues:

> It is to say 'I am Scottish', when Scottishness means everything that I am; I substantiate the otherwise vacuous national label in terms of my own experience, my reading of history, my perception of the landscape, and my reading of Scotland's literature and music, so that when I 'see' the nation, I am looking at myself. (1996: 805)

Scotland is not a figment of the nationalist imagination: 'the histories, literatures, folklores, traditions, languages, music, landscapes, and foods of Scotland are social facts on which individuals draw in providing themselves with a shared vocabulary. That is how culture works' (A. Cohen, ibid.). And, we might add, why Scotland is not England, and vice versa. Those who would oppose the constitutional project of independence are forced to deny the cultural power of being Scottish, and/or assert that of being British. In so doing, they, perforce, play the same game, asserting that *my* nation-ness trumps yours, but, in truth, playing by similar rules. Both play the game of 'othering', thus showing that all identities, and not simply national ones, are contrastive. Nor is it sufficient to assert that 'you were content once'; to which the answer comes: 'yes, but that was then, and this is now'. We are not the people our parents and grandparents used to be. And nations have a habit of living through quite contrasting times. 'We' are ostensibly not the people of fourteenth-century wars of independence; nor of nineteenth-century church–state–empire when to be Scottish and to be British were, as far as we can tell, complements, not antitheses, of each other. However, as Benedict Anderson observed, nations move calendrically through time, changing shape and form as they adapt to new conditions of existence.

That is because national identity may be personal, but it is also institutional. It lives through governance, whether this is church, school, law court, and the panoply of institutional actors which speak on our behalf; and *we*, fundamentally, are *they*, and they are us. They make us, but we in turn make them as they adapt to new times on our behalf. This makes Scotland an imagined community; not insofar as there is only one single and required community, but in the sense that there are several, which play out and reflect who we are and want to be. And as Michael Anderson (2018) has pointed out, there are plural *Scotlands*, not simply in demographic terms, but socially, economically, culturally. Moreover, as Anthony Cohen observed, local experience mediates national identity; there is a Glasgow way of being Scottish, an Aberdeen way, a Shetland way, and so on (A. Cohen, 1982).

Identities resemble cultural containers which social actors imbue with significant meanings. In short, they have to do with claims people make about others, as well as judgements made about who does or does not 'belong'. Identities are not wished upon people willy-nilly; rather, they are the active products of how people interact with others. The argument has been made many times that in the broadest of terms, national identity is a matter of the personal and the political (with a small p). It is both the fragility but also the robustness of national identity, generated as deeply personal, but sustained by institutional apparatus, that makes Scotland, and all nations, *'willensnations'*.

In Chapter 2, we saw that Scotland fits the bill of nation, (civil) society and even state to a considerable degree. And yet, as we saw in the previous chapter, there has long been a fear that somehow, in cultural terms, it does not exist, or is at existential risk, or is so deeply marred that it cannot make the next step to 'independence', whatever that may mean and entail.

CHANGING SCOTLAND

To reiterate the argument running throughout this book: fundamental changes took place in Scotland from the final decades of the twentieth century. They were not unique to Scotland, and represented the end of *Les Trente Glorieuses*, such as it was. The impact of these changes, common to most advanced industrial societies, including England and Wales on this island, produced different political and cultural outcomes. Social structural changes are almost glacial in their dynamics, even though, as in the case of demography, they have an impact on aggregate patterns which can appear as quite dramatic. A case in point is the fall in the number of births in Scotland after the mid-1970s, even though these resulted from decisions by couples to have children, or indeed not to have them. There is also considerable interaction between social factors, one being the increasing number of young women staying on in education, and thereby postponing the age of marriage, or cohabitation.

Relatedly, changes in industrial and occupational structures, and particularly the expansion of white-collar work together with the decline of manual working-class jobs, altered the nature and shape of the social class structure. This, in turn, was both cause and effect of social mobility through higher education, opening up opportunities for young women in particular. Furthermore, the shake-out of 'traditional' communities tied to single industries like coal-mining and steel-making generated geographical mobility, and new communities which detached from older patterns of culture and politics. These also altered the relationships between men and women, reflected in patterns of child-rearing and social care. More babies are now born 'out of wedlock' than to married couples, but in stable relationships which frequently lead to marriage or civil partnerships, to what in German is called 'companionship of shared responsibility' (*Verantwortungsgemeinschaft*).

Taken together, what we are seeing is a radical transformation in social relations and patterns of solidarity. These also have an effect on how people do their politics and worship, the relative demise of denominational patterns whereby the church which people attended was a good predictor of how they would vote; coupled with the loosening of links between social class and support for political parties. As social changes became more transparent, and even problematic, social researchers became attuned to picking them up, and so we began to get systematic data collection and analysis exploring social change. Many of these changes were embedded in the long post-war period, only properly researched in its later phases once these changes became plain and problematic. The assumptions immediately post-war were less easily researched because they were taken for granted.

Taken in the round, we can see just how interactive these changes were: demographic, social, economic and political, with an impact on how people described their national identity, singular or plural, and how they did their politics. The overall effect was to transform Scotland, dating broadly from the late 1960s and early 1970s, and which, fifty years later had clearly shaped the country in new ways. We had ceased to be the people our ancestors were; and by the end of the twentieth century, the setting up of a Scottish parliament meant that Scotland was not the place it had once been. Above all, recovering a directly elected Scottish parliament right at the end of the twentieth century has arguably been the most significant institutional change in our lifetimes. What difference has it made? What do people think of it so far?

A Parliament o' Oor Ain

Let us take stock of twenty-five years of a devolved Scottish parliament, for this will help to predicate how we might construe the future. The political scientist Michael Keating has written that 'the very width of support [for devolution] disguised a lack of depth or conviction. Devolution appealed to a wide swathe of opinion, from unionists for whom it was a reluctant concession, to those for whom it was a precursor to independence' (Keating, 2021: 121). To what extent has it held?

What does public opinion over the twenty-five years of devolution make of it?[1] What does it look like over the long term?

Asked throughout the lifetime of the parliaments since 1999, or, in the case of our second measure, from 2004, three questions provide a public assessment of the devolved parliament and its governments:[2]

- Does the Scottish parliament give ordinary people more or less say on how Scotland is governed?
- How good would you say the Scottish government is at listening to people's views before taking decisions?
- How much do you trust Scottish government to work in Scotland's best interests?

Having a Say

With the exception of 1999, when hopes were high based on little or no evidence, there was scepticism but little hostility towards the parliament. For the first few years, majority opinion was that it made little or no difference to giving 'ordinary people' a greater say. The cross-over in public opinion such that the parliament gave people more say in how Scotland was governed took place in the middle years, notably from 2007 when the SNP took control by forming a minority government, and a clear opinion that it was giving ordinary people more say dates from around the independence referendum in 2014. This continued through the period of the Brexit referendum in 2016, and the Covid-19 pandemic in 2020. Only in the Covid and post-Covid years did the gap between 'more say' and 'no difference' narrow.

'Good at Listening'

Our second measure relates to assessments from 2004 about governments being good (or bad) at listening before making decisions. The survey time series is shorter, from 2004, but the trend is clear: Scottish governments are 'quite good' at listening to people before making decisions, at least from 2007 until the early years of the second decade. Being 'good at listening' is, of course, a relative judgement, and we can compare people's responses in Scotland to Scottish and UK governments[3] over the period, this time dividing responses into positive ('very good' or 'quite good') and negative ('not very good' or 'not good').

The differences once more are clear: Scottish governments get a consistently better rating than UK governments in terms of being good at listening to people, even when, as in later years, the trendlines are downward in both cases.[4]

Trust

The third measure is whether people trust a Scottish government to work in Scotland's best interests. We live in times when the business of government is a tainted trade. It does not appear to be so in Scotland. Throughout the period of devolved government since 1999, the main response is that people trusted the Scottish government 'most of the time', followed by 'some of the time'. We get a better view of trends if we combine the responses: 'most of the time', and 'just about always', and juxtapose them to 'only some of the time', and 'almost never'. Once more, positives outweigh the negatives, except in 2023 when there is a cross-over. Levels of trust in the Scottish government are consistently higher than for the UK government, the median difference being 37 percentage points, ranging from a high of 53 in 2011, to a low of 28 in 2023, but still a substantial gap in favour of the Scottish parliament. Leaving aside the anticipatory response in 1999 before the parliament had begun to function, we find a gap opening up around 2007 between the optimists and the pessimists, when the first SNP government was elected. This trend was sustained (and widened) at the time of the Brexit referendum in 2016, and maintained on a ratio of 2 to 1 throughout the Covid-19 pandemic.

So who are the optimists and who the pessimists when it comes to making judgements about the Scottish government? Those more likely to think that it listens to people tend to be younger rather than older; SNP party identifiers rather than Conservatives; 'Scots' rather than 'British'; in favour of independence; and people expressing a 'high interest' in politics. Similarly, those more likely to think the Scottish government can be trusted to make fair decisions are men rather than women; young rather than old; those with more education; SNP identifiers; those with high interest in politics; and self-identifying 'Scots' rather than 'British'.

We can be more precise about what sorts of people rate Scottish government positively by identifying those factors which have *most* effect on people's opinions, all things considered.[5] The analysis was carried out using the Scottish Social Attitudes survey data for 2023, which saw a significant dip in optimism and positive assessments of Scottish government.[6] To take an example: those most likely to trust the Scottish government are SNP voters, those favouring independence, and those saying they are Scottish not British; and we would expect there to be considerable overlap between these determinants. In terms of trusting the Scottish government, the key factors are: being in favour of independence, having 'liberal' (rather than 'authoritarian') values, being young (under 30), being on the Left rather than the Right in terms of social attitudes, having high levels of interest in politics, as well as being educated to degree level. Our other two measures, 'giving ordinary people a say', and thinking the Scottish government is 'good at listening' are influenced by similar factors, notably being in favour of independence, being 'liberal', and having high levels of political interest. The influences, however, are not identical, and we would not expect them to be, because they tap into different dimensions: trust, listening and having a say. Thus, being on the Left figures in 'giving ordinary people a say', while thinking of yourself as Scottish not British has a significant impact on thinking the Scottish government is 'good at listening', as does being young. Similarly, having a Higher Education degree has a significant impact on 'trust', but not as regards 'giving people a say' and being 'good at listening'. In general, however, the more likely you are to have these characteristics, the more 'optimistic' you are about the Scottish government. They predispose you to be favourable rather than determine that you are; think of it as a matter of significant propensities.

Exploring a Conundrum

At the end of the first period of devolved government, between 1999 and 2003, we spotted something we called the 'devolution conundrum': that despite people recognising the limitations of a devolved parliament, they were much more likely to credit its achievements at the expense of Westminster, and to blame the latter for its failures. We wrote at the time '… there has been some fall in trust in [the parliament's] ability to look after Scotland's long-term interests, while almost half think the new parliament should not have been built. On the other hand, there is continued consistent support for devolution as the preferred constitutional option for Scotland.' (Park and McCrone, 2006: 27). The conundrum lay in the allocation of credit and blame to different levels of government, Scottish or British, and in those early years 'it is Westminster rather than Holyrood that is blamed for shortcomings, and the latter which gets any credit going'. (ibid. 27); hence, the conundrum.

In three policy areas – standards in the health service, quality of education and general standard of living – people were more likely to blame Westminster for falling standards, and to credit Holyrood with any improvements, even where, like standard of living, Westminster would ostensibly have more influence over outcomes. Thus, those who considered that educational standards between 1999 and 2003 had fallen were more likely to blame Westminster (45 per cent) than Holyrood (25 per cent). Those who thought educational standards had improved, on the other hand, were more likely to credit the Scottish Executive (the Scottish government) than the UK government (by 43 per cent to 31 per cent).

These were early, even halcyon, days for devolution, but by 2015, and despite changes of government from Labour/Liberal Democrat to SNP in 2007, we found much the same results. These surveys focused on three policy areas: the health service, the general standard of living and the Scottish economy. Arguably, only the first of these is the prime responsibility of the Scottish government. The results were unequivocal, and reprised the earlier surveys: optimists credited Holyrood, pessimists blamed Westminster, despite the fact that the health service is a directly devolved responsibility. As regards the general standard of living, arguably more closely related to taxation and macro-economic policies, the responsibilities of Westminster, people were more likely to blame the UK government for deteriorating standards of living, while the Scottish government got more credit than Westminster for improving the standard of living (McCrone, 2019a).

A similar pattern related to the Scottish economy: of those who thought it had got stronger over the previous year, 54 per cent credited the Scottish government, three times more than they did the UK government. A similar proportion – 3:1 – attributed blame to Westminster among those who thought the

Scottish economy had grown weaker. While we might expect that blame, rather than credit, is more likely to attach to the familiar (Holyrood) than the far-away (Westminster), this does not appear to have happened. Recall, too, that there was a Labour/Liberal Democrat 'Executive' between 1999 and 2007, and an SNP government thereafter, so the pattern holds regardless of which party is in power. In other words, the Scottish government seemed to benefit from people in Scotland thinking of it as 'theirs'.

The conundrum held, furthermore, when questions related to the degrees of 'trust' in levels of government. Thus, among those who thought that 'government' was good at listening to people's views before making decisions, 64 per cent credited the Scottish government (and only 18 per cent the UK government), while among those who thought 'government' was bad at listening, 82 per cent blamed Westminster, but only 36 per cent Holyrood. Similar patterns occurred on trusting 'government' to work in Scotland's long-term interests: 73 per cent would trust the Scottish government all or most of the time, while they would trust the UK government rarely or never (75 per cent). Similar ratios were found as regards trusting 'government' to make fair decisions; the Scottish government got the credit ('a great deal' or 'quite a lot'), while the UK government got the blame; in each case ratios of between 2:1 and 3:1 in favour of Holyrood.

Such high levels of trust in the Scottish government, certainly vis-à-vis the UK government as it is perceived in Scotland might seem at odds with the commonly perceived notion that governments everywhere have fallen into disrepute.[7] People in Scotland, at any rate, have the alternative of blaming the UK government for their ills, and insofar as Brexit was an anti-government movement, in England at least, there is a sense in which people in Scotland see 'Government' as 'government', the essence of Scottish civil society rather than rulership.

The Covid-19 pandemic provided the biggest challenge facing governments everywhere. It also meant that face-to-face social surveys, such as the Scottish Social Attitudes survey, were suspended until it was judged safe to carry them out. When fieldwork re-commenced in late 2021 to early 2022, it turned out that the 'devolution conundrum' still operated, the systematic association of the UK government with 'decline', and the Scottish government with 'improvement'. Thus, the Scottish government were credited with improvements, in NHS standards (60 per cent), and even as regards the Scottish economy (45 per cent), whereas the UK government got the blame for falling standards (respectively, 28 per cent and 31 per cent).

Manifestly, these results in 2021–2 were adumbrated by the Covid-19 experience. What is interesting, however, is how that experience is reflected in people's judgements about competence or otherwise. Thus, the most significant factor in accounting for 'trust to work in Scotland's best interests' is a positive view of how well the Scottish government handled the pandemic[8] (by a factor of 10). The same is true in explaining 'being good at listening before taking decisions' (by a factor of 22), and thinking that 'Scottish parliament gives people more say in how Scotland is governed' (by a factor of 11); and a satisfaction with the National Health Service in Scotland (by a factor of 4).

The 2023 Scottish Social Attitudes survey was the first to use online survey methodology, 'push-to-web' techniques, rather than face-to-face interviewing, thus making comparison with previous survey results difficult. To permit such comparability, a split-sample was offered the older set of response questions, while the other half received the new set. While the latter were more likely to allocate any blame between the Scottish and the British governments equally (42 per cent), of those offered the old question, almost half (47 per cent) blamed the UK government, and 32 per cent the Scottish government, results comparable to previous surveys where blame attached significantly more to Westminster than Holyrood.[9]

These trend data might suggest that they are simply a function of shifting support for political parties, and in particular the electoral success of the SNP since 2007, as they have been in continuous office since then. A better way of accounting for the trends would be to see a positive view of devolution, and the success of the SNP, as correlates rather than causes, given that all parties who have been in government get the devolution dividend. After all, in the (in)famous words of Walter Scott's character, Mrs Howden: 'when we had a King, and a chancellor and Parliament – men o' oor ain, we could aye peeble them wi' stanes when they werena guid bairns – But naebody's nails can reach the length o' Lunnon.'[10] The immediacy and propinquity of politics matter.

When all is said and done, and over a decade of Scottish Social Attitudes surveys, we find consistent associations between political and social factors, and judgements about the competence or otherwise of Scottish governments on the one hand, and UK governments on the other (McCrone, 2025). Recall, too, that Labour was in power at Westminster from 1997 until 2010, followed by a Conservative-Liberal Democrat coalition until 2015, and thereafter a Conservative government until 2024. Hence, responses to 'UK government' in the survey questions are not to be taken as simply contra *parti-pris*.

Looking across the array of results, it is striking that social class has no significant effect, that higher income levels are more likely to be associated with trust in Scottish government, as are higher levels of education, and those with greater interest in politics. In other words, it is the better-off, the better-resourced and arguably the better-informed, who place greater trust in Holyrood. Those most likely to put their faith in Westminster, on the other hand, do so for reasons of 'politics', whether constitutional or party political, but generally evince less interest in politics as such.

Now and Then

Twenty-five years on, then, have people's wishes been fulfilled? Back in 1997, what was striking was how socio-demographic variables such as sex, age, education and social class did not account for much of the variation in attitudes to devolution (Brown, Paterson and McCrone, 1999). Yet neither did feeling 'strongly Scottish' account for key variations in these attitudes to devolution. Being Scottish was so ubiquitous that, in and of itself, it did not explain variations in listening and trust. This is not to imply that feeling Scottish is unimportant; to the contrary, because it matters to so many people across the spectrum, from Right to Left, it does not operate to discriminate their attitudes to Scottish government. In any case, personal national identity is refracted through civil institutions, a point made in relation to the 1997 Scottish referendum, that 'our findings on expected benefits show a strong faith that Scottish social institutions can work in harmony with the new Parliament' (ibid. 128). This is because the political aspects of Scottish national identity are mainly about loyalty to key institutions.

Taking stock of the Scottish parliament and government twenty-five years on, conventional socio-demographic factors still explain relatively little as to how people judge governing institutions. Age, sex, social class, income and education, as well as national identity, do not, in themselves, account for much variation in respect of key attitudes to devolution, but neither did they do so in 1997 before it all began. Those who judge the Scottish government to be good at listening to people are significantly more to the Left,[11] and significantly more liberal.[12] These are the Left-leaning liberal middle classes in the main, who support self-government. Those more likely to credit the UK government when it comes to listening are significantly more to the Right.[13]

In 1997, we wrote:

> Scots are not nationalists for expressive reasons: identity matters less to politics than effective government. But, equally, they are nor anti-nationalist either. Because the option of Independence will not go away – and because it does not provoke deep animosity among the majority – for the foreseeable future Scottish politics will continue to be dominated by the question of how the country is governed. (Brown, Paterson and McCrone, 1999: 162–3)

That turns out to be a conclusion which still holds a quarter of a century later.

Others make similar judgements about the efficacy of devolution. As in our analysis, Alex Scholes, writing online in *What Scotland Thinks* in late 2022, found that party preference was an important discriminator as regards policy areas, such that SNP supporters were more likely to accord 'blame' to Westminster, and 'credit' to Holyrood, and that Conservative supporters did the reverse.

We can, then, sum up how people in Scotland judge their parliament after twenty-five years: not at all bad, and certainly much better than Westminster. That may be a low bar, but it is a significant one, at a time when parliamentary democracy in general is under threat globally (Runciman, 2019; Müller, 2022). It is also one which, by and large, holds whichever party is in (Scottish) government; and only the Conservatives have never been. Why so positive, or at least less negative? Because, for good or for ill, the parliament is 'ours'. People in Scotland have taken to self-government, even of the devolved sort. Regaining a parliament in 1999, it seems, allows not only *peeblin' wi' stanes*, but for a modest degree of approbation. The question is: what comes next?

THINGS FALL APART: CAN THE CENTRE HOLD?

The Irish poet William Butler Yeats famously posed this question in his poem *The Second Coming* in 1920, when it was clear that some form of independence for Ireland was in the offing, though it was quite unclear what form and shape the new state would take. The convention has been to write comparisons between Scotland and Ireland out of the picture. After all, the claim that Ireland was a colony of England holds much more water than to say the same of Scotland, although some have tried (Michael Hechter tried to invoke 'internal colonialism' in his 1975 book of that name).

The comparisons fall upon stony ground because their economic histories are markedly different. Put simply, most of Ireland, apart from the north-east corner around Belfast, was never thoroughly industrialised as was Scotland, and we saw in Chapter 5 how closely Scotland's industrial structure paralleled the British structure. Ireland virtually made the leap from pre-industrial society to a post-industrial one. Scotland, on the other hand, has been concerned from the mid-twentieth century with dealing with the after-effects of thoroughgoing industrialisation in the nineteenth century, and as a result the political economies of the two countries do not resemble each other. Religion, which became such a rallying point in Ireland against the union state, was never the defining issue in Scotland once the Treaty of Union, and in particular the grandiloquent 'Protestant Religion and Presbyterian Church Act' of 1707 was promulgated. Scotland was arguably a more integral part of the British state than (most of) Ireland ever was. The two countries simply had different trajectories, even though for more than one hundred years they belonged to the same, attenuated, British state. And yet, the UK is one of the few states in Europe which has seen serious secession of territory in modern times. As Michael Keating has pointed out: 'It is an extraordinary historical amnesia that allows the UK to present itself as a model of stability and territorial integrity in spite of being one of only two western European nations to experience secession in the 20th century' (Keating, 2021: 199).

Volte Face

This is the point where we turn conventional wisdom on its head, and argue that the peculiarities belong to the British state, rather than to Scotland. We can consider Scotland to be 'normal' in that it is a small, western European territory which found itself in, and took advantage of being part of, a global British empire from the late eighteenth century until the mid-twentieth century. It prospered economically, as well as culturally, exporting Scottish values and ideas to all corners of empire (Crawford, 1992). When those conditions ceased to exist in the final quarter of the twentieth century, then the 'marriage of convenience', the *raison d'être* of Union, also ceased to be. The task, then, is not to explain why Scotland is 'different', even abnormal, but to account for the 'abnormalities' of the British state.

The contradictions, arguably, lie at the centre of that British state, not with the so-called 'Celtic fringe', a term which makes a virtue of the peripherality of 'not-England'. Michael Keating's argument is pertinent here. The problem of Union is not the peripheries, but the centre; a rigid insistence that the fundamental principle of authority is the centralised 'monarchy-in-parliament', the assumption that the UK is a 'Westphalian' state, subsuming power, dominion and sovereignty at the centre, while never taking the required steps to be such a thing in formal terms. The aim of Union, Keating observed, was not 'nation-building' within, but the pursuit of military, religious and dynastic security without, by means of trade and empire. There has been no thoroughgoing programme of cultural integration to create a unitary 'demos' as in other European states. He sums it up as follows: 'the UK is not a state, unitary or federal, but a union, and as such does not necessarily need a hard core or sovereignty or purpose' (Keating, 2021: 50). Furthermore, it follows that:

> (m)aintaining unions is ... a specific form of statecraft, sensitive to variety and the contested and negotiated nature of claims to authority. These cannot be reduced to a single principle or hierarchy of principles, to provide undisputed legitimacy. The relationship among the constituent units is always open to argument, institutional dynamics and power. (ibid. 19)

Our research on sovereignty in Scotland underscores this point (McCrone and Keating, 2021, 2023). Since Brexit 2016, we have entered a battle of sovereignties – Scottish and British – between two apparently antithetical conceptions of sovereignty, reflected in political struggles between nationalists and unionists.

The question of sovereignty, however, has never been resolved anent Scotland. On the one hand, there is the belief that the Westminster parliament is absolutely sovereign and supreme; on the other, that it is a union of nations, bound by the terms of Union and periodically renegotiated. Brexit 2016 destabilised the devolution compromise and posed questions about sovereignty that had long lain dormant but were rekindled by devolution. Brexit 2016 showed up the contradictions within the British state: that it behaved as if it were a unitary state, and yet could not face up to the challenge of being a union state. The UK government, especially between 2019 and 2024, pursued a strict 'sovereigntist' line, seeking to remove any real or symbolic constraints from Europe, even at considerable economic cost. The Scottish government, for its part, has continued to pursue Scottish sovereignty in the form of independent statehood, but in the context of a supranational Europe, and while recognising continued interdependency with the United Kingdom.

Our surveys showed that even among Scottish sovereigntists and British unionists, the two polar positions on the *subject* of self-determination, there is considerable nuance and complexity about the *object*, such that sovereigntists are willing to accept sharing with the UK, even post-independence, while unionists accede that many decisions should be the responsibility of the Scottish government. There is still a large measure of support for options that mix and match elements of Scottish sovereignty and British union in different ways. We encounter considerable nuance and sophistication in the Scottish population which is not matched by 'muscular unionism', as practised by UK governments since 2015, and arguably for much longer than that. Consider: for the forty-five-year period between 1979 and 2024, all but thirteen of those years (that is, less than one-third) have seen Conservative governments at Westminster largely based on English votes in a first-past-the-post electoral system. Furthermore, these governments have been indubitably of the political Right, set in train by Mrs Thatcher and her successors, employing neo-liberal policies and slogans, with a veneer of 'English nationalism' as a conservative ideology (McCrone, 2023).

The historian Colin Kidd has made the point[14] that 'despite devolution and the [Scottish] referendum scare of 2014, unitarists – English nationalists as well as "muscular unionists" – continue to treat the UK as England writ large'. He comments:

> Anglocentric chauvinism was long hardwired into constitutional interpretation. According to Stephen Tierney [one of the book's contributors], the constitution's Whiggish interpreters bear considerable responsibility for the current predicament of the United Kingdom. There has been no serious attempt to understand the 1707 Treaty of Union as a fundamental 'transformation' rather than merely a geographical 'extension' of the English state. Instead, the post-1707 British Parliament is casually assumed to be 'the inheritor, or indeed the same body as its English predecessor, essentially incorporating the Scottish Parliament'. Tierney reminds us that the modern Scottish challenge to the Diceyan state has taken two very different forms: most obviously the secessionist claim to Scottish independence, but also the project to redescribe the UK, shorn of a constricting doctrine of legislative supremacy, as a 'plurinational' union-state. (Kidd, 2024: 33)

The problem of the Other

The second decade of the twenty-first century brought many of these contradictions to a head. Not only was a system of devolved government in place at the turn of the century in Scotland, Wales and Northern Ireland, but two referendums, on Scottish independence in 2014, and Brexit in 2016, crystalised those contradictions. On the morning after the Scottish referendum, the Prime Minster David Cameron announced that having seen off the Scottish threat to the Union, it was now England's turn for attention. He said: 'I have long believed that a crucial part missing from this national discussion is England. We have heard the voice of Scotland – and now the millions of voices of England must also be heard. The question of English votes for English laws – the so-called West Lothian question – requires a decisive answer.' (https://www.gov.uk/government/news/scottish-independence-referendum-statement-by-the-prime-minister).

Cameron's proposal, 'English votes for English laws' (known as EVEL), that legislation involving England required only English MPs to vote for it was short-lived, lasting from 2015 until 2021, when it fell into desuetude because it was unworkable in a unitary British House of Commons. The afterlife of the proposal, however, infused Conservative politics, especially in the brief period of office (2019–22) held by Cameron's successor, Boris Johnson. Electoral success in the British general election of 2019 was one in which 'being English' proved to be an effective rally-call for (northern) English votes, the so-called 'red wall' joined to the 'blue wall' in the south, producing a sort of purple confection. It turned out that mobilising English nationalism, partly in opposition to devolved parliaments in Scotland, Wales and Northern Ireland, on the grounds of 'what about us?', did not carry much political weight. Furthermore, there was no huge increase in demand for a separate English parliament as opposed to a UK one. According to the definitive British Social Attitudes survey, 18 per cent of people in England wanted an 'English parliament' in 1999, rising to 29 per cent in 2009, but falling back to 22 per cent in 2020. All in all,

> The Conservatives, with UKIP, a more radical English party hard on its heels, were better able to appeal to people in England on the basis of being English. 'Take Back Control' was a wolf-whistle for English nationalism. Its 'other' was not the smaller countries of these islands but 'Europe', imagined as the significant other in this slogan. (McCrone, 2023: 611)

With hindsight, the inherent contradictions of 'English nationalism' – it is in cultural terms an elegiac backward-looking confection, led by a party of privilege and in power, and a political movement of the post-Brexit moment – do not gainsay the crisis of the British state. Such political-cultural events as those experienced in 2014 and 2016, and throughout that decade, bring into focus the crisis of the centre. As Colin Kidd observed, the constitution's Whiggish interpretation bears much of the responsibility for the current predicament of the UK.

Nationalist Troubles

At the time of writing (2024), the crisis of the Scottish National Party distracts somewhat from this predicament, reflected in its loss of Westminster seats at the 2024 British general election. It seems that the SNP has become 'just another party', in Ben Jackson's words (Jackson, 2023), hobbled by scandals, policy errors and internal divisions, with its leader, Nicola Sturgeon, having departed the stage, and subsequently also her successor, Humza Yousaf, who lasted barely a year. Having been in power continuously from 2007, the party had hitherto three advantages: it was not encumbered by the baggage of having been in government before; it retained its 'separateness' from the British state and political system such that it was as much 'movement' as 'party'; and it was structured around loyalty to a common cause – independence – at which point, there was a question as to whether, if and when that was achieved, the party would have accomplished its primary aim, folded its tents and left the political scene (Foley et al., 2023).

The heightened political context of the two referendums, on independence in 2014, and Brexit in 2016, gave the SNP a momentum which governing parties usually do not have. It ran, however, into significant road-blocks, notably the refusal of UK government to permit a second referendum on independence, reinforced by a legal-constitutional ruling of the UK Supreme Court that permitting such a thing was in the hands of British, not Scottish, government. Furthermore, as James Mitchell observed: 'The central paradox of Scottish politics has been that in the desire to find an alternative system we have ended up with a system of government that is essentially the same as the Westminster system' (*Scottish Left Review*, 2022[15]). The SNP's inability to construct a routine game-plan for government, reinforced by centralising power to itself, and a failure to work out what independence would mean in fiscal-economic terms meant that it ended up in a political cul-de-sac. Gerry Hassan observed that by 2023 Scottish government had been reduced to a mini-version of Westminster and Whitehall, and a form of leadership under Sturgeon which was part-presidential and part-presentational (Hassan, 2023). Above all, reconciling being a political party as well as a social movement, especially post-2014, has meant that like Syriza in Greece, Podemos in Spain, and Five-Star Movement in Italy, it 'exaggerated hopes raised by the party's growth, and its limited capacity to accomplish even modest demands for change' (Foley, Montgomery and Kerr, 2023: 546).

Nevertheless, while opinion poll support for the SNP was little more than one-third (36 per cent in October 2023, and 30 per cent of the vote in the British general election of 2024), support for independence stood at almost 50 per cent, another Scottish political conundrum, but neither unusual nor unexpected in Scottish politics (https://www.whatscotlandthinks.org/2023/10/mr-yousafs-conference-challenge/). Detaching support for constitutional change from party politics is not a new phenomenon in Scotland. It was, after all, 'civil society' which took control of the campaign for Home Rule in the 1990s through the medium of the Scottish Constitutional Convention; just as the Scottish Covenant in 1949, devised by John MacCormick, was an all-party movement. Lindsay Paterson's analysis has pointed to 'a liberal and left leadership of the independence movement among people well-educated and having a Scottish identity' (Paterson, 2023b). Thus, 'if the SNP declines, that same educated judgement is perfectly capable of shaping the Independence movement in new ways, building indeed on a rhetoric of betrayal that could be as readily directed at the old SNP as at unionists.' (ibid. 534)

And yet. Iain Docherty has pointed out that, while the crisis engulfing the SNP has the hallmarks of a strategic surprise for a party which has won all elections in Scotland in the last decade, it was no surprise at all in the context of the 2014 referendum – a defeat not a victory for nationalists – the Brexit 2016 vote which placed Scotland on the losing side, and the draining fiscal and health crises of Covid-19 from 2020. There remains, however, the key question: 'how sustainable is the UK as a coherent political economy given its deep-seated structural crisis?' (Docherty, 2023: 566). He argued that 'moving the dial on public attitudes to the economics of independence is … probably the most important task facing the SNP if it is to generate the consistent 60 per cent levels of support for Yes' (ibid. 568). Rather than Scottish independence being dead, 'to focus on the economic sustainability of the UK is where the potential for a possibly decisive surprise in Scottish constitutional politics resides' (ibid. 569).

This is because, for centuries, the UK's political economy 'is structured around an extreme core-periphery model that mobilises natural resources and human capital from the periphery to sustain high standards of living, especially for the elite, in the metropolitan core' (ibid. 570). In that regard, the debate about Scotland's place in the Union is one expression of a much wider question of inter-regional inequalities within the UK. The question is less that of the UK being 'greater England' than of 'greater London'. One can imagine a UK updated and reformed, with a written constitution, federalised government, PR elections, as well as devolved regions in England, but it is hard to visualise that happening unless one takes the view that only the extent of the crisis will usher in radical change. The optimistic view is that this is the route-map to fundamental constitutional and social change. The pessimistic view is that, such is the scale of the crisis, muddling along is the likely option to be taken. The election of a Labour government in 2024 might seem a way out of the constitutional impasse, but there is little expectation that radical institutional change is in the offing. Significantly, the constitutional crisis seems the greater in the two territories which voted in favour of Remain in 2016: Northern Ireland (56 per cent) and Scotland (62 per cent). The routes out of their respective Unions might seem theoretically easier as a result of striking divergence from the British centre, but in practice have become more difficult because it raises the matter of where the boundaries are, notably with 'Europe'.

Europeans Now

In the meantime, Scots have quietly become Europeans (see Chapter 5). In 2016, they voted to Remain in the European Union by 62 per cent to 38 per cent; England voted to Leave by 53 per cent to 47 per cent. We can argue about what being European means, but Scots have shifted a long way since the 1975 referendum, when they were much more lukewarm, voting 58 per cent to join – less enthusiastic than the UK as a whole, which voted by 67 per cent to 33 per cent.[16] The contrast with England is clear. Being strongly 'European' produced comparably high proportions of Remain voting in both countries in 2016, while 'weak' Europeans in England were significantly more likely to vote Leave than their counterparts in Scotland. Similarly, the 'strongly British' in Scotland were far more likely to describe themselves as 'strongly European' than similar people in England. While 'national identity' in Scotland has little discriminating effect on 'being European' (people describing themselves as 'mainly Scottish' are just as likely to say they are weak Europeans as strong), being English had a major effect in that the more English were far more likely to be weak Europeans.

In England in 2016, being English became a key marker of *not* being European, while in Scotland, being Scottish is so pervasive an identity as to have had no *discriminating* effect on explaining the Brexit vote. The infusing of 'European' with such political content in the two countries was bound to raise its salience, even though how it plays into being Scottish and being British is not straightforward. Nevertheless, being Scottish and being British, something of an identity alliance, were pushing in the same direction to bring about a strong Remain vote. It was as if the political mesh reinforced the 'European' vote; being Scottish ran on the weft, and being British ran on the warp, so as to produce and sustain a strong Remain vote. Plainly, Scotland was not the country it had been fifty years previously in the 1970s when our story began. Being taken out of the EU against the popular will was reinforced by the refusal by the British state, Westminster and the UK Supreme Court between them to countenance another referendum on Scottish independence, despite the changed material and constitutional circumstances.

Territorial identities operate in context. They tell us how and why their substance matters; they are frames through which we make sense of the world. In Scotland, being European signifies certain values which matter to people. They interplay with other territorial identities, but also with wider aspects of social identities: being young, educated, liberal, 'nationalist', both Scottish and British. Being European (or not) tells us something about key social, political and cultural processes, and provide frameworks for understanding, and ultimately social and political action. With hindsight, the 2016 Brexit vote, with its different outcomes north and south of the border, have become suffused with new political and cultural meanings (McCrone, 2019b). 'Being European' has entered the politics of Scotland and England, and relations within the British state are changed utterly.

TRANSFORMATIONS: THE DEMISE OF OLD CERTAINTIES

Consider, then, how Scotland has changed in fifty years. Recall the observation by Phillips and his colleagues (Chapter 5) that 'industry was never a neutral, descriptive term for a particular type of economic activity. It also carried connotations of progress, modernity and effective nationhood ... Scotland's economic history had embedded a widespread notion of the country as an "industrial nation" (Phillips, Wright and Tomlinson, 2023: 41). So much attached to and depended on that characterisation of Scotland that its demise brought consternation, even denial, but for some, also liberation.

The end of heavy industry, especially coal-mining and steel-making, but much more besides, undermined the masculinist culture upon which notions of Scotland were based. In particular, the role of women was transformed. This meant not only the opening-up of formal employment in service jobs, but the reordering of social relations, staying on in education, and the rebalancing of gender relations, without implying that equal opportunities for men and women had been achieved. Recall, too, the end of the 'marriage bar', which was formally made illegal by the Sex Discrimination Act 1975. It now seems incredible that women had to leave employment as teachers on marriage – though still reflected in the residual ubiquity of 'Miss' as a formal address for women teachers – and in clerical employment by local and central authorities.

The transformation of family forms, and with that, relations between men and women in households, discussed in Chapter 4, is a reflection of economic change, the opening up of employment and educational opportunities, as well as cultural and political shifts. In truth, such structural changes were not unique to Scotland. The rise in married women's employment, the ideology of companionate marriage and partnerships and new models of motherhood were to be found in England and elsewhere (Sutcliffe-Braithwaite and Thomlinson, 2022). Thus, sex is no longer a significant discriminating variable in shaping opinions and values between men and women, despite abiding social and personal inequalities between the sexes.

Furthermore, 'work' is no longer the preserve of men with hammers and shovels. Scotland, in that regard, is no longer a 'working class' society in terms of its employment structure. It has three more or less equal parts: one-third in managerial and professional jobs; one-third in administrative and service jobs and one-third in manual employment. This is not to say that social class does not matter, for we have seen that, relative to England, there is greater propensity throughout the class structure to self-describe as 'working class'. This reinforces the point that social class is as much a matter of culture as it is of structure.

We might assume that Scotland and its economy have been hollowed out by globalisation; that local control of its indigenous staple industries, heavy engineering, shipbuilding, textiles, once dominated by local capitalists, has come to an end. Up until 1914 under the aegis of the British empire, the world had been their oyster. All of Scotland's major industries were heavily dependent on international – imperial – markets. As economic historian Jim Tomlinson has pointed out, 'we can argue that by 1913 Scotland probably had the most globalised economy in the world' (Tomlinson, 2014: 172). What it did not have was much 'community of fate':

> The economic livelihoods of Dundonians rested largely on the monsoon in Asia, the intensity of Calcutta competition in jute and the state of the American market; that of Glaswegians rested on global levels of trade feeding through to demand for ships, and fluctuations in the world market for capital goods. (ibid.)

It was, in fact, *de*-globalisation between the wars which led to industrial decline, and attempts by the state, first Conservative and then Labour, to restructure the Scottish economy, notably through the Scottish Office. Public ownership was one response; state inducement to foreign capital, mainly American, was another. One such, badged as Silicon Glen, was built on a base of defence industries such as Ferranti in east Scotland, and Barr and Stroud in the west, and prospered briefly from the 1970s until the end of the century, when footloose capital and much cheaper labour in Eastern Europe and Asia drew away such investment. The post-1979 Thatcher government put an end to such corporatist thinking as there was, and as a result, industrial employment in Scotland fell as a share of total employment from 42 per cent to 11 per cent over sixty years.

A key feature of the last half-century has been the growth of public sector employment such that the historic differential in unemployment rates in Scotland vis-à-vis the UK has diminished significantly. In that regard, says Tomlinson, the growth of public sector employment has been a significant component of de-globalisation. De-industrialisation also undermined the influence of 'unionist' solutions achieved through the organised labour movement, especially with neo-liberal Conservative governments in power from 1979 to 1997. Labour unionism had lost its clout, and capacity to deliver. Tomlinson concluded:

> from a globalised industrial economy, reaching its peak in the years before 1914, Scotland has become a significantly post-industrial economy with strong de-globalising elements. A much greater amount of the forces acting upon the Scottish economy than ever before is now internal; above all, political decisions made about public spending in Edinburgh, within some constraints imposed from London, matter a great deal. (2014: 176)

There is, however, one final material turn to make: the transformation of the energy economy. Consider this: 'wind power accounted for 55 per cent of Scotland's [electricity] generation in 2022, the greatest proportion of any nation and more than double the proportion of England and Wales wind generation' (Rees, 2023). Over the period from 2018 to 2022, renewable generation in Scotland increased by 30 per cent. The closure of coal-fired power stations, Kincardine in 1997, Cockenzie in 2013, and Longannet in 2016, and of nuclear generation at Hunterston B in 2022,[17] means that renewable generation now has a greater share than fossil fuels. And weather to the contrary, Scotland has had by far the greatest increase in solar generation, up 19 per cent between 2018 and 2022, compared with 10 per cent in England. Renewable electricity has virtually tripled. Between 2008 and 2018, while unabated fossil fuel generation has decreased by 70 per cent (Webb and Lunn, 2021), Scottish energy efficiency policy has diverged from that set by UK government such that more than half of public housing is now rated EPC C or higher,[18] compared with just over one-third of owner-occupied stock.

And oil? It has come and largely gone,[19] although the UK government continues to claim it is important for energy security, despite 80 per cent of North Sea oil and gas being exported,[20] and issued in 2024 new licences for offshore oil and gas exploration, running against the political tide. The North Sea Transition Deal is not in line with the Climate Change Commission's recommendations for reaching net-zero emissions by 2050, nor the UK's international pledge to cut emissions by 68 per cent by 2030, compared with 1990 levels (Webb and Lunn, 2021). The Climate Change Commission's Sixth Carbon Budget pointed out that 60 per cent of changes needed to relate to human behaviour as regards heating and transport which are heavily dependent on oil and gas, and which account for 75 per cent of energy use. So far, so material.

Not Reading the Papers

These changes in the material base of Scotland have been framed by changing cultural forms. Consider, for example, the virtual demise of the newspaper industry which had once been so significant in transmitting social change. James Kellas, writing in the mid-1970s, had observed:

> All Scottish [news]papers are part of the economic log-rolling of the Scottish interest groups (among them trade unions, employers' associations, and the Scottish Council (Development and Industry)) who seek further government-aided development in Scotland. The political affiliation of the papers then becomes somewhat irrelevant. (Kellas, 1975: 175–6)

All were united in support of the Scottish growth project, shifting the Scottish economy away from heavy industries. It turned out that, in the long duration, it was not simply the economy which was transformed, but the newspapers themselves. Between 1973 and 2015, *The Scotsman* lost 72 per cent of sales; *The Herald*, 62 per cent; *The Daily Record*, 69 per cent; *The Dundee Courier*, 65 per cent; and the Aberdeen *Press and Journal* (*P&J*), a mere 48 per cent. By 2022, the BBC journalist Douglas Fraser[21] noted that sales of *The Herald* were less than 13,000 per day; *The Scotsman* managed a mere 7,000; *The Courier*, 19,000; *The P&J*, 24,000; and *The Daily Record*, which sold over 100,000 in 2018, was down to half that number by 2024.

Plainly, seekers after news and comment were going elsewhere, notably online with all that entailed, or indeed, not at all. In the new media environment, traditional newspapers are 'replaced by a horizontal online network of content-generating users, bloggers, social networkers, citizen journalists, media literate activists and all those who can, because of the communication technology at their disposal, now contribute to the globalised public sphere. They read, but they also write'.[22] Thus were the means of cultural reproduction transformed in the half-century since the 1970s. The other cultural mainstream had been religion.

And No Longer Doing God

If communicating with others is one thing, communicating with one's God is another. Steve Bruce has observed that: 'Even in the 1960s a church affiliation was assumed by the armed forces, schools and hospitals: those who had no particular affiliation were logged as Church of Scotland for chaplaincy purposes' (Bruce, 2017: 351). By 1974, only a quarter of the adult Scottish population said they had no religion. By 2011, it had doubled to half the population. Ten years later, it was close to 60 per cent. Furthermore, *practising* religion is very low, even among those who profess to have one: almost half of believers report that they never go to church (Scottish Social Attitudes survey, 2021). It matters not which denomination we are considering: the figures are little different for members of the Church of Scotland, Catholics, or other Christians.[23] More than two-thirds of those brought up in one or other denomination said they never attended church. The writing had been on the wall much earlier. Of those asked in 1974 about their religiosity, over half (53 per cent) said 'very much so' but only when they were children; a mere 26 per cent expressed that view when they became adults. What we see in looking at religious practice and beliefs is a process of generational atrophy. Not only does a much higher proportion of people say that they were not brought up in any religion, but that the drop-off rate of those who were is steep. Historically religion had been one of the key props of Scottish identity, reflected in voting patterns and social behaviour; yet more evidence that Scots were no longer the people they once had been. Bruce concluded:

> By far the most significant change over the twentieth century has been the rise of religious indifference ... Liberty has trumped rectitude and personal autonomy has trumped obedience ... Secularisation need not mean the end of religion but it does undermine shared religion. With the state and the public sphere religious neutral, religion has become a thoroughly private matter: a sphere in which the individual consumer is sovereign. (2017: 368)

CONCLUSION: A WAGER ON HISTORY

To return to W. B. Yeats: 'Surely some revelation is at hand; Surely the Second Coming is at hand.' To which our reply might properly be: not necessarily. Consider once more the epigraph by Neal Ascherson with which this chapter began. Ascherson might appear to be hedging his bets, union or independence, but the argument of this book is that outcomes cannot be predicted, and in any case, what constitutes 'union' or 'independence' are nowadays considerably moot. The electoral successes of the Scottish National Party since 2007 might seem to lay a path to inevitable 'independence', whatever that might constitute, while success for Labour in 2024 might imply a drawing back into 'devolution', once more, whatever that might constitute. We run the risk of teleological history, reading backwards into the past to explain current, and future, events.

The fact that we are able to show that support for Scottish sovereignty is a dominant but not a majority position does not infer that this constitutes support for 'independence'. It is perfectly logical, as Ascherson's epigraph implies, that one can support the principle of sovereignty while recognising that the practical conditions for independence are not to hand; that 'now is not the time'. History, after all, is littered with such examples. Neal Ascherson observed that 'there is something wrong with academic studies of nationalism. They define the subject too tightly and force it into Procrustean categories' (Ascherson, 2002: 273). Furthermore, he observed, 'small countries with dangerous neighbours have always concluded that personal freedom and national independence hang together' (ibid.). The point is not, of course, that England is any more a 'dangerous neighbour' for Scotland as it was in the fourteenth century – involving in Ascherson's words '... what it feels like to see foreign troops riding down the street' – but that decisions made there have implications north of the border. Such was the impact of a declaration to leave the European Union in 2016, to which Scotland had no recourse. Whatever the political-constitutional impacts, we can say unequivocally that the past has become a poor predictor of Scotland's future.

Changed utterly, to borrow from Yeats, might seem an exaggerated way of accounting for a Scotland changed radically over the past fifty years. And yet in terms of social, political and economic structures that has been the case. The task of this book has been to account for those changes, and to follow them through an analysis of who we are and who we have become. The future is in people's hands wherever that might lead.

NOTES

1. A fuller analysis of these data appears in 'What do we think of it so far? Twenty-five years of Devolution', in *Scottish Affairs* (McCrone, 2025).
2. I am grateful to the Scottish Centre for Social Research, who carried out these surveys for the Scottish government, for permitting me to use the data. Further analysis can be found in Scottish Social Attitudes 2015: Attitudes to Government, the National Health Service, the Economy and Standard of Living, Social Research 2016: <https://www2.gov.scot/Publications/2016/03/5843/downloads>. For 2023, see <https://www.gov.scot/publications/scottish-social-attitudes-survey-2023-attitudes-government-economy-health-service/>.
3. Respondents in Scotland were asked how they assessed the Scottish government and the UK government in these respects. The responses to the latter are *not* those of people in the UK as a whole, but of people in Scotland.
4. The companion survey, British Social Attitudes, did not ask a question about giving 'ordinary people a say', so comparable data for Scotland and UK are not available.
5. We can do this by using the statistical measure, regression analysis, which identifies which factors have greatest predictive power. This is especially useful when correlations between a variety of putative causes and effects are high.
6. This has the merit of not only being more up-to-date, but taking place in more pessimistic times. Regression analysis, however, on previous years shows similar effects.
7. By way of comparison, the British Social Attitudes 2011 survey, which covered Britain as a whole, found that only 14 per cent trusted parliament at Westminster 'a great deal or quite a lot', and 49 per cent 'not very much' or 'not at all'. When asked 'do you trust British governments in general?', 16 per cent trusted them 'a great deal or quite a lot', and 45 per cent 'not very much' or 'not at all'. In 2022, only 12 per cent of the British public said they trusted political parties. More than two in three people, 68 per cent, said they distrusted political parties, which were the least trusted of any UK public institution (ONS, reported in *Financial Times*, 1 March 2024). The British Social Attitudes survey for 2024 reported that 45 per cent of respondents trusted British governments 'almost never', the lowest figure ever recorded in British Social Attitude surveys (<https://natcen.ac.uk/publications/bsa-41-five-years-unprecedented-challenges>).
8. This analysis was carried out by Scottish government statisticians based on the Scottish Social Attitudes survey 2021–2, and using

linear regression modelling to produce odds-ratios. A factor of 10, for example, means that people believing that the Scottish government had handled Covid-19 well were ten times *more* likely to think that the Scottish Government could be trusted to work in Scotland's best interests than those who thought it handled the pandemic badly. Such modelling has the merit of highlighting the most significant variable(s) out of a set of significant associations, and therefore can be considered the most significant 'cause'. For further details, see <https://www.gov.scot/publications/scottish-social-attitudes-2021-22>.
9. Full details are given in <https://www.gov.scot/publications/scottish-social-attitudes-survey-2023-technical-report/pages/3/>.
10. Mrs Howden made her famous statement at the failure to hang Captain Porteous (in Scott's novel (1982) [1818], *The Heart of Midlothian*, London and Glasgow: Collins, pp 45–6).
11. On the Left-Right scale, where 1 is left and 5 is right, they have a mean score of 2.32, compared with 2.45 who think the Scottish government is not good at listening, a significant difference at the .019 level).
12. This refers to a liberal-authoritarian scale. The lower the score, the more liberal are people's views. They score 3.39 compared with 3.52, also statistically significant, at .005.
13. A mean of 2.76 on 'good at listening', and 2.28 on 'not good at listening', a significant difference at the .000 level.
14. Kidd's review is of Peter Cane and Harshan Kumarasingham (eds) (2023), *The Cambridge Constitutional History of the United Kingdom*, 2 vols, Cambridge: Cambridge University Press, p. 1178.
15. For 'The Scottish Question Revisited', see <https://reidfoundation.scot/publications__trashed/the-scottish-question-revisited-pamphlet/>.
16. And England in 1975 was even more pro-European than Scotland, voting 69 per cent Yes, and 31 per cent No.
17. This leaves Torness on the east coast, with Hunterston A on the west having amalgamated with Hunterston B in 1990.
18. EPC stands for Energy Performance Certificate issued by governments (see <https://www.scottishepcregister.org.uk>).
19. Kemp (2011) and Kemp (2012).
20. <https://eciu.net/media/press-releases/2024/british-fuel-from-new-north-sea-licences-would-make-up-less-than-1-of-a-tank-of-petrol>.
21. Douglas Fraser 'Fading Newsprint: Scotland's newspapers struggle on', 8 March 2023. (<https://www.bbc.co.uk/news/uk-scotland-64888510>).

22. Scottish Universities Insight Institute (SUII), 'Mapping Futures for News: Trends, Challenges and Opportunities for Scotland', Nov 2010: ii. Ironically, in 2024, SUII itself ceased production.
23. The media has made much of Scottish census data for 2022 purporting to show that fewer Scots profess a religion than in England and Wales. The problem is that Scottish and English (and Welsh) census data are not comparable because different questions were asked, the English and Welsh question offering 'Christian' while the Scottish question more helpfully disaggregated Church of Scotland, Roman Catholic and other Christian. We should be sceptical of media claims.

Bibliography

Alston, D. (2021) *Slaves and Highlanders: Silenced Histories of Scotland and the Caribbean*, Edinburgh: Edinburgh University Press.
Anderson, B. (1996) *Imagined Communities: Reflections on the Origin and Spread of Nationalism*, London: Verso.
Anderson, M. (2012) 'The demographic factor', in T. M. Devine and J. Wormald (eds), *The Oxford Handbook of Modern Scottish History*, Oxford: Oxford University Press.
Anderson, M. (2018) *Scotland's Populations from the 1850s to Today*, Oxford: Oxford University Press.
Anderson, R. D. (1985) 'In search of the "lad o'parts": the mythical history of Scottish education', *History Today*, 19.
Anderson, R. D. and S. Wallace (2015) 'The Universities and National Identity, c.1830–1914', in R. D. Anderson et al. (eds), *The Edinburgh History of Education in Scotland*, Edinburgh: Edinburgh University Press.
Ascherson, N. (1988) *Games with Shadows*, London: Radius.
Ascherson, N. (2002) *Stone Voices: The Search for Scotland*, London: Granta Books.
Ascherson, N. (2022) 'Endpiece', *Scottish Historical Review*, CI(3), 532–6.
Barnett, A. (1997) *This Time: Our Constitutional Revolution*, London: Vintage Books.
Bealey, F. and J. Sewel (1981) *The Politics of Independence: A Study of a Scottish Town*, Aberdeen: Aberdeen University Press.
Beaune, C. (1985) *Naissance de la Nation France*, Paris: Gallimard.
Bechhofer, F. and D. McCrone (2009) 'Being Scottish', in F. Bechhofer and D. McCrone (eds), *National Identity, Nationalism and Constitutional Change*, London: Palgrave Macmillan.
Billig, M. (1995) *Banal Nationalism*, London: *National Identity, Nationalism and Constitutional Change*, London: Palgrave Macmillan.
Beveridge, C. and R. Turnbull (1989) *The Eclipse of Scottish Culture: Inferiorism and the intellectuals*, Edinburgh: Polygon.

Blaikie, A. (2010) *The Scots Imagination and Modern Memory*, Edinburgh: Edinburgh University Press.
Brand, J. (1978) *The National Movement in Scotland*, London: Routledge.
Braudel, F. (2009) 'History and the Social Sciences: the *Longue Durée*', *Review*, 32(2), 171–203.
Breitenbach, E. and F. Wasoff (2007) 'A gender audit of statistics: comparing the position of women and men in Scotland', Edinburgh: Scottish Executive Social Research.
Brown, A., D. McCrone and L. Paterson (1999) *The Scottish Electorate: The 1997 General Election and Beyond*, London: Palgrave Macmillan.
Broun, D. (1994) 'The origins of Scottish identity', in C. Bjørn, A. Grant and K. J. Stringer (eds), *Nations, Nationalism and Patriotism in the European Past*, Copenhagen: Academic Press, 35–55.
Broun, D. (1998) 'Defining Scotland and the Scots before the Wars of Independence', in D. Broun, R. J. Finlay and M. Lynch (eds), *Image and Identity: The Making and Remaking of Scotland Through the Ages*, Edinburgh: John Donald, 4–17.
Broun, D. (2003) 'The Declaration of Arbroath: Pedigree of a Nation', in Geoffrey Barrow (ed.), *The Declaration of Arbroath: History, Significance*, Edinburgh: Society of Antiquaries of Scotland.
Broun, D. (2015) 'Rethinking Scottish Origins', in S. Boardman and S. Foran (eds), *Barbour's Bruce and its Cultural Contexts*, Martlesham, Suffolk: Boydell and Brewer.
Broun, D. (2023) 'Scottish independence and British identity: a Medieval Perspective', TC Smout lecture, St Andrews University, 9 November (mimeo).
Brown, C. (1990) 'Each take of their several way? The Protestant churches and the working classes in Scotland', in G. Walker and T. Gallagher (eds), *Sermons and Battle Hymns: Protestant Popular Culture in Modern Scotland*, Edinburgh: Edinburgh University Press.
Bruce, S., T. Glendinning, I. Paterson and M. Rosie (2004) *Sectarianism in Scotland*, Edinburgh: Edinburgh University Press.
Bruce, S. (2017) 'Have Scots Become a Godless People?' in D. McCrone (ed.), *The New Sociology of Scotland*, London: Sage.
Bukodi, E., J. H. Goldthorpe, L. Waller and J. Kuha (2015) 'The mobility problem in Britain: new findings from the analysis of birth cohort data', *British Journal of Sociology*, 66(1), 93–117.
Calder, A. (1994) *Revolving Culture: notes from the Scottish Republic*, London: Taurus.
Calhoun, C. (1993) *Habermas and the Public Sphere*. Cambridge, MA: MIT Press.
Carruthers, G. (2009) *Scottish Literature*, Edinburgh: Edinburgh University Press.
Caughie, J. (1982) 'Scottish Television: What would it look like?', in

McArthur, C. (ed.), *Scotch Reels: Scotland in Cinema and Television*, London: BFI Publishing, 112–22.
Checkland, S., and O. Checkland (1984) *Industry and Ethos: Scotland 1832–1914*, London: Edward Arnold.
Cohen, A. (1982) *Belonging: Identity and Social Organisation in British Rural Cultures*, Manchester: Manchester University Press.
Cohen, A. (1986) *Symbolising Boundaries: Identity and Diversity in British Cultures*, Manchester: Manchester University Press.
Cohen, A. (1994) *Self Consciousness: An Alternative Anthropology of Identity*, London: Routledge.
Cohen, A. (1996) 'Personal nationalism: a Scottish view of some rites, rights and wrongs', *American Ethnologist*, 23(4), 802–15.
Cohen, A. (2000) 'Peripheral Vision: nationalism, national identity and the objective correlative in Scotland', in A. Cohen (ed.), *Signifying Identities: Anthropological Perspectives on Boundaries and Contested Values*, London: Routledge.
Cohen, R. (1994) *Frontiers of Identity: The British and the Others*, London: Longman & New York: Addison Wesley.
Colley, L. (1992) *Britons: Forging the Nation, 1707–1837*, New Haven: Yale University.
Condor, S., S. Gibson and J. Abell (2006) 'English identity and ethnic diversity in the context of UK constitutional change', *Ethnicities*, 6, 123–58.
Craig, C. (1983) 'Visitors from the stars: Scottish film culture', *Cencrastus*, 11, 6–11.
Craig, C. (1987) 'Twentieth century Scottish literature: an introduction', in C. Cairns (ed.), *The History of Scottish Literature, Volume 4, The Twentieth Century*, Aberdeen: Aberdeen University Press.
Craig, C. (1996) 'Absences', in *Out of History: Narrative Paradigms in Scottish and British Culture*, Edinburgh: Polygon.
Craig, C. (1999) *The Scottish Modern Novel*, Edinburgh: Edinburgh University Press.
Craig, C. (2001) 'Constituting Scotland', *The Irish Review* (28), 1–27.
Craig, C. (2018) *The Wealth of the Nation, Scotland, Culture and Independence*, Edinburgh: Edinburgh University Press.
Craig, D. (1961) *Scottish Literature and the Scottish People, 1680–1830*, London: Chatto and Windus.
Crawford, R. (1992) *Devolving English Literature*, Edinburgh: Edinburgh University Press.
Crick, B. (1992) *In Defence of Politics*: London: Weidenfeld and Nicolson.
Curtice, J. (2017) 'Why did Brexit not work for the Conservatives?', https://ukandeu.ac.uk/why-did-brexit-not-work-for-the-conservatives/.
Damer, S. (2020) *Scheming: A Social History of Glasgow Council Housing, 1919–1956*, Edinburgh: Edinburgh University Press.

Davie, G. (1961) *The Democratic Intellect: Scotland and Her Universities in the Nineteenth Century*, Edinburgh: Edinburgh University Press.
Davies, N. (2011) *Vanished Kingdoms: The History of Half-Forgotten Europe*, Harmondsworth: Penguin.
Davis, H. (1969) *Beyond Class Images: Explorations in the Structures of Social Consciousness*, London: Croom Helm.
Devine, T. (2016) *Independence or Union: Scotland's Past and Scotland's Present*, London: Allen Lane.
Devine, T. (ed.) (2015) *Recovering Scotland's Slavery Past: The Caribbean Connection*, Edinburgh: Edinburgh University Press.
Dickson, T. (1980) *Scottish Capitalism: Class, State and Nation From Before the Union to the Present*, London: Lawrence and Wishart.
Docherty, I. (2023) 'On Surprises, Strategy, the Economy and What Comes Next for Scottish Independence', *Political Quarterly*, 94(4), 565–74.
Donaldson, W. (1986) *Popular Literature in Victorian Scotland*, Aberdeen: Aberdeen University Press.
DuGay, P. (1997; 2013) *Doing Cultural Studies: The Story of the Sony Walkman*, London: Sage.
Durkheim, E. (2001 [1912]) *Elementary Forms of the Religious Life*, Oxford: Oxford University Press.
Engender (2014) 'Gender Inequality and Scotland's Constitutional Futures' (http://www.engender.org.uk/content/publications/Gender-equality-and--Scotlands-constitutional-futures.pdf).
Ernaux, A. (2008) *Les Années*, Paris, Gallimard.
Ferguson, W. (1998) *The Identity of the Scottish Nation*, Edinburgh: Edinburgh University Press.
Finlay, R. (1994) 'Controlling the Past: Scottish historiography and Scottish identity in the 19th and 20th centuries', *Scottish Affairs*, 9, 127–42.
Foley, J., T. Montgomery and E. Kerr (2023) 'The Antinomies of Insurgency: The Case of the Scottish National Party', *Political Quarterly*, 94(4), 535–46.
Fournier, M. (2013) *Émile Durkheim: A Biography*, Cambridge: Polity Press.
Fourastié, J. *Les Trente Glorieuses, ou la révolution invisible de 1946 à 1975*, Paris: Fayard.
Gamble, A. (1988) *The Free Economy and the Strong State*, London: Macmillan.
Gellner, E. (1983) *Nations and Nationalism*, Oxford: Blackwell.
Gellner, E. (1994) *Encounters with Nationalism*, Oxford: Basil Blackwell.
Gibbs, E. (2021) *Coal Country: The Meaning and Memory of Deindustrialization in Postwar Scotland*, London: University of London Press.
Gildea, R. (2024) *Backbone of the Nation: Mining Communities and the Great Strike of 1984–85*, London: Yale University Press.

Goldthorpe, J., D. Lockwood, F. Bechhofer and J. Platt (1969) *The Affluent Worker in the Class Structure*, Cambridge: Cambridge University Press.

Goldthorpe, J. (1980) *Social Mobility and Class Structure in Modern Britain*, 1st edn, Oxford: Oxford University Press.

Goldthorpe, J. (1987) *Social Mobility and Class Structure in Modern Britain*, 2nd edn, Oxford: Oxford University Press.

Gordon, E. and E. Breitenbach (1990) *The World is Ill-Divided: Women's Work in Scotland in the Nineteenth and Early Twentieth Centuries*, Edinburgh: Edinburgh University Press.

Grant, A. (1994) 'Aspects of National Consciousness in Medieval Scotland', in C. Bjørn, A. Grant and K. Stringer (eds), *Social and Political Identities in Western History*, Copenhagen: Academic Press, 68–95.

Grassic Gibbon, L. (1971) [1932] *Sunset Song*, London: Hutchinson and Co.

Gray, A. (1981) *Lanark: A Life in Four Books*, Edinburgh: Canongate Press.

Greenfeld, L. (1993) *Nationalism: Five Roads to Modernity*, Cambridge, MA: Harvard University Press.

Guinjoan, M. and T. Rodon (2015) 'A Scrutiny of the Linz-Moreno Question', *Publius: The Journal of Federalism*, 46(1), 128–42.

Gutmann, A. (1987) *Democratic Education*, Yale: Princeton University Press.

Hall, S. (1992) 'The Question of Cultural Identity', in S. Hall, D. Held and T. McGrew (eds), *Modernity and Its Futures*, London: Polity Press, 273–316.

Hames, S. (2020) *The Literary Politics of Scottish Devolution: Voice, Class and Nation*, Edinburgh: Edinburgh University Press.

Harrison, L. (2017) 'That famous manifesto': The Declaration of Arbroath, Declaration of Independence, and the power of language', *Scottish Affairs*, 26(4), 435–59.

Harvie, C. (1988) 'Industry, religion and the state of Scotland', in D. Gifford (ed.), *The History of Scottish Literature, volume 3, the Nineteenth Century*, Aberdeen: Aberdeen University Press, 23–42

Hassan, G. (2024) 'From Donald Dewar to Humza Yousaf: the role of Scotland's First Ministers and the Importance of Political Leadership', *Political Quarterly*, 94(4), 556–64.

Hassard, J. (1990) (ed.), *The Sociology of Time*, London: Palgrave Macmillan.

Hastings, A. (1997) *The Construction of Nationhood: Ethnicity, Religion and Nationhood*, Cambridge: Cambridge University Press.

Hearn, J. (2000) *Claiming Scotland: National Identity and Liberal Culture*, Edinburgh: Polygon.

Hearn, J. (2015) 'Demos before Democracy: ideas of nation and society in Adam Smith', *Journal of Classical Sociology*, 15(4), 396–414.

Hechter, M. (1975) *Internal Colonialism: The Celtic Fringe in British National Development, 1536–1966*, London: Routledge and Kegan Paul.

Hechter, M. (1982) 'Internal Colonialism revisited', *Cencrastus*, 10, 8–11.

Hobsbawm, E. and T. Ranger (eds) (1984) *The Invention of Tradition*, Cambridge: Cambridge University Press.

Hrytsak, Y. (2023) *Ukraine: The Forging of a Nation*, London: Sphere books.

Jackson, B. (2023) 'Introduction: Scottish Politics after Sturgeon', *Political Quarterly*, 94(4), 515–17.

Jenkins, R. (2008) *Social Identity*, 3rd edn, London: Routledge.

Keating, M. and D. Bleiman (1979) *Labour and Scottish Nationalism*, London: Macmillan.

Keating, M. (2020) 'Scotland as a political community', in *The Oxford Handbook of Scottish Politics*, Oxford: Oxford University Press.

Keating, M. (2021) *State and Nation in the United Kingdom: The Fractured Union*, Oxford: Oxford University Press.

Kellas, J. (1973) *The Scottish Political System*, 1st edn, Cambridge: Cambridge University Press.

Kellas, J. (1975) *The Scottish Political System*, 2nd edn, Cambridge: Cambridge University Press,

Kellas, J. (1978) *Modern Scotland: The Nation since 1870*, London: Pall Mall Press.

Kellas, J. (1984) *The Scottish Political System*, 3rd edn, Cambridge: Cambridge University Press.

Kellas, J. (1989) *The Scottish Political System*, 4th edn, Cambridge: Cambridge University Press.

Kemp, A. (2011) *The Official History of North Sea Oil and Gas, vol. 1*, London: Routledge.

Kemp, A. (2012) *The Official History of North Sea Oil and Gas, vol. 2*, London: Routledge.

Kenny, M. (2014) *The Politics of English Nationhood*, Oxford: Oxford University Press.

Kidd, C. (1993) *Subverting Scotland's Past: Scottish Whig Historians and the Creation of an Anglo-British Identity, 1689–c.1830*, Cambridge: Cambridge University Press.

Kidd, C. (2008) *Union and Unionisms: Political Thought in Scotland, 1500–2000*, Cambridge: Cambridge University Press.

Kidd, C. (2024) 'Highbrow Mother Goose', *London Review of Books*, 46(4) (review of P. Cane and H. Kumarasingham, *The Cambridge Constitutional History of the United Kingdom*, 2 vols, Cambridge: Cambridge University Press).

Lawrence, J. (2019) *Me, Me, Me: The Search for Community in Post-War England*, Cambridge: Cambridge University Press.

Lee, C. (1995) *Scotland and the United Kingdom: The Economy and the Union in the twentieth century*, Manchester: Manchester University Press.

Lenman, B. (1977) *An Economic History of Modern Scotland*, London: Batsford.
Leyland, A., R. Dundas, P. McLoone and F. A. Boddy (2007) 'Inequalities in mortality in Scotland, 1981–2001' (MRC Social and Public Health Sciences Unit: http://www.inequalitiesinhealth.com).
McArthur, C. (1982) (ed.), *Scotch Reels: Scotland in Cinema and Television*, London: BFI Publishing.
McArthur, E. (2013) *Scotland, CEMA, and the Arts Council: Background, Politics and Visual Arts Policy*, London: Routledge.
McCartney, G., C. Collins, D. Walsh and G. D. Batty (2011) 'Accounting for Scotland's excess mortality: towards a synthesis', April, Glasgow Centre for Population Health.
MacCormick, N. (1999) *Questioning Sovereignty*, Oxford: Oxford University Press.
McCrone, D. (1992) *Understanding Scotland: The Sociology of a Stateless Nation*, London: Routledge.
McCrone, D. (2001) *Understanding Scotland: The Sociology of a Nation*, London: Routledge.
McCrone, D. (2010) 'Recovering Civil Society: does sociology need it?', in P. Baert et al. (eds), *Conflict, Citizenship and Civil Society*, London: Routledge.
McCrone, D. (2017), 'Explaining Brexit North and South of the Border', *Scottish Affairs*, 26(4), 391–410.
McCrone, D. (2019a) 'Peeble them wi' stanes: twenty years of the Scottish Parliament', *Scottish Affairs* 28(2), 125–51.
McCrone, D. (2019b) 'Who's European? Scotland and England compared', *Political Quarterly*, 90(3), 515–24.
McCrone, D. (2020) 'Declaring Arbroath: *atque supra cresidam*', in K. P. Müller (ed.), *Arbroath 1320–2020*, Frankfurt: Lang.
McCrone, D. (2023) 'The rise and rise of English nationalism?', *Political Quarterly*, 94(4), 604–12.
McCrone, D. and F. Bechhofer (2015) *Understanding National Identity*, Cambridge: Cambridge University Press.
McCrone, D. and M. Keating (2021) 'Questions of sovereignty: redefining politics in Scotland?', *Political Quarterly*, 92(1), 14–22.
McCrone, D, and M. Keating (2023) 'Exploring Sovereignty in Scotland', *Political Quarterly*, 94(1), 26–35.
McCrone, D. (2025) 'What do we think of it so far? Twenty-five years of Devolution', *Scottish Affairs*, 34(1), 14–36.
McCrone, D. and J. Todd (2025) 'A tale of two islands: exploring national identity processes in Scotland and Ireland', in P. Gillespie, M. Keating and N. McEwen (eds), *Political Change across Britain and Ireland: Identities, Institutions and Future*, Edinburgh: Edinburgh University Press.
McGuinness, D. et al. (2012) 'Socio-economic status is associated with

epigenetic differences in the pSoBid cohort', *International Journal of Epidemiology*, 41, 151–60.

McIlvanney, W. (1977) *Laidlaw*, London: Coronet Books, Hodder and Stoughton.

McKay, A. (2013) 'The debate over Scotland's future: do women care?' (https://www.opendemocracy.net/ourkingdom/ailsa-mckay/debate-over-scotland's-future-do-women-care).

Mackenzie, W. (1978) *Political Identity*, London: Palgrave Macmillan.

McPherson, A. and C. Raab (1988) *Governing Education: A Sociology of Policy Since 1945*, Edinburgh: Edinburgh University Press.

Malešević S. (2011) 'The chimera of national identity', *Nations and Nationalism*, 17(2), 272–90.

Mason, R. (2014), 'Beyond the Declaration or Arbroath: Kingship, Counsel and Consent in Late Medieval and Early Modern Scotland', in Steve Boardman and Julian Goodare (eds), *Kings, Lords and Men in Scotland and Britain, 1300–1625: Essays in Honour of Jenny Wormald*, Edinburgh: Edinburgh University Press, 265–82.

Maxwell, S. (1976) 'Can Scotland's political myths be broken?', *Q*, 19 November, 5.

Michels, K (2022) (ed.), *Epigenetic Epidemiology*, New York: Springer International Publishing.

Middlemas, K. (1979) *Politics in an Industrial Society: The Experience of the British System Since 1911*, London: Harper Collins.

Middlemas, K. (1986) *Power, Competition and the State: Britain in Search of Balance, 1940–61*, London: Palgrave Macmillan.

Miller, W. (1981) *The End of British Politics? Scots and English Political Behaviour in the Seventies*, Oxford: Clarendon Press.

Miller, D. (1995) *On Nationality*, Oxford: Oxford University Press.

Miller, K. (1970) *Memoirs of a Modern Scotland*, London: Faber and Faber.

Mills, C. W. (1959) *The Sociological Imagination*, Oxford: Oxford University Press.

Mitchell, J. (2022) 'A Scottish Question time for Scottish Questions', in *Scottish Left Review* (https://scottishleftreview.scot/complexities-inform-mature-discussion-on-scotlands-constitutional-future/).

Moore, C. and S. Booth (1989) *Managing Competition: Meso-corporatism, Pluralism and the Negotiated Order in Scotland*, Oxford: Clarendon Press.

Moore, M. (2006) 'Nationalism and Political Philosophy', in G. Delanty and K. Kumar (eds), *The Sage Handbook of Nations and Nationalism*. London: Sage Publications, 94–103.

Morton, G. (1999) *Unionist-Nationalism: Governing Urban Scotland, 1830–1860*, East Linton: Tuckwell Press.

Muir, E. (1980) [1935] *Scottish Journey*, Edinburgh: Mainstream Publishing.

Müller, J.-W. (2022) *Democracy Rules*, London: Penguin.
Nairn, T. (1968) 'The Three Dreams of Scottish Nationalism', *New Left Review*, 1 (48), 3–18.
Nairn, T. (1977) *The Break-Up of Britain*, London: New Left Books.
Nairn, T. (1988) *The Enchanted Glass: Britain and its Monarchy*, London: Verso.
Nairn, T. (1995) '*La société civile: un mythe écossais*', *Liber*, 24 October.
Nairn, T. (1997) *Faces of Nationalism: Janus Revisited*, London: Verso Books.
Nairn, T. (1997) 'From civil society to civic nationalism: evolutions of a myth', in *Faces of Nationalism*, London: Verso Books, 73–89.
Nairn, T. (2004) '*Break-Up*: Twenty-Five Years On', in *Scotland in Theory*, Scottish Cultural Review of Language and Literature (SCROLL), 1, 17–33.
Park, A. and D. McCrone (2006) 'The Devolution Conundrum?', in C. Bromley and J. Curtice (eds), *Has Devolution Delivered?* Edinburgh: Edinburgh University Press.
Paterson, L. (1994) *The Autonomy of Modern Scotland*, Edinburgh: Edinburgh University Press.
Paterson, L. (2004) 'The modernising of the democratic intellect: the role of English in Scottish secondary education, 1900–1939', *Journal of Scottish Historical Studies* 24(1), 45–79.
Paterson, L. (2015) 'Utopian Pragmatism: Scotland's Choice' *Scottish Affairs*, 24(1), 22–46.
Paterson, L. (2017) 'Scottish Education and Scottish Society', in D. McCrone (ed.), *The New Sociology of Scotland*, London: Sage.
Paterson, L. (2023a) *Scottish Education and Society Since 1945: Democracy and Intellect*, Edinburgh: Edinburgh University Press.
Paterson, L. (2023b) 'Independence is not Going Away: The Importance of Education and Birth Cohorts', *Political Quarterly*, 94(4), 526–34.
Paterson, L. (2023c) 'Doubtful nationalists and uncertain unionists: the middle ground of the debate about Scottish independence', mimeo.
Paterson, L. (2023d) 'Education and support for Scottish Independence, 1979–2016', *Journal of Educational Policy*, 38(3), 521–42.
Paterson, L., F. Bechhofer and D. McCrone (2004) *Living in Scotland: Social and Economic Change Since 1980*, Edinburgh: Edinburgh University Press.
Petrie, D. (2000) *Screening Scotland*, Basingstoke: Palgrave Macmillan.
Petrie, M. (2022) *Politics and The People, 1945–79*, Edinburgh: Edinburgh University Press.
Petrie, M. (2023) 'Politics, the Constitution and the Independence Movement in Scotland since Devolution', *Political Quarterly*, 94(4), 581–25.
Poggi, G. (1978) *The Development of the Modern State*, London: Hutchinson.

Polanyi, K. (1944) *The Great Transformation*, New York: Farrar and Rhinehart.

Pulzer, P. (1967) *Political Representation and Elections in Britain*, London: Routledge.

Phillips, J., V. Wright and J. Tomlinson (2023) *Deindustrialisation and the Moral Economy in Scotland since 1955*, Edinburgh: Edinburgh University Press.

Rees, A. (2023) 'Electricity generation and supply in Scotland, Wales, Northern Ireland, and England, 2018 to 2022', https://assets.publishing.service.gov.uk/media/6762f0be3229e84d9bbde81a/Electricity_generation_and_supply_in_Scotland_Wales_Northern_Ireland___England_2019_to_2023.pdf

Robinson, E., C. Schofield, F. Sutcliffe-Braithwaite and N. Thomlinson (2017) 'Telling Stories about Post-War Britain: Popular Individualism and the "Crisis" of the 1970s', *Twentieth Century British History*, 28(2), 268–304.

Runciman, D. (2019) *How Democracy Ends*, London: Profile Books.

Scholes, A. and J. Curtice (2020) 'The changing role of identity and values in. Scotland's politics', https://www.whatscotlandthinks.org/analysis/the-changing-role-of-identity-and-values-in-scotlands-politics/

Scholes, A. (2022) https://www.whatscotlandthinks.org/2022/10/attitudes-towards-the-scottish-and-uk-governments-is-there-still-a-halo-effect/

Scott J. and E. Clery (2013) 'Gender roles: an incomplete revolution?', *British Social Attitudes*, 30, 115–39.

Smith, A. (1986) *The Ethnic Origins of Nations*, Oxford: Basil Blackwell.

Smith, A. (1996) 'Nations and their pasts', *Nations and Nationalism*, 2(3), 358–65.

Smith, G. (1919) *Scottish Literature: Character and Influence*, London: Macmillan.

Smout, T. C. (1987) *A Century of the Scottish People, 1830–1950*, Glasgow: Collins.

Smout, T. C. (1994) 'Perspectives on the Scottish Identity', *Scottish Affairs*, 6, 101–13.

Stenhouse, D. (2004) *On the Make: How the Scots Took Over London*, Edinburgh: Mainstream.

Stringer, G. and A. Grant (1995) 'Scottish Foundations', in A. Grant and G. Stringer (eds), Uniting the Kingdom? *The Making of British History*, London: Routledge, 85–108.

Sutcliffe-Braithwaite, F. (2018) *Class, Politics, and the Decline of Deference in England, 1968–2000*, Oxford: Oxford University Press.

Sutcliffe-Braithwaite, F. and N. Thomlinson (2022) 'Vernacular Discourses of Gender Equality in the Post-War British Working Class', *Past and Present*, 254, 277–313.

Thomas, W. I. (1921) *The Child in America*, New York: Knopf.

Therborn, G. (1983) 'Why some classes are more successful than others', *New Left Review*, March–April, https://newleftreview-org.eux.idm.oclc.org/issues/i138/articles/goran-therborn-why-some-classes-are-more-successful-than-others

Thompson, E. P. (1963) *The Making of the English Working Class*, Harmondsworth: Penguin.

Thompson, E. P. (1965) 'The Peculiarities of the English', *The Socialist Register*.

Thompson, E. P. (1971) 'The Moral Economy of the English Crowd in the Eighteenth Century', *Past and Present*, 50, 76–136.

Todd, J. (2018) *Identity Change After Conflict: Ethnicity, Boundaries and Belonging in the Two Irelands*. London: Springer/Macmillan.

Tomlinson, J. (2014) 'Imagining the economic nation: the Scottish case', *Political Quarterly*, 85(2), 170–7.

Young, H. (1989) *One of Us*, London: Macmillan.

Webb, J. and R. Lunn (2021) 'Energy', https://rse.org.uk/wp-content/uploads/2022/04/RSE-AP-TP-Facing-Up-to-Climate-Change-10-Years-On-Energy-2021.pdf

Weber, E. (1977) *Peasants into Frenchmen: The Modernization of Rural France, 1870–1914*, London: Chatto and Windus.

Wetherall, M. (2009) *Theorizing Identities and Social Action*, London: Palgrave Macmillan.

Williams, G. A. (1991) *When was Wales?*, London: Penguin.

Williams, R. (1974) *Television: Technology and Cultural Form*, London: Routledge.

Williams, R. (1977) *Marxism and Literature*, Oxford: Oxford University Press.

Wimmer, A. (2002) *Nationalist Exclusion and Ethnic Conflict: Shadows of Modernity*, Cambridge University Press.

Wimmer, A. (2011) 'A Swiss anomaly? A relational account of national boundary-making', *Nations and Nationalism*, 17(4), 718–37.

Wimmer, A. and N. Glick Schiller (2002) 'Methodological nationalism and beyond: nation–state building, migration and the social sciences', *Global Networks*, 2(4), 301–34.

Index

Act of Settlement 1690, 177
age, 9
Alston, D., 37n
Ancram, M., 58–9
Anderson, B., 27–8, 210, 225, 243
Anderson, M., 41, 75, 78, 82, 96, 100, 105, 243
Anderson, R., 136–7, 235
Ascherson, N., 218, 241, 268
Autonomy of Modern Scotland, The (Paterson), 212–13, 231

Backbone of the Nation (Gildea), 122–3
Barnett, A., 150
Beveridge, C. and R. Turnbull, 218
Billig, M., 61
biography, 3–5, 71–2
birth rate, 75, 80–4
Blaikie, A., 227–8, 238
Bogdanor, V., 144
Brand, J., 63
Braudel, F., 2–3
Break-up of Britain, The (Nairn), 25, 215

Brecht, B., 229
Brexit referendum, 65, 204n, 261
 and education, 54–5
 and national identity, 158, 161, 168, 170, 190–1
 and sovereignty, 193, 256
British general elections, 173, 174–6, 179, 180–1
 Conservative vote share, 184
 Labour vote share, 186
 Liberal/Lib-Dem vote share, 183
 SNP vote share, 189
British nationalism, 59–60
British nationality / citizenship, 149–50
British state, 255; *see also* United Kingdom (UK)
British unionists, 194, 195, 196, 198, 232, 256
Britishness, 23–4
Broun, D., 14, 15, 20, 22–3
Brown, A., L. Paterson and D. McCrone, 253
Brown, G., 220, 233

Bruce, S., 63, 267
Burns, R., 143, 223

Calder, A., 228
Caledonian Antisyzygy, 25, 203, 213
Calhoun, C., 31
Callaghan, J., 180
Cameron, D., 190, 257
Campaign for a Scottish Assembly (CSA), 187
capitalism, 43, 112
Cartwright, A., 124
Catholics, 63–4, 135–6, 267
Caughie, J., 117
change see cultural change; demographic change; economic transformation; industrial transformation; political change; social change
chronological age, 9
citizenship, 46, 143–5
civil society, 28–30, 208, 238
 and nationalism, 30–3
class consciousness, 137, 139
Class, Politics and the Decline of Deference in England, 1968–2000 (Sutcliffe-Braithwaite), 6
class structure see social class
clock-time, 3
Clydesidism, 117–18, 119, 125, 219–22
Coal Country (Gibbs), 120, 122
coal mining, 113, 115, 116, 122–5, 127, 130
co-habitation, 85
Cohen, A., 149, 168, 209, 236, 242

Cohen, R., 145
Colley, L., 24
communalism, 235
Condor, S., 150
Conservative party, 47, 54, 175, 177–8, 183–5, 200, 201
 1970 British general election, 173
 2024 British general election, 179
 October 1974 election, 57, 61, 138
 referendum decade, 191–2
 Thatcher government, 45, 58–60, 120, 121, 180
constitutional preferences, 162–3, 190–1; see also Brexit referendum; Scottish independence referendum
Cooper, T., 1st Baron Cooper of Culross, 18–19, 22
Corby, 11
corporatism, 44–5
covenants, 236
 Scottish Covenant 1949, 186, 202, 236, 260
Covid-19, 89, 95–6, 250–1
Craig, C., 25, 27, 117–18, 119, 210, 214, 220–2, 223–4, 230
Craig, D., 211–12, 216, 221
Crawford, R., 222–3, 225, 227, 230
Crick, B., 31, 215
cultural change, 8, 266
cultural deformation, 212, 213–14
 and modernity, 216–19

cultural formations, 117
  Clydesidism, 117–18, 119, 125, 219–22
cultural intimacy, 228
cultural pessimism, 25–6, 207–8, 237
  shift away from, 229–31
  see also cultural deformation
cultural tropes, 119, 126;
  see also Clydesidism; kailyardism; tartanry
culture, 209–10
  and social class, 55–6
  see also Scottish culture
Curtice, J., 54–5

Damer, S., 106
Davie, G., 218–19
Davis, H., 56
death, causes of, 90, 91, 96
death rate, 75; see also mortality
Declaration of Arbroath, 16–19, 236
deindustrialisation, 40, 41, 106, 115, 116–25, 129–30, 263–5
democratic deficit, 32, 234
Democratic Intellect, The (Davie), 218–19
demographic change, 72–9, 101–7
  birth rate, 75, 80–4
  and education, 86
  and gender, 85–8
  household size, 84–5
  life expectancy, 11n, 81–2, 89–95
  migration, 72–5, 76–9
  mortality, 96–8: Glasgow effect, 98–100; infant mortality, 82
devolution, 32, 47, 147, 193
  Scottish parliament, 245–54
  see also Home Rule
devolution conundrum, 248–50
Devolving English Literature (Crawford), 222–3
Dewar, D., 1, 201
division of labour, 88, 123, 125, 128
Docherty, I., 260
Doing Cultural Studies (Du Gay), 106
domestic labour, 88
Donaldson, W., 217
Dr Jekyll and Mr Hyde (Stevenson), 213
dream pathology, 211
Du Gay, P., 106
Durkheim, E., 29, 72

ecological fallacy, 100–1
economic activity *see* labour force participation
economic transformation, 114–25; *see also* deindustrialisation; industrial transformation
education, 226–7
  and demographic change, 86
  higher education, 53, 86, 198
  and social mobility, 53–6, 135–6
egalitarianism, 235
Elliot, W., 178

emigration, 76; *see also* out-migration
employment, 114
  moral economy of, 121–2, 125
  see also labour force participation; labour market
energy economy, 265–6
England, 24, 66
  Brexit referendum, 54
  immigration, 78–9
  individualism, 6–7, 59
  national identity, 65, 150, 262
  population dynamics, 73–4, 75–6
  social mobility, 51, 52
  union with, 22–3, 26–7, 176, 177, 216, 255
English language, 225, 226–7
English literature, 222–3, 226
English parliament, 258
'English Votes for English Laws' (EVEL), 257
Englishness, 168
epigenetics, 99–100
equal citizenship, 46
Eriksen, T., 148
European identity, 166–7, 261–2
Ewing, W., 27

Ferguson, B., 21, 218
fertility *see* birth rate
Finlay, R., 23
Fourastié, J., 10
France, 10, 40
Franklin, B., 3
Fraser, D., 43, 266

Gaidhealtachd, 22, 36n, 172n
Gamble, A., 60, 184
Geertz, C., 169, 209
Gellner, E., 28
gender
  and demographic change, 85–8
  and division of labour, 88, 123, 125, 128
  and labour force participation, 49, 87–8, 114, 128–9, 130, 263
Gender Equality Index, 88
Gibbs, E., 120, 122, 125
Gildea, R., 122–3, 124, 126
Glasgow, 40, 41–2, 63
Glasgow effect, 97, 98–100
globalisation, 264–5
Goldthorpe, J., 51, 52, 135
Goodhart, D., 202
Gordon, E. and E. Breitenbach, 118
Grant, S., 16, 20
Grassic Gibbon, L., 39
Gray, Alister, 128, 222
Gray, Alexander, 13
gross domestic product (GDP), 114–15
Gutmann, A., 54

Hames, S., 229
Harrison, L., 17
Harvie, C., 213, 217
Hassan, G., 259
Hassard, J., 3
Hearn, J., 30, 236, 237, 238n
Herdman, J., 221, 230
higher education, 53, 86, 198
Highlandism, 217

History of England, A (Hume), 24, 223
Home Rule, 179, 182–3, 186–8, 200–1, 201, 204; *see also* devolution
household size, 84–5
housework, 88
housing, 41–2, 105–6
How I Killed Margaret Thatcher (Cartwright), 124
Hume, D., 24, 223

Identity of the Scottish Nation, The (Ferguson), 21
immigration, 76–9, 101, 102–3
In Defence of Politics (Crick), 31
individualism, 6–7, 59, 72
industrial specialisation, 112–14
industrial transformation, 42–7, 244, 262–3, 264–6; *see also* deindustrialisation; economic transformation
industrialisation, 121, 254
infant mortality, 82
inter-generational social mobility, 52, 131–2
Inverness, 103
Ireland, 24, 51, 67, 144, 182, 225, 239n, 254

Jackson, B., 248
Jacobite legacy, 23–4
Jenkins, R., 148
Johnson, B., 258
Johnston, T., 40

kailyardism, 214, 217–18, 227–8
Keating, M., 34, 46, 67, 173–4, 176, 177, 245, 254, 255
Kellas, J., 56, 63, 201, 266
Kelly, P., 187, 201
Kenny, M., 168
Keynes, J. M., 222
Kidd, C., 177, 232, 257

labour, division of, 88, 123, 125, 128
labour force participation, 49, 87–8, 114, 128–9, 130, 263
labour market, 49–50, 113, 114, 115–16; *see also* service sector
Labour party, 124, 175, 200, 201
  1970 British general election, 173, 174
  1997 British general election, 180–1
  2024 British general election, 179
  and devolution, 186–8
  referendum decade, 192
  and Scottish National Party (SNP), 58, 125
  sovereigntists v. unionists, 194–5
  state intervention, 45, 46, 47
Labour supporters, 196–8
'lad o' pairts', 136–7, 209, 235
Laidlaw (McIlvanney), 42
Lanark (Gray), 128
landscape, 228–9

Lang, I., 231
language, 33–4, 224–7
Lawrence, J., 6, 59
Lenman, B., 112
Les Trente Glorieuses, 10, 40, 41
Leyland, A., 96
Liberals/Liberal Democrats, 177–8, 182–3, 187, 200
life expectancy, 11n, 81–2, 89–95
Linz, J., 62, 156
Linz-Moreno measure, 156, 157, 159, 163, 168
Literary Politics of Scottish Devolution, The (Hames), 229
literature, 6, 25, 216, 221–2, 222–4
longue durée, 2, 39

McArthur, C., 117, 119
MacCaig, N., 229
MacCormick v. Lord Advocate, 18–19
MacDiarmid, H., 213
McGahey, M., 124
McIlvanney, W., 21, 42, 61, 146, 169, 230
McKay, A., 88
Mackenzie, B., 148
Macmillan, H., 10–11
Macpherson, J., 21
McQuarrie, S., 185
Making of the English Working Class, The (Thompson), 48
Malešević, S., 147
manual workers, 50, 52, 57, 127, 128, 130, 132

marriage, 82
marriage bar, 263
Maxwell, S., 126
'Me, Me, Me: The Search for Community in Post-war England' (Lawrence), 6, 59
Middlemas, K., 44
migrants, 146
migration, 40–1, 72–5, 76–9; see also immigration; out-migration
Miller, B., 178
Miller, D., 147, 148
Mills, C. W., 3–4
miners' strike, 124, 126
mining, 113, 115, 116, 122–5, 127, 130
Mitchell, J., 259
modernity, 216–19
Moore, C., 45
Moore, M., 145
moral economy thesis, 121–2, 125
morbidity, 97–8
Moreno, L., 156
Moreno scale, 62; see also Linz-Moreno measure
mortality, 96–8
  Glasgow effect, 98–100
  infant mortality, 82
Morton, G., 176, 231–2
Muir, E., 25, 221
Mundell, D., 232

Nairn, T., 25, 41, 207–8, 211–17, 218, 227, 230, 237
nation, 29, 149
  Scotland as, 27–8, 210, 241–2

nation-states, 33–5, 241
National Health Service (NHS), 74
national identity, 19–20, 145–52, 168–70, 210, 242–3, 252
  and Brexit, 158, 161, 168, 170, 190–1
  changes to, 61–6, 159–63
  and citizenship, 144
  in England, 65, 150, 262
  and European identity, 166–7, 261–2
  importance of, 152–8
  and landscape, 228–9
  and the referendum decade 2011–21, 163–7
  v. class identity, 139
  see also Scottish identity / Scottishness
nationalism, 29, 46, 61, 211–12, 215, 220–1
  and civil society, 30–3
  and social change, 56–61
  see also unionist-nationalism
nationality, 144–5
  and European identity, 166–7
net migration, 40–1, 72–5, 76–8
newspaper industry, 266
non-manual workers, 50, 57; see also service sector; white-collar work
North Sea Oil, 46, 215, 265
Norther Ireland, 166, 261
nostophobia, 221
nuptiality, 82

occupational distribution, 115–16, 129–30; see also labour market
occupational transition, 47, 49
O'Hagan, A., 229–30
'Old and New Scottish Nationalism' (Nairn), 212
origin myth-stories, 20–2
O'Rourke, D., 230
Othering, 26, 243
out-migration, 40–1, 73–4, 78, 98–9; see also emigration

Paterson, L., 86, 135, 139, 154, 169, 177, 198, 202, 203, 212, 219, 226–7, 232, 233–4, 260
personal troubles, 4–5
Peterhead, 58
Petrie, D., 119
Petrie, M., 178–9
Phillips, J., V. Wright and J. Tomlinson, 115, 120, 121, 262
'Pictomania', 21
Pinkerton, J., 21
place, sense of, 16
Poggi, G., 44
political change, 174–82
Political Identity (Mackenzie), 148
political values, 234–6
Politics and The People (Petrie), 178
population dynamics, 72–9, 101–7
  birth rate, 75, 80–4
  and education, 86

population dynamics (*cont.*)
   and gender, 85–8
   household size, 84–5
   life expectancy, 11n, 81–2, 89–95
   migration, 72–5, 76–9
   mortality, 96–8: Glasgow effect, 98–100; infant mortality, 82
pragmatism, 203, 232–3
Presbyterianism, 177
primary industry, 116
privatisation, 106
Protestantism / Protestants, 24, 63
public issues, 4–5
public sector employment, 264

re-development, 41–2
re-housing, 41–2
referendums, 165; *see also* Brexit referendum; Scottish independence referendum
Reformation, 211
regional specialisation, 112–14
religion, 24, 63–4, 135–6, 177, 254, 267
Robbins report, 53
Robinson, E., 6, 59
Romanticism, 211

Salmond, A., 58, 179, 182, 188
Scholes, A., 253
Scholes, A. and J. Curtice, 165–6, 190
Scotch Myths tradition, 119
Scotch Reels (Caughie), 117

Scotch Reels (McArthur), 119
Scotland
   as dream country, 211–15
   early history, 14–19, 26
   as nation, 27–8, 210, 241–2
   origin myth-stories, 20–2
   as society, 13, 28–30
   as state, 30–3; *see also* Scottish Office
   union with England, 22–3, 26–7, 176, 177, 216, 255
Scotland Act 1998, 193
Scots, 15–16, 149–52; *see also* Scottish identity / Scottishness
Scots Imagination and Modern Memory, The (Blaikie), 227–8
Scotsman, The, 231
Scott, W., 213, 217, 231, 233, 251
Scottish Claim of Right, 187, 193
Scottish Constitutional Convention, 181
Scottish Covenant 1949, 186, 202, 236, 260
Scottish culture, 209–11
   Clydesidism, 117–18, 119, 125, 219–22
   cultural deformation, 212, 213–14: and modernity, 216–19
   cultural pessimism, 25–6, 207–8, 237: shift away from, 229–31
   language, 224–7
   literature, 222–4
   and social class, 55–6
   see also Scottish tropes

Scottish Election Surveys, 56, 62
Scottish Household Survey, 85
Scottish identity / Scottishness, 14, 15, 19–20, 24, 242–3; *see also* national identity; nationality
Scottish independence referendum, 32, 165–6, 190, 191, 192, 195, 233–4, 257–8
  and Brexit referendum, 202
  and national identity, 65, 144, 161, 169–70
  and social class, 138
Scottish Literature and the Scottish People (Craig), 216
Scottish National Party (SNP), 46–7, 125, 173, 175–6, 178–9, 180, 188–9, 201–2
  decline in support, 258–60
  and Scottish independence referendum, 191
  support by social group, 56–8, 181–2, 200
Scottish nationalism *see* nationalism
Scottish Office, 32–3, 40, 45–6, 121, 178, 264
Scottish parliament, 245–54
Scottish Social Attitudes Surveys, 152–3, 189, 193–4, 198, 248, 251
Scottish sovereigntists, 194, 195–6, 255–6
Scottish tropes, 119, 126; *see also* Clydesidism; kailyardism; tartanry
Scottish Unionist Party, 63, 177–8
Screening Scotland (Petrie), 119
Second Coming, The (Yeats), 254
secondary industry, 116
sense of place, 16
Sermon on the Mound, 184–5
service sector, 47, 49, 115, 116, 128; *see also* non-manual workers; white-collar work
Smith, Adam, 29–30
Smith, Anthony, 28
Smith, G., 25, 203, 213
Smout, C., 16, 24, 112, 151–2
social change, 2, 3, 5–9, 39–47, 106, 244–5
  and industrial transformation, 42–7
  and Scottish nationalism, 56–61
social class, 48–56, 64, 126–31, 136–9, 140, 263–4
  and gender, 86
  and morbidity, 97–8
  and Scottish National Party (SNP), 56–8
  see also social mobility
social deprivation, 95, 98
social mobility, 50–3, 131–5
  and education, 53–6, 135–6
social-time, 3
social values, 234–6

society
  Scotland as, 13, 28–30
  v. biography, 3–5, 71–2
sociological imagination, 4
Solution, The (Brecht), 220
sovereignty, 192–9, 203, 241, 255–6, 268
specialisation, industrial, 112–14
state intervention
  industrial transformation, 44–7
  re-housing, 41–2
state, Scotland as, 30–3; *see also* nation-states; Scottish Office
Stone Voices (Ascherson), 241
structural change, 5–8; *see also* social change
Sunset Song (Grassic Gibbon), 39
Sutcliffe-Braithwaite, F., 6, 48, 202
Sutcliffe-Braithwaite, F. and N. Tomlinson, 123
Switzerland, 34

tartanry, 212, 214, 217–18
'Telling Stories about Post-War Britain' (Robinson), 6
Thatcher government, 45, 58–60, 120, 121, 180
Thatcher, M., 58–9, 72, 107n, 184–5, 256
Therborn, G., 48
Thompson, E. P., 48, 136, 140
Thomson, D. C., 228
'Three Dreams of Scottish Nationalism, The' (Nairn), 211
time, 2–3
Todd, J., 66, 149
Tomlinson, J., 264, 265
traditions, 236
  Scotch Myths tradition, 119
Treaty of Union 1707, 22, 23, 26–7, 30, 176–7, 192, 216, 236
Trevor-Roper, H., 21, 217–18
tropes, 119, 126; *see also* Clydesidism; kailyardism; tartanry
trust, 247–8, 250–1

Ukraine, 20, 241
union with England, 22–3, 26–7, 176, 216, 255; *see also* Treaty of Union 1707
unionist-nationalism, 176, 231–2
unionists, 194, 195, 196, 198, 232, 256
United Kingdom (UK), 34, 45, 66–7, 147, 260–1; *see also* British state
universities, 53; *see also* higher education
utopianism, 203, 232–4

values, 234–6
Voice Over (MacCaig), 229
voting behaviour, 149–50, 177–8; *see also* British general elections

Wales, 7
  deindustrialisation, 115
  employment, 113

immigration, 78–9
population dynamics, 73, 74, 75–6
social mobility, 51, 52
Wealth of the Nation, The (Craig), 220, 222
Welsh language, 225
Welsh Office, 33
Wetherall, M., 146
'What Scotland Thinks' website, 165–6, 253

white-collar work, 49–50, 127, 128; *see also* non-manual workers; service sector
Whitman, W., 223
Williams, R., 106, 117, 236
Wimmer, A., 34–5, 242
Wright, K., 173
Wrong, D., 72

Yeats, W. B., 254, 267

EU representative:
Easy Access System Europe
Mustamäe tee 50, 10621 Tallinn, Estonia
Gpsr.requests@easproject.com

www.ingramcontent.com/pod-product-compliance
Lightning Source LLC
Chambersburg PA
CBHW071659170426
43195CB00039B/2237